1987

University of St. Francis
GEN 327.09 O599

W9-AEP-643

3 0301 00064445 6

THE CONDUCT OF EAST-WEST RELATIONS IN THE 1980s

At a time when the state of East-West relations is generally acknowledged to be at a low point and when West-West relations have been going through a particularly difficult period also, the IISS devoted its 1983 annual conference to analysis and prescription - analysis of the reasons for the chill and prescriptions for improvement. The papers presented at the conference covered the Soviet Union itself and its relations with its Allies in Eastern Europe, the state of the Western Alliance, the nature of the military relationship between East and West, the purely European dimension of the East-West relationship, economic relations (including questions of technology transfer and sanctions), the complex question of how the Third World impinges on East-West relations and aspects of public opinion and its impact on policy. The presenters were chosen not just for their wide experience in these fields but also in such a way as to provide a comprehensive selection of viewpoints. The conclusions that emerge give full expression to the complexity of the issues at stake but generally conclude that there is no obvious reason why things should get worse. Despite assertions made in the 1970s in some quarters that détente was irreversible, the process has most clearly been reversed, at least between the super powers, but that may have been replaced by a more realistic appraisal of the need to make some basic accommodation and restore dialogue.

Robert O'Neill, editor, is Director of The International Institute for Strategic Studies.

THE CONDUCT OF
EAST–WEST RELATIONS
IN THE 1980s

Edited by

ROBERT O'NEILL

ARCHON
BOOKS

LIBRARY
College of St. Francis
JOLIET, ILLINOIS

© The International Institute for Strategic Studies 1985

All rights reserved. No part of this publication may be
reproduced or transmitted, in any form or by any means,
without permission

First published in the United Kingdom in 1985 by
The Macmillan Press Ltd
London and Basingstoke
and in the USA by
Archon Books, an imprint of
The Shoe String Press, Inc.
995 Sherman Avenue
Hamden, Connecticut 06514

Printed in Great Britain

ISBN 0-208-02084-5

Library of Congress Cataloguing in Publication Data
Main entry under title:
The Conduct of East-West relations in the 1980s.
Includes bibliographical references and index.
1. World politics – 1975-1985 – Congresses. 2. United
States – Foreign relations – Soviet Union – Congresses.
3. Soviet Union – Foreign relations – United States –
Congresses. 4. International relations – Congresses.
5. International economic relations – Congresses.
I. O'Neill, Robert John.
D839.2.C64 1984 327'.09'048   84-21609
ISBN 0-208-02084-5

327.09
0599

CONTENTS

122,997

Soviet Union Nationalities

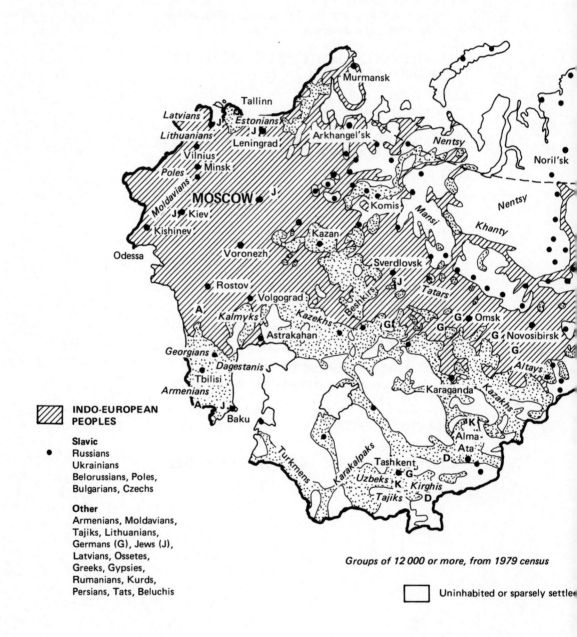

Murmansk

Tallinn

Latvians J *Estonians*
Lithuanians J
Leningrad
Arkhangel'sk

Vilnius

Poles Minsk

Nentsy

Noril'sk

MOSCOW J

Moldavians

J Kiev

Komis

Mansi

Nentsy

Kishinev

Kazan

Khanty

Odessa

Voronezh

Sverdlovsk

Rostov

J

Bashkirs

Tatars

Volgograd

A

Kalmyks

Kazekhs

G

G

G Omsk

G

G Novosibirsk

G

Astrakahan

Karaganda

Kazakhs

Altays

Georgians

Dagestanis

Tbilisi

Armenians

A J

Baku

K

Alma-
Ata

Turkmens

Karakalpaks

Tashkent

G

D

Uzbeks K *Kirghis*

Tajiks D

INDO-EUROPEAN PEOPLES

Slavic
- Russians
  Ukrainians
  Belorussians, Poles,
  Bulgarians, Czechs

Other
Armenians, Moldavians,
Tajiks, Lithuanians,
Germans (G), Jews (J),
Latvians, Ossetes,
Greeks, Gypsies,
Rumanians, Kurds,
Persians, Tats, Beluchis

Groups of 12 000 or more, from 1979 census

Uninhabited or sparsely settled

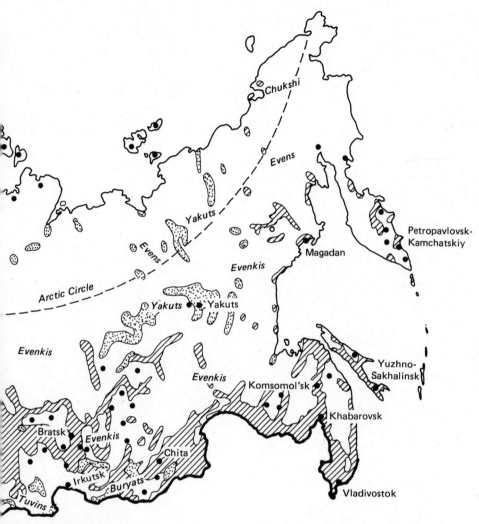

Chukshi

Evens

Yakuts

Evens

Arctic Circle

Evenkis

Yakuts Yakuts

Evenkis

Magadan

Petropavlovsk-
Kamchatskiy

Yuzhno-
Sakhalinsk

Evenkis

Komsomol'sk

Khabarovsk

Bratsk

Evenkis

Chita

Irkutsk Buryats

Tuvins

Vladivostok

CAUCASIANS
Georgians, Dagestanis (Avars,
Lezgins, Dargins, Laks,
Tabassarans, Rutuls, Tsakhurs,
Aguls), Chechens, Kabardians,
Ingush, Adygeys, Abkhaz, Cherkess,
Abazins

PALEO-SIBERIAN PEOPLES
Chukchi and others

SEMITIC PEOPLES
A Assyrians

SINO-TIBETAN PEOPLES
D Dungans

KOREANS
K Koreans

 **URALIC AND ALTAIC, CAUCASIAN
PEOPLES**

Turkic
Uzbeks
Kazakhs, Tatars, Kirghiz, Chuvash,
Bashkirs, Karakalpaks
Azerbaijanis, Turkmens
Kumyks, Uighurs, Gagauz, Tuvins,
Karachays, Turks, Khakas, Balkars,
Nogays, Altays, Shors

Other
Mordvins, Estonians, Udmurts, Maris,
Buryats, Yakuts, Komis, Hungarians,
Komi-Permyaks, Kalmyks, Karelians,
Finns, Nentsy, Evenkis, Khanty, Evens

Introduction

DR ROBERT O'NEILL

In planning the Conference at which these Papers were presented, we wished to provide participants (and readers) with information and opinion on what appears to be the major crisis of the 1980s, that in East–West relations. Since the late 1970s, and particularly since the Soviet invasion of Afghanistan, tensions have risen steadily between the United States and the Soviet Union. These tensions have flowed on into relations between NATO and the Warsaw Pact generally, and even wider, involving other allies and friends of each super-power and even many of the 'non-aligned' states.

These tensions mounted considerably in 1983, culminating in the deployment of American cruise and *Pershing* II missiles in Western Europe and Soviet abrogation of the arms-control negotiations on intermediate range nuclear forces. They also extend into many other areas: strategic weapons deployments; East–West trade; technology transfers from the West; regional confrontations in Central America, Lebanon, Southern Africa and in several parts of Asia; and the possible military use of space. The picture is not one of total gloom: agreement was reached finally at the CSCE Review Conference in Madrid in late 1983, and there has been some slight narrowing of differences in the Vienna negotiations on Mutual Balanced Force Reductions. None-the-less the trends are much more strongly negative than positive and the future of East–West relations is therefore one of the most vital for consideration by all who are interested in international security.

The analysis presented here begins by considering the Soviet Union, her essential aims (particularly in relation to Western security interests) and the challenges she is likely to present in the 1980s. The focus of analysis then moves to the nature of the Soviet Union herself, her structural economic, internal political and social problems, confronting the apparent paradox of a state which in military terms only is a super-power: in most other dimensions she is of tertiary importance or less. President Andropov, despite his poor health, had to shoulder an extremely difficult task while the Reagan Administration declared its aim of reducing the degree of external assistance which the Soviet Union had received in the past in attempting to resolve some of these problems. The question arises therefore as to whether the Soviet Union will be able to meet her essential objectives in the 1980s and 1990s and, if not, will the world be more secure or less secure?

In the light of these assessments of the nature of the Soviet Union and her challenges to the West, consideration is given to the goals of the latter group. How far is it in Western interests to put pressure on the Soviet Union by non-military and military means? How responsive is the Soviet leadership likely to be to a more moderate approach? The age of detente might be regarded generally as long past, but there are some dimensions of co-operation, especially between Eastern and Western European nations, which testify that a new Cold War has not come to dominate all aspects of East–West relations.

The growth in tensions between the two major alliance groups has, of course, implications for relations within those Alliances, particularly the more polycentric West. Sharp differences of policy on major issues such as economic relations have caused serious dissent within the North Atlantic Alliance. Other problems such as differences in emphasis on arms-control policies, the public debate on security issues and disagreements on the nature of Soviet aims in other parts of the world have made it timely to consider the future of the Alliance itself in the coming decade.

Against the background of these themes covered by the four plenary Papers of the Conference, more detailed consideration is given to specific problems of East–West relations in the twelve committee Papers presented here. We have endeavoured to present views which, while not necessarily being totally opposed, are drawn from different sectors of expert opinion on each topic. Sometimes the division of labour is between a European view and an American, sometimes it is between different sectors of opinion within each of these two groups; in one it is between regional specialists from widely differing parts of the world. Finally, to give readers something of the flavour of the debates which took place on each Paper, a conference report is included, which, while preserving necessary confidentiality of opinions expressed by participants, sets out the key factors which specialists from the West and many developing countries found in September 1983 to be the main issues for debate.

It is hoped that this collection of Papers, like its predecessors, will have value beyond ere consideration of the major problems of the year of the Conference on which it was based. The difficulties of East–West relations are, for the most part, not transitory in nature, and they must be studied and debated at length before workable, lasting solutions will be found. It is hoped that these Papers might represent another step on what is likely to prove a long path.

The Soviet Union: Her Aims, Problems and Challenges to the West

PROFESSOR ZBIGNIEW BRZEZINSKI

This Paper will examine the distinctive nature of the Soviet Union as a world power and assess the special character of the Soviet challenge to the international system. The basic theses of this analysis can be stated briefly at the outset:

- That the expansionism of the Soviet imperial system is a unique organic imperative produced by the sense of territorial insecurity on the part of the system's Great Russian national core;
- That as a result of the Great Russian stake in the imperial system a genuine evolution of the Soviet system into more pluralistic forms is not likely in the foreseeable future;
- That the political priorities and bureaucratic distortions of the Communist system confine the Soviet Union to the role of a one-dimensional military world power;
- That the Soviet Union – which now has military global reach but which lacks political global grasp – feels herself both too strong internationally to accommodate to the *status quo* and too weak domestically not to fear it;
- That as an organically expansionist, but one-dimensional military world power lacking the capacity to effect a genuine revolution in the world system, the Soviet Union is confined to the essentially negative role of disrupter of wider and more co-operative international arrangements;
- That a major disruption of the international political system could occur as a consequence of Western failure to offset Soviet military power while not coping effectively with the mushrooming crises in the strategically and geopolitically central zones of the Middle East and Central America.

A Uniquely Organic Imperialism

The Soviet Union is the political expression of Russian nationalism. The Great Russians dominate the multinational Soviet Union, populated by some 270 million people; and through the power and resources of that Union, they dominate in turn a cluster of geographically contiguous states numbering approximately an additional 115 million people. In effect, about 135 million Great Russians exercise political control over a political framework that cumulatively encompasses some 385 million spread over much of the Eurasian Continent.

This is not to say that the system is one of simple national oppression. The Great Russians rule as much by co-optation as by suppression. The historical record of Russian imperial preponderance is replete with examples of successful co-optation, corruption, and integration of foreign elites, of the gradual absorption politically and even culturally of ethnically-related peoples, of the creation of a sense of a larger community. Nonetheless, in the background of this process is the reality of Moscow's power, which is applied ruthlessly whenever a given nation chooses to resist domination and especially if it seeks to detach itself from the Russian-dominated larger whole.

The distinctive character of the Russian imperial drive is derived from the interconnection between the militaristic organization of Russian society and the territorial imperative which defines its instinct for survival. As often noted by both Russian and non-Russian historians, from time immemorial Russian society expressed itself politically through a state that was mobilized and regimented along military lines, with the security dimension serving as the central organizing impulse. The absence of any clearly definable national boundary made territorial expansion the obvious way of assuring security, with such territorial expansion then breeding new conflicts, new threats, and thus a further expansionary drive. A relentless historical cycle was thus set in motion: insecurity generated expansionism; expansionism bred insecurity; insecurity, in turn, would fuel further expansionism.

Russian history is consequently a history of sustained territorial expansionism. This sustained expansion from the north-east plains and forests of Muscovy has lasted – almost on a continuous basis – for more than 300 years. It has involved a push westwards against major power rivals, resulting in the eventual expulsion of Sweden from east of the Baltic and in the partition of the Polish–Lithuanian Republic; it has involved the persistent drive southwards, culminating – in the wake of defeats inflicted on the Ottoman Empire – in the subordination of the Ukrainian Cossacks and the Crimean Tatars and in the absorption of several Caucasian nations and of Muslim central Asia; it has involved a steady stream of settlers, penal colonists, and military explorers eastwards, along the brim of the Chinese empire, all the way to Kamchatka. Such territorial expansion is doubtless – both in scale and in duration – one of the most ambitious examples of a relentless imperial drive in known history.

The Russians have come in this manner to control the world's largest real estate. They do so by the relatively dense inhabitation of its inner core – the large area known as European Russia – and by settling in smaller but still politically significant numbers in strategically significant colonial outposts in the Baltic region (including Kaliningrad), parts of Byelorussia, East Ukraine, the north-east shore of the Black Sea, large parts of Kazakhstan, and along a great security belt spanning the trans-Siberian Railroad all the way to the Soviet Far East. The empty vastness of Siberia has thus been effectively sealed off and remains available for gradual colonization.

In the process, the Russians have come to dominate the weaker peoples inhabiting some of these territories, by subordinating them politically, co-opting them culturally, and even sometimes decimating them biologically. The non-Russian nations are controlled from the centre and prevented from coalescing against the politically dominant Great Russians, who populate the strategically located central inner core of the multinational state.

The Russian imperial system – with its mixture of co-optation, subordination, and strategic settlement – thus emerged in a manner that differs profoundly from the experience of other recent empires. Naval expansion to remote lands, followed by limited settling, was not the method. The Russian method was much more organic – a process of steady seepage into contiguous territory, with the atavistic instinct for survival dictating the perceived need to acquire more land, with 'insecurity' being translated into persistent expansion. As as a result, and contrary to many journalistic clichés, Russia historically was not so much a victim of frequent aggression but rather the persistent aggressor herself, pressing from the centre in this or that direction, whenever opportunity beckoned. Any list of aggressions committed in the last two centuries against Russia would be dwarfed by a parallel list of Russian expansionist moves against her neighbours. The vaunted Russian sense of insecurity exists – but not because Russia was so frequently attacked but because her organic expansion has prompted, and was prompted by, territorial acquisitiveness, with its inevitably antagonistic ripple-effects.

An additional, and enduring, consequence of such sustained territorial expansion has been the emergence of an imperial consciousness among the Great Russian people. Such a notion of 'imperial consciousness' is difficult to define, but difficulty of definition is not a negation of the phenomenon. There is something strikingly imperial in the insistence of the Russians describing themselves as the 'Big Brother' of the other dominated peoples, in the spontaneous determination to build huge Russian orthodox cathedrals in the very centres of dominated capitals (as in Helsinki and Warsaw – and even to replace the Warsaw *Sobor*, which the newly emancipated Poles blew up in 1919, thirty years later with the monumental Stalin Palace of

Culture), in the deeply-rooted feeling that somehow the non-Russian nations of the Soviet Union and of Eastern Europe must be retained as part of Mother Russia's special domain. Anyone who has seen, or read reports of, how the Soviet ambassadors stationed abroad handle their periodic joint sessions with fellow ambassadors from the Warsaw Pact obtains a first-hand insight into imperial and hierarchical relations.

Great Russian imperial consciousness is a complex web of religious messianism, which has long associated Moscow with the Third Rome, of nationalistic instincts for survival and power, and of the more recent universalistic ideological zeal. In addition, territorially expansive insecurity has been reinforced by the Communist obsession with internal and external enemies, reinforcing an already existing paranoiac attitude towards the outside world. This complex web of motivations has helped to generate and sustain a world outlook in which the drive to global pre-eminence, for decades measured by competition with the US, has become the central energizing impulse. That impulse sustains the predatory character of Great Russian imperialism.

It is this drive towards global pre-eminence as well as the vested interest in the imperial system that inhibits the prospects of a qualitatively significant evolutionary change in the character of the Soviet system. Without Soviet intervention, Czechoslovakia under Dubcek or Poland under Walesa probably would have become social democratic republics, with Communist totalitarianism effectively dismantled.

But Soviet intervention occurred for the very same reason that internal evolution towards greater political pluralism within the Soviet Union will be intensely, and probably even more successfully, resisted for a very long time to come. The reaction against peaceful change in Eastern Europe stemmed from the same impulses which make Great Russians fear any significant relaxation of central Moscow control. A genuinely far-reaching decentralization of the Soviet system, even if only economic, would pose a mortal danger to Great Russian imperial control, and thus, in the Russian psyche, eventually to the security of the Great Russian people. After all, what does 'only economic' decentralization mean in political terms insofar as the Soviet Union is concerned? Inevitably, it would have to mean a greater degree of autonomy for the non-Russians who would be then in a position to translate greater economic self-determination into growing political self-determination.

To the majority of the Great Russians that is a highly threatening prospect. *Any* significant national self-assertion on the part of the non-Russians also constitutes a challenge to Russian territorial pre-eminence and could possibly even pose a biological threat to Great Russian national survival. Where would genuine decentralization, the acceptance of more democratic norms, the institutionalization of pluralism eventually lead? Where, indeed, could one even draw proper lines between the Great Russians and the others, given the demographic intermingling of the recent decades? There would be escalating tensions, eventually even head-on conflicts in a variety of areas: in some of the Baltic Republics which have been heavily settled by unwelcome Great Russians; in the culturally co-mingled areas of Byelorussia and the Ukraine; certainly on the fringes of the Caucasian and Central Asian Republics.

The dismantling of the overseas British and French Empires did not mean the end of either Britain or France. The dismantling of the territorially contiguous Russian Empire could even threaten Russia herself, given the absence of natural frontiers. The difficulties the French faced in Algeria would be dwarfed on the peripheries of the purely Great Russian lands. Any attempted disentangling along national lines would be messy and bloody, and awareness of that prospect makes almost every Great Russian instinctively wary of tolerating any significant devolution of Moscow's central control. The instinct for survival gives the autocratic, highly-centralized, and imperial Soviet system unusual staying power, neutralizing the kind of inner self-doubt and imperial fatigue that induced the British and French to accede to the dismantling of their Empires.

5

A One-Dimensional World Power of a New Type

Western observers of the Soviet system have been loath to concede that the political centralism of the Soviet system has staying power and that the Russian imperial impulse is vitally inherent to that system. It is certainly more reassuring to believe that both conditions are evanescent: that the system will mellow because of either containment or economic development (or a combination of both), and that its imperial drive will wane with the allegedly inevitable fading of Marxist zeal. The transformation of the system and the waning of its imperial ambitions will thus relieve the West of the obligation of having to face up to the much more difficult dilemma of determining how to historically co-exist in the nuclear age with a powerful and closed political system motivated by vague but highly unsettling global goals.

But what if the Soviet system does not mellow, and what if her military power continues to grow? Rarely, if ever, do Western observers address themselves to the international implications of this issue, except occasionally from the extreme right perspective, cast usually in highly Manichaean and moralistic terms. Yet the issue demands attention and, above all, sober realization that for many decades to come an uneasy historical – but not entirely peaceful – co-existence with a militarily powerful Soviet Union may continue to teeter on the edge of the nuclear abyss.

The point of departure for a realistic appraisal of the relationship must be recognition of the special character of the Soviet system as a world power. The Soviet Union is a world power of a new type in that her might is one-dimensional, with the result that she is essentially incapable of sustaining effective global dominance. The fact of the matter is that the Soviet Union is a global power only in the military dimension, but in no other. She is neither a genuine economic rival to the United States nor – as once was the case – even a source of a globally interesting ideological experiment. This condition imposes a decisive limitation on the Soviet capability to act in a manner traditional to world powers or claimants to the status of world power.

Traditionally, both the dominant world military power, as well as its principal rival, possessed relatively matching political and socio-economic systems, each with the capability for sustained and comprehensive pre-eminence. From the late Middle Ages on, naval power has been the central instrument for exercising global military reach, and the powers exercising it (to the extent that such global reach can be said to have existed in the age of slow communications and weapons of limited lethality) and their principal rivals were – broadly speaking – Portugal and Spain (during much of the sixteenth century); followed by the Netherlands and France (during the seventeenth century); by Britain, and then first France and later Germany (during the eighteenth, nineteenth and part of the twentieth centuries); and finally by the United States and the Soviet Union (during the second half of the twentieth century). In all cases until the most recent, the contest was between powers at a comparable level of development, with the rival quite capable of providing also wider commercial and political leadership as a supplement to its military pre-eminence. In effect, the rival, in displacing the pre-eminent global power, could both provide and sustain equally comprehensive leadership.

The unusual quality of the Soviet global challenge is that the Soviet Union is manifestly unequipped to provide constructive and sustained leadership in the event that she should succeed in unseating the United States as the leading world power. The Soviet Union could not provide global financial leadership. Her economy could not act as the locomotive for global development and technological innovation. Her mass culture has no wider appeal (and her leading intellectuals and artists have been steadily fleeing the Soviet Union). In brief, American displacement could not be followed by a Soviet replacement.

The main reason for this condition is to be found in the Russian Communist system itself. Its bureaucratization, centralization, and dogmatization of decision-making have stifled socio-economic initiative to an unprecedented degree. As a result, the Soviet record in all the non-military dimensions of systemic performance ranges from the average to the mediocre. It still takes literally a *political* decision at the highest level for the Soviet economic system to produce some item that is generally competitive worldwide. Soviet economic performance over the years has required social sacrifice altogether disproportionate to the actual output. Perhaps never before in history have such a gifted people, in control of such abundant resources, laboured so hard for so long to produce relatively so little.

Comparative studies of socio-economic development, as for instance by Professor Cyril Black of Princeton, show that today the Soviet Union occupies in world rankings of social and economic indices a place roughly comparable to that which it held at the beginning of this century. Black's conclusion was that 'In the perspective of fifty years, the comparative ranking of the USSR in composite economic and social indices *per capita* has probably not changed significantly. So far as the rather limited available evidence permits a judgment, the USSR has not overtaken or surpassed any country on a *per capita* basis since 1917 with the possible exception of Italy, and the nineteen or twenty countries that rank higher than Russia today in this regard also ranked higher in 1900 and 1919. The *per capita* gross national product of Italy, which is just below that of the USSR today, was probably somewhat higher fifty years ago'.[1]

In other words, the extraordinary sacrifices, the unprecedented loss of life, the sustained social deprivation that every Soviet citizen has felt have yielded results comparable to those achieved by other societies at much smaller social cost. Moreover, the pace of Soviet economic development after World War II has been only average, despite the fact that initially the Soviet Union had the statistical advantage of recovering from an artifically low plateau generated by wartime devastation. In 1950, the Soviet GNP accounted for about 11% of the global product; three decades later it is still 11%. No wonder that Soviet propagandists now prefer not to recall Khrushchev's challenge of 1960

to surpass the United States in absolute production by 1970 and in relative *per capita* production by 1980.

The picture is just as bleak in the social and cultural dimensions of Soviet life. Recent studies point to a decline in male longevity, to the poor state of Soviet health care, to increasing infant mortality, and to the spread of alcoholism. Intellectual and artistic life has become stifled; social innovation has been shackled by bureaucratic inertia. In brief, the Soviet Union is not a society capable of projecting world-wide an appealing image, a condition essential to the exercise of global leadership.

The main effect of this poor performance is two-fold. First of all, it magnifies the traditional Russian and the doctrinaire Communist suspicions regarding the outside world. That world is perceived as bent on dismantling Moscow's empire and on promoting an anti-Communist counter-revolution. The outside thus continues to look threatening to the USSR, despite the Soviet attainment of the status of a global military super-power. Though the Soviet Union takes great pride in her new military prowess, and has used it to claim co-equal status with the United States, in the Soviet perception of the world the US looms as a giant, with her finances, communications, and mass media enveloping the world with many tentacles. American technology (for instance, currently micro-electronics) keeps on providing the American military establishment with new capabilities which the Soviets take more than seriously. In the Far East, there looms the potential for a Chinese–Japanese constellation, while in the West there is always the magnetic pull on Eastern Europe of a Europe that has not fully resigned itself to an indefinite post-Yalta division.

All of that enhances Soviet paranoia and contributes directly to the second major effect of the one-dimensional character of Soviet global power. It generates an erratic pattern of accommodation and competition with the United States, in which on the one hand the Soviet Union seeks to attain a condominium with Washington and yet on the other fears becoming locked into the role of the junior

partner in effect committed to the maintenance of the global *status quo*. That *status quo*
Moscow rejects for it would not only perpetuate American preponderance but – in
Soviet eyes – it would serve as the
point of departure for policies designed to
promote 'peaceful evolution' of a contained
Soviet Union, i.e. her political subversion.

As a result, the promotion of regional
conflicts, the inhibition of wider and more
genuinely international co-operation, and
opposition to what is called 'world order' are
strategies that the Kremlin finds compatible
with its own one-dimensional global military
power. That military power permits the
USSR to play a wider role in keeping with
the Soviet imperial consciousness, it reduces
the fear that regional conflicts could precipitate a head-on collision with the United
States, and it enables the Soviet Union to use
military leverage to undermine American
pre-eminence in areas hitherto considered as
safe US havens. Particularly important and
effective in this respect is the Soviet ability
(in excess of the American) to deliver
promptly from her large inventories huge
amounts of military equipment to Soviet
clients and would-be friends. In effect,
a policy of gradual undermining of American
global pre-eminence is a key aspect of the
historical self-definition of the Soviet Union
as a global power.

And that leads to a broader conclusion
still: the real danger to the West is not that
the Soviet Union will someday succeed in
imposing a *Pax Sovietica* on the world.
Rather, it is that the Soviet Union, as a
one-dimensional world power committed to
the disruption of the existing arrangements,
because such disruption is essential to the
displacement of the US, will contribute
decisively not to a world revolution in
existing international arrangements but to
greater global anarchy from which all will
suffer.

A Partially Revised Perspective on the Soviet Challenge

Implicit in the foregoing conclusion are some
revisions of the prevailing Western view
regarding the nature of the Soviet threat. In
the immediate post-World War II era, the
West was preoccupied with the fear that vast
Soviet armies would pour westwards, literally
swamping Western Europe. Internal high-
level American discussions – as recent
studies by Professor D. A. Rosenberg show[2] –
focused heavily on the question of how the
US should respond, given her limited but
monopolistic nuclear arsenal. Berlin became
the symbolic lynchpin of Western resolve,
with the blockade providing an American–
Soviet test of wills.

Western, and notably US, anxiety mounted
further after the Communist invasion of
Korea, leading for the first time to comprehensive US nuclear war planning and
to the creation of the SAC (Strategic Air
Command) as the principal means of massive
retaliation. In the late 1950s, Khrushchev's
missile boasting precipitated more intensified
US efforts to offset the allegedly emerging
Soviet advantage, resulting by the early 1960s
in a considerable US strategic superiority.
However, by the late 1970s and early 1980s,
with the US homeland also fully vulnerable
to a Soviet attack, the Soviet Union was
again perceived as being on the verge of
obtaining a politically significant military
edge, with President Reagan even explicitly
proclaiming that the Soviet Union is already
strategically superior to the United States.

In fact, during much of the post-war era
the Soviet challenge to the West – contrary to
prevailing perceptions – was not primarily
military, and even now the much more
important military dimension of the Soviet
threat needs to be seen in a broader political
framework. During the immediate post-war
years, Stalin did engage in some peripheral
probes designed to establish the resilience of
the new geopolitical realities, but his challenge was not primarily a military one.
Indeed, the West greatly over-estimated the
existing Soviet military capabilities, in
apparent ignorance of the large-scale demobi-
lization of the Red Army. To be sure,
the West, and especially the US, disarmed
most hastily, but the West confronted an East
that was socially exhausted and militarily
also readjusting to a peacetime status.

The primary challenge in those years was
in fact ideological–political. The Soviet
Union emerged from World War II with

unprecedented prestige. She was hailed and idealized in the West, and not only by fellow travellers. Many in the West so desperately wanted to believe that the USSR would remain also a post-war ally that they bent over backwards to see the Soviet point of view on the contentious international issues. Moreover, to the populations of war-devastated countries, the Soviet Union projected the image not only of a victor but also of an apparently successful socio-economic system. It was that image that generated the ideological support and invited political imitation. An enormous American effort, above all the Marshall Plan, was required to neutralize that appeal – and it was on this front, and not purely on the military level, that the initial historical confrontation occurred. This is not to deny the importance of NATO, or of the Korean War in the containment of the Soviet Union, but it is to postulate that the political–ideological dimension was then critical in the rivalry.

The next crucial phase in the Soviet challenge occurred during the late 1950s and early 1960s. Khrushchev's policy of premature globalism, based on deliberately falsified claims of missile superiority, collapsed during the Cuban crisis of 1962. Khrushchev's challenge was predicated, however, also on a more generalized historical vision in which economic optimism was the decisive element. The Soviet leader's vulgar 'We will bury you' was not – as it was widely perceived at the time – a physical threat but a historic gauntlet, derived from misplaced confidence that American economic stagnation and Soviet economic dynamism would result in the emergence by the 1970s of the Soviet Union as the world's pre-eminent economic power.

That did not happen. In 1980 the Soviet Union was as behind the United States as it had been a quarter of a century ago. It is also now behind Japan. The vaunted techno-logical race ended with the American flag on the moon. Today the Soviet economy is widely perceived as being, if not in crisis, then at least non-innovative and confronting increasingly difficult trade-offs. Soviet agriculture is clearly an undisputed failure. The Soviet system more generally has lost its ideological appeal and that, too, detracts from Soviet global influence.

By the 1980s, however, Soviet military power had acquired, for the first time, genuine global reach, compensating thus for the lack of systemic appeal. This new condition was clearly gratifying to the Soviet leaders, and anyone who has dealt with them can testify to their pride at the Soviet Union's new status as a global super-power.

But global reach is not the same thing as global grasp. The Soviet challenge today, as already noted, is one-dimensional and therefore it cannot be the point of departure for either comprehensive global leadership, or even for an enduring global partnership with the United States. The ambivalent condition of one-dimensional power induces an outlook on the world which is a combination of possessive defensiveness and disruptive offensiveness.

To be sure, it is quite doubtful whether the Soviet leaders operate on the basis of some broad revolutionary blueprint or that they even have a systematic long-term strategy. In real life, most decision-makers are so compelled to respond to circumstances and to cope with a myriad of specific issues that they simply lack the time and the intellectual inclination to engage in any systematic long-term definition of policy goals. Doubtless the Soviet leaders are no exception. But the Soviet leaders do operate in the context of an orientation in which the retention of what the USSR controls and the disruption of what the US seeks to organize provide lodestars for more specific tactics and strategies.

It is important to recall here that there is a basic difference between a genuinely revolutionary world power and a disruptive world power. Napoleonic France threatened not only the *status quo*; France's socio-economic development was such that France could serve as the centre of a new international order that would have emerged if Napoleon had prevailed over Britain and Russia. In that sense, France was a genuinely revolutionary power. To an ominous degree, both Hitler's Germany and Tojo's Japan had also the revolutionary potential for creating a new international system, in the event that German and Japanese arms had won victory.

In contrast, the Soviet Union is limited to a disruptive, but not a truly revolutionary role. She is confined to that role by the nature of her one-dimensional power and also by the character of nuclear weapons. Nuclear weapons eliminate the possibility of a central war serving as the revolutionary cataclysm. Until the advent of the nuclear age, a world power could be displaced by its rival through a head-on military confrontation, with military victory then translated into premier status by the exercise of the other attributes of national power, such as the economy, finances, science, and national culture. The nuclear age has had the effect of making these other means of exercising world domination also become the more critical instruments for *achieving* such world domination.

Yet it is in these other attributes of power that the Soviet Union is most deficient. Moreover, there is no reason to believe, given the inherent limitations of the Soviet system, that this situation will soon alter to the Soviet Union's benefit. The Soviet Union is thus condemned to seeking global status neither by head-on nuclear collision nor by a peaceful socio-economic competition. The only way open to it is that of attrition and gradual disruption of stable international arrangements so that the US suffers directly and indirectly.

The most effective way of pursuing such a strategy of disruption is to achieve and maintain sufficient military power to deter US reactions and to intimidate the friends of the US, while encouraging trends hostile to American interests in those particular strategically vital areas which possess the greater potential for a dynamic shift in the global political-economic balance. Today, these areas are, above all, the Middle East and Central America.

Accordingly, what happens in these two strategically and geopolitically sensitive zones will determine the longer-range pattern of the American–Soviet relationship and define the Soviet global role. A progressive deterioration of the political stability of the Middle East, combined with the gradual political re-entry of the Soviet Union into a region from which it has been excluded since 1973, could have far-reaching implications for American relations with both Europe and the Far East. The strategic salience of this region is such that any qualitatively important decline in American influence, especially if matched by a corresponding rise in Soviet political presence, is bound to have far-reaching and worldwide strategic consequences for the nature of the American–Soviet global equation.

Similarly, how the United States handles her new dilemmas in Central America, and in the longer run also the US–Mexican relationship, is bound to affect the global balance, and therefore also the Soviet world role. As in the Middle East, it is again not so much a matter of what the Soviet Union may be doing as of how the United States conducts herself, either by commission or by omission. If American policy results in the Americanization of socio-political conflicts to such an extent that the western hemisphere is increasingly turned against the United States, and the American–Mexican problems become consequently so complicated that the United States loses the capacity for helping constructively in the resolution of Mexico's internal problems, the result will be a far-reaching decline in American global standing.

That, in turn, would reinforce the Soviet imperial consciousness and the expansionary impulse, while strengthening further the existing structure of Soviet power and the basic character of the system. Indeed, it is appropriate to recall in this connection that insofar as Russian historical experience is concerned, internal political change of truly significant character has tended to occur only in the wake of external defeats, whereas external successes have tended to reinforce centralism and ideological control. Moreover, as Arnold Horelick has shown in a recent RAND study, an improved Soviet domestic performance also tends to encourage a more assertive external behaviour and the surfacing of greater external ambitions.[3]

In contrast, external setbacks have induced profound reassessments of Russian internal policies and have occasionally produced even significant systemic changes. Thus, despite the internal weakness of the Tsarist regime, its pervasive corruption and its mindless bureaucracy, the basic structure of its power endured for a long time – and collapsed finally only because of the massive military defeat inflicted upon it during the three devastating years of World War I. Moreover, the occasional periods of internal reform that occurred during the 1980s and in the first decade of the twentieth century followed immediately upon external defeats suffered by Russia in the Crimean conflict and in the Russo/Japanese War respectively. The great Russian historian, V. O. Kluchevsky (as cited in Horelick's Paper) notes that 'a Russian war carried to a successful issue has always helped to strengthen the previously compounded order', but 'progress in Russia's political life at home has always been gained at the price of Russia's political misfortune abroad'.

By having become a global military power, the Soviet Union has *de facto* broken through the US policy of geographic containment. At the same time, by expanding her exposure at a time when her own capacities are still very one-dimensional, the Soviet Union is exposing herself to the possibility of over-extension and even eventually to some major external misfortune, because of some protracted military-political misadventure. And in that respect the Soviet strategy of deliberate exploitation of global turbulence could turn out historically to have been a case of playing with fire.

The policy implications that follow from the foregoing analysis can be posited briefly as the following:

- The military dimension of the East–West competition, notably of the US–Soviet rivalry, is negatively of critical importance. Although the rivalry is not likely to be finally resolved by a clash of arms, the West must exercise every effort to make certain that the Soviet Union does not gain a military edge which would enable it to attempt political intimidation.
- Arms-control arrangements should be assessed primarily in terms of their contribution to the maintenance of a stable East–West military balance. That is their central role. Arms control, moreover, should be pursued without historical

illusions regarding the impact of any agreement on the character of the Soviet system and its relationship with the West, for the long-term political rivalry will not be ended even by a comprehensive arms-control arrangement.
- A major Soviet external misfortune is likely to have the most immediate impact on Eastern Europe. This region is manifestly restless and resentful of Soviet control. Any sign of Soviet weakness, any prolonged and debilitating Soviet foreign entanglement will be exploited to break the weakest link in the Soviet imperial chain. Moreover, it is a region that is most susceptible to Western ideas and culturally attracted by Western Europe. It offers, therefore, a topical focus for Western policies designed to dilute the Soviet imperial impulse.
- Western, and especially American, efforts to maintain and promote regional stability, notably in such vital areas as Central America and the Middle East, are going to be decisive in determining whether Soviet global influence expands, to the detriment of international stability. American passivity in the Middle East and US over-engagement in Central America are the most immediate geo-political dangers.
- The positive task of shaping a wider international system that genuinely embraces the newly emancipated Third World, and thus replaces the narrower European world order that collapsed in the course of World War II, will have to be pursued for quite some time to come without constructive Soviet involvement. The Soviet Union – too strong not to be a rival, yet feeling herself too weak to be a partner – cannot be counted upon to become a true participant in the constructive global process since her systemic interests are diametrically opposed to the preservation of the *status quo* in a world which the Soviet Union can disrupt but not dominate.
- Historical co-existence with the Soviet Union will remain dominated by the largely negative task of avoiding a nuclear catastrophe. It will be Western acts, of commission or omission, that will ulti-

mately determine whether that historical co-existence – a co-existence that at best for a long time to come will be pre-cariously peaceful – will eventually produce a more harmonious relationship or deteriorate into wider global anarchy.

NOTES

[1] Cyril E. Black, 'Soviet Society: A Comparative View', in A. Kassoff, *Prospects for Soviet Society* (London: Pall Mall Press, 1968), pp. 42–3.

[2] David Alan Rosenberg, 'The Origins of Overkill: Nuclear Weapons and American Strategy, 1945–1960', *International Security*, Spring 1983, pp. 3–71.

[3] Arnold L. Horelick, 'External Implications of Soviet Internal Development', prepared for the RAND–SWP Conference, 24–27 June 1983 (Santa Monica, Ca: RAND Corporation, 1983).

Andropov's Burden: Socialist Stagnation and Communist Encirclement

PROFESSOR SEWERYN BIALER AND PROFESSOR JOAN AFFERICA

The unrelenting drive of Soviet leaders to sustain and advance Soviet power in the global arena during this decade will encounter formidable obstacles both internally and externally. Whether Soviet power will grow, both in absolute terms and in relation to that of her principal Western adversary, will depend of course on the complex interaction of Soviet developments with circumstances beyond Soviet control, not the least of them being the changing international environment and the capacity of the United States to mobilize, expand and utilize effectively her own vast resources. The growth of Soviet power will also depend, however, on how successfully the new leadership in Moscow responds to the more predictable, well-defined and immediate problems under its direct authority.

Soviet power cannot grow unless Soviet leaders arrest the profoundly adverse trends in their domestic, economic, social and political environment; unless they manage despite these trends to sustain their military build-up; unless they contain and minimize the repercussion of actual and potential disaffection within their 'internal' and 'external' empires; unless they stabilize their periodically explosive relations with the People's Republic of China; unless they evolve a coherent, imaginative and active foreign policy to replace the failed detente with the US. Moreover, all these dilemmas must be confronted at a highly vulnerable time, when not only has a new leader to consolidate his authority, but all governing heirarchies must undergo the far-reaching replacement of leading elites within a relatively brief time.

Socialist Stagnation

The profound economic, social and political problems bequeathed by Brezhnev to Andropov are, in the final analysis, systemic and represent the cumulative effects of inherent weakness in basic Soviet structures. The most immediate problems are economic in nature. They will inevitably bear heavily on society and policy. Without decisive action by the leadership, they promise to become even more acute as the 1980s progress. If they are not in my view as catastrophic as some analysts in Washington would have us believe, they are far from being as routine as Soviet leaders would have us believe. For many decades the political 'superstructure' has shaped the socio-economic 'base' in the Soviet Union. Now the time has come for the 'base' to take its revenge on the 'superstructure'.

Soviet economic problems are well-known to specialists. Some have their sources in the economy's maturity, some are directly connected to the archaic and cumbersome economic system, some are the consequence of specific policies and their inertial continuation, some are exogenous. The familiar list includes a planning system geared to one indicator, size of output, in which prices, costs and profits provide no true measure of performance on the micro- or macro-level, and managerial and incentive systems that reward primarily quantity not quality of production. It includes: the scarcity of investment capital; the limits on ability to earn hard currency for technological imports; unfavourable demographic trends that bring fewer newcomers annually to the labour force; the inability of agriculture to keep pace with population growth; the lack of a satisfactory infrastructure; the exhaustion of cheap abundant raw materials; the slow and uneven growth of energy resources; and the backwardness of the machine-building industry. Given all these problems, it is projected

13

that the Soviet gross national product will grow in this decade at the low rate of 2–3% annually, according to optimistic estimates. Even more significant is the low quality of both the inputs and outputs of that growth.

The essence of the matter for Soviet leaders is not that there are now more economic problems than at many other troubled times in the past, but that these problems are qualitatively different today in two important respects. First, the economic problems of today are those associated with stagnation; the economic problems of yesterday were those associated with growth. Second, closed now to Soviet leaders is the sole means that the system used to provide to combat problems – the crash mobilization of people, capital and resources. What is needed in place of *extensive* sources of growth are *intensive* sources – high technology, high quality, and high labour productivity. To mobilize these new sources of growth would require major reforms. The alternative is a 'muddling down' of economic performance.

Economic stagnation fosters social instability, not an uncommon condition in Soviet historical experience. Until now, challenges to social stability have been successfully resolved in every period of Soviet development. Stalin dealt with the threat from the countryside in a radical and brutal way by crushing the independent peasantry and establishing a coercive rural system that effectively ended opposition. For his successors, the main potential threat to social stability came from the 'intelligentsia' and youth and from emerging open dissent. Soviet leaders have successfully isolated the dissenters who constitute domestically an insignificant force. The new 'intelligentsia' remains clearly within the system – career-orientated and materialistic – while the youth, unlike that of any other industrial country, has not made its 'revolution'.

In the 1980s the potential danger to social stability may come primarily from a more critical stratum, the industrial workers. The factors which have assured labour peace will be considerably weakened in this decade. The repressive police state will most probably become even stronger and more active. Yet it is difficult to predict how urban workers will react to stagnation or decline in their standard of living which has been steadily rising in the last two decades. Their plight would be further exacerbated by any serious industrial reform which would bring them austerity while at the same time exacting improved performance. Finally, the inter-generational mobility of workers into middle and professional classes is declining and will continue to decline owing to competition from the quite large middle class, the stagnation or even decrease of educational expenditures, and the low level of economic growth.

Another potential source of social instability emanates from the non-Russian nations of the Federation. Here too the many factors which have assured social peace will be considerably weakened in the 1980s as the economic base erodes. The nationality problem will not, however, constitute a main source of social instability in this decade in my view, even if in the long run it remains potentially the most resistant to enduring resolution and the most destructive to the existing system.

Economic and social problems will in all likelihood intensify already serious political problems generated by the legacy of political Stalinism and the complex succession process. The new leadership must contend with age-old (Russian and Soviet) problems of social discipline and bureaucratic inertia and corruption. In recent years social discipline has deteriorated to a remarkable extent, even by Soviet standards. One finds surging absenteeism, unacceptably high worker turnover, substandard quality of production, rampant alcoholism, and outright theft that amounts to a secondary redistribution of national income. Some Soviet sociologists and economists wonder whether official attempts to stimulate a greater sense of responsibility and improved work habits can at all impress the present generation of workers.

The bureaucratic stagnation of recent years had no close parallel in the past Soviet history except perhaps the last years of Stalin's rule. The already cumbersome process of decision-making became even more intractable during Brezhnev's decline. Bureaucratic routine prevailed at every level. At the centre, crucial decisions (regarding energy supplies, for example) were delayed too long. Other costly policies (agricultural investment, for example) were pursued without alteration, although they yielded few of the expected results. The stability of cadres was higher than at any previous period as the aging and aged elite barred the path upwards to an entire layer of middle-aged officials in middle positions. Meanwhile, clientalism, patronage and corruption on a vast scale pervaded the entire Party–State apparatus from Moscow to the smallest district.

Another potential source of political instability lies in relations among the various elites and bureaucracies. Here too the factors which have assured political peace will be considerably weakened with sagging economic growth. Inevitable scarcities and austerity will undermine the enduring equilibrium of the Brezhnev years as competition over growth resources divides spokesmen for the military and civilian sectors, for agriculture and industry, and for the territories of European Russia, Ukraine, Siberia and Central Asia.

Not least of the political problems of the 1980s will follow decisions on economic reform. So far the systemic crisis facing Soviet leaders today is one of effectiveness, not survival. Only when actual survival is at issue will Soviet leaders find acceptable the high political cost of radical reform. Their dilemma is, however, that a high political price will be exacted from each of the principal choices with regard to the economy: radical reform; rejection of radical reform; and even an attempt to introduce a consistent series of limited reforms within the existing economic system. Reforms would require a politically dangerous withdrawal of subsidies from basic commodities. They would engender strong opposition from middle-rank officials and managers who have learned to live with the existing system and to take advantage of it. The political repercussions of limited reform, not to speak of radical reform, are perhaps the key domestic political dilemma of the 1980s.

Andropov's Baptism
What can one learn of Andropov's approach to this staggering constellation of problems

during his period as General Secretary? Most striking is the now flagging campaign that Andropov launched soon after taking office. It pursued three directions, each calculated to demonstrate that the Soviet Union is 'moving again', even if no substantial changes were taking place. The first direction was greater candour in relations between leadership and population concerning the country's problems. The second direction sought to convince the public that the new leader was hard at work, on top of his job, and capable of resolving the difficulties inherited from his predecessor. The third and most impressive direction sought to enforce greater discipline in the workplace and society at large as well as to reduce blatant corruption.

Even more important were the deeper currents of activity that suggested preparations for change. These currents affected personnel, institutional functions, and ideological orientation. Andropov's appointments indicated several main objectives: to strengthen the central party and state apparatus in Moscow; to move loyalists into key positions; to initiate the renovation of the highest ranks; and to forestall a repetition of his own success story by placing professional policemen and not political leaders in control of the coercive apparatus.

Andropov's reapportionment of functions within the party-state machine indicated these main objectives: to limit drastically the role of the central party bureaucracy in day-to-day supervision of government economic agencies and to concentrate their energies on the preparation of strategic economic decisions; to increase control over state agencies by the Presidium of the Council of Ministers and by strategic placement in the state apparatus of party and KGB personnel; and to diminish the weight of the professional military in military-economic decision-making by ensuring the independence of the staff of the Supreme Defence Council, hitherto under direct military supervision.

Andropov's ideological adjustments prepared justifications for organizational-administrative and economic changes. The two most important new formulae concerned 'the potential for growth in socialist society' and 'contradictions in the development of mature socialist societies'. The former alleged socialist superiority over capitalism a 'potential' which will not be realized unless wisely exploited by the directors of socialist society and vigorously pursued by the workers. The second argued that constant contradictions between the potential of Soviet development and the actual growth and development of the means of production, especially with regard to new technology, can only be overcome by continuous adjustment and reform of economic mechanisms and organization so as to take full advantage of the unrealized potential inherent in the socialist organization of labour.

Yet there was no sign that Andropov intended a radical reform of the economic system. The reforms initiated or signalled were well within the bounds of the existing system. Perhaps the most far-reaching may yet occur in agriculture where the 'contract brigade' tested in Georgia will in all probability be adopted throughout the USSR this autumn (1983). Conversations with Soviet officials confirm that there are no plans for radical decentralizing reforms that even approach the Hungarian model which is not considered relevant to Soviet conditions.

One should not easily dismiss, however, the modest programme of reform described in the speeches by Andropov and his associates and discussed in professional journals. Economic performance can be improved marginally, even without radical reform, at least in the first years because the economic system and political-economic relations within it display so much slack, irrationality, and unused potential that a determined leadership can mobilize in-system reserves of growth to considerable effect. Yet in the long run, limited reforms suffer from three inherent defects. First, rather than providing the stimulus to change the system, they are absorbed by it. Second, they are being introduced at a time when the economy lacks those very reserves that would assure their greater effectiveness. Third, their manner of introduction – the creation of hot-house conditions limited to given regions or branches of the economy – exaggerate their beneficial impact and cannot be replicated throughout the entire economy.

If the succession process is not yet complete, it is true that Andropov did consolidate his position much faster than either of his two predecessors. The expectations of the political elite and the evidence of his professional experience suggested, however, that he had no opportunity to undertake his principal measures for coping with the lack of social discipline, bureaucratic inertia, and economic reform.

Domestic Problems and Soviet Power
It remains to consider how Soviet domestic problems will affect the growth of Soviet power in this decade. Very probably, both economic and military power will advance at lower rates than during Brezhnev's first decade. The drop in an annual growth rate to about 2.5% will vastly complicate decisions concerning the level and distribution of funds for military growth. The leadership's dilemma is not guns versus butter. It is the choice between growth of current direct expenditures on arms and upkeep of military forces versus growth of large-scale investment in military-industrial plants to support future military growth. To maintain both at 1970s levels is not possible economically and politically. Andropov, it would appear, leaned towards preservation of military investment growth even if growth of direct military expenditures must be curtailed. Any future choice will obviously depend on the Soviet evaluation of the East–West military balance.

Major impediments to sustained, high-quality military development abound. If they do not originate on the demand side, from cuts in military spending, they may on the supply side, from the inability of the economy to deliver the necessary resources. The continued separation of military and civilian sectors also militates against technologically-advanced military growth. The technological base of the economy is too small and narrow to support large-scale military progress at reasonable cost. No longer open to Soviet leaders is the traditional route to success in the military area – concentration on very few priorities regardless of cost. The number of priorities is growing, the strength of competing claimants is increasing, and the width of the technological gap between military and

16

civilian sectors makes very difficult the transfer of resources. Finally, the quality of the Soviet Armed Forces may be seriously impaired by the combined effect of long-neglected health services, low educational levels, and a shift in the ethnic mix of Soviet recruits toward non-Slavic minorities. Political tensions may result from the association of Slavic officer and non-Slavic draftee, while the Armed Forces in general may become less reliable as a major socializing agency in the Party–State.

This assessment should not persuade us that the Soviet leaders will fail to match American efforts in a continuing or accelerating arms race. It does however demonstrate that the economic, social and political costs of the arms race to the Soviet Union will be much higher than in the past. It suggests that Soviet leaders may prove more responsive to serious proposals on decelerating the pace of arms production. For now and for the immediate future, Soviet leaders are clearly preoccupied with major domestic problems. This situation reinforces the basic mode of retrenchment characteristic of Soviet foreign policy in recent years. The retrenchment, however, does not depend on internal sources alone. It reflects as well the failure as yet to conceive an alternative to the coherent foreign policy structured around detente with the United States, the need to perpetuate detente with Western Europe, the reluctance to test Reagan's hard line, and, not the least, the consequences of 'communist encirclement'.

Communist Encirclement
At Stalin's death in 1953, his successors inherited the concept of the dread 'capitalist encirclement' which constituted the well-spring of Soviet military and foreign policy. To the degree that fear of the consequences of capitalist encirclement has receded with the growth of Soviet power in subsequent decades, another set of problems, which may be termed 'Communist encirclement', has become more central in policy formulation.

This second encirclement may be envisaged as four concentric arcs at different spatial and political distances from vital Soviet interest, each of which generates over time problems of varying intensity and danger. The first arc, nearest to the centre both physically and politically, encompasses the Soviet 'internal empire', the belt of non-Russian nations dominating the periphery of the USSR. The second arc includes the Soviet 'external empire', the phalanx of East European nations which owe their existence and survival as Communist states to Soviet force, threatened and actual. (Cuba and Vietnam should, in my view, be regarded as separate cases.) The third arc, farther yet from the centre, holds the People's Republic of China, the colossus risen from an authentic revolution to provide a long-range threat on the Soviet Eastern border. The fourth arc, farthest from the centre, collects those remains of a once cohesive international movement dominated from Moscow, the many Communist parties which now exhibit a troublesome autonomy. This Paper will focus on the second and third arcs.

The Second Arc: The Eastern European Empire
Historically, one cardinal axiom governs the Soviet approach to her Eastern European empire: while tactical evaluations and practical policies vary, the strategic-political orientation remains basically unchanged. Soviet leaders from Stalin to Andropov have not faltered in their determination to preserve and dominate the 'external empire'. It is a total commitment that differs little from total commitment to the integrity of the 'internal empire'.

Security interests alone cannot explain the depth of Soviet determination to maintain the Eastern European Empire regardless of cost. Soviet leaders of course regard as imperative the retention of this extensive buffer zone between the USSR and Western Europe and the ability to mobilize the military and economic potential of Warsaw Pact members as a counter-balance to NATO. But these security considerations do not require the high level of Soviet control over social and political developments in Eastern European countries. If security interests do not account for the depth of commitment, neither does the utility of Eastern Europe in advancing Soviet global ambitions – for example, the dispatch of Eastern European security and military forces to the Third World.

The key explanation goes beyond pragmatism and instrumentality to the very normative and ideological foundations of Great Russian and Communist control within the imperial power itself. Victory in World War II was the key to legitimizing Soviet rule at home, and control over Eastern Europe was the major spoil of war. Determination to retain the Eastern European empire creates a fundamental bond between the Soviet government and its Great Russian and other Slavic populations. It constitutes a key justification for the pre-eminent role of the political leadership and Party elite within the complex elite structure. To say it simply, preservation of the Eastern European Empire remains one of the basic foundations that legitimizes Soviet rule of the country and the Party's dominance within the elite.

Loss of control over Eastern Europe, not to mention the disintegration of the 'external empire', moreover, could and would probably strengthen centrifugal tendencies within the 'internal empire'. Therefore, the key question concerning Soviet policy in this area is not whether, when and how the Soviet Union will relinquish her hold but what means she will choose to preserve her domination and how successful she is likely to be.

Soviet policies and experience in Eastern Europe after 1953 permit us to generalize about the nature and extent of Soviet controls over society, polity and economy in the area. The position of the Soviet Union has been intransigent with regard to maintaining the monopoly of power by Communist Parties, the highly monolithic and orthodox character of these Parties, and their organization in accordance with the Leninist principles. The Soviet Union has insisted that the security and armed forces of the satellite nations be subordinated to a dual system of native Party supervision and direct control by the Soviet security and military command. They have unswervingly placed communications media under strict Party control and have monitored with special care breaches in censorship and criticism of the Soviet Union. They have not permitted any autonomous organizations of a political character to exist, let alone challenge, the Party's monopoly.

In the post-Stalin decades, Soviet controls have been relaxed in some areas, particularly in regard to economic organization and reform. The Soviet Union has reluctantly tolerated if not encouraged economic experimentation, leaving initiatives in this area to native Party leaders. They have limited the extent to which they have attempted to harness satellite economies to the service of Soviet goals. Economic integration of Eastern European economies with the Soviet economy is not far advanced. The Soviet Union has also tolerated relaxation of restraints on private if not political freedoms, again on the decisions of local Party leaders. And, until the Polish events of this decade, direct daily supervision of satellite party activities was less stringent than under Stalin.

With regard to foreign policy, the satellites enjoyed only marginal opportunities for initiative and freedom of manoeuvre. The relative independence of Romanian foreign policy was rather exceptional and derived from the strategic marginality of Romania to the Soviet Union, from compensating orthodoxy of the Romanian internal regime, and, simply, from the 'guts' of Romania's 'supreme leader', Ceausescu.

The extent and flexibility of Soviet controls relate directly not only to given issues but also to given countries. Most central here is the question of actual or potential opposition to Soviet *diktat*. The Hungarian system differs from the Czechoslovak today because of willingness to fight Soviet tanks. Poland's historical pugnacity surely influenced Soviet hesitation to terminate dual power and the choice of an internal solution over invasion. It will surely affect Soviet toleration of any relatively liberal Polish 'road to socialism' that might emerge from the present stalemate. Two other variables also affect Soviet control: the unity of satellite leaders and the authority of the chiefs in resisting Soviet pressure (witness the cases of Gomulka in 1956 and Ceausescu today); and the strategic importance of the satellite to the USSR both militarily and politically (witness the GDR).

Surveying the general situation in Eastern Europe today, after three decades of Soviet

18

domination, one must conclude that the Soviet 'external empire' has peaked; its decline has commenced. However Soviet leaders themselves evaluate the trends, evidence of decline may be found in areas economic, military, political and ideological.

The Economic Perspective

From the economic point of view, most Western and many Soviet economists concur that, with regard to direct exploitation, Eastern European countries have become a burden for the Soviet Union. (Of course, in a broader sense, by dictating the parameters of the economic systems in Eastern Europe, the Soviet Union has been and is exploiting Eastern Europe.) Not only would the Soviet Union have received higher prices in world markets for raw materials now sold to satellites highly dependent on them for economic development, they would also have earned the hard currency to purchase highly essential advanced technology. At present the Soviet Union routinely accepts from Eastern Europe, in exchange for its raw materials, inferior goods unsuitable for sale in world markets, all the more so during periods of depression. Furthermore, it would appear that Eastern European countries do not bear their proportional share of military expenditures as members of the Warsaw Pact.

Reliability as Allies

From the military point of view, not only is the potential contribution of Eastern European countries to Soviet conventional war capabilities very limited; it is probably by now a minus factor. In case of war, the Soviet Union could probably rely only on select Eastern European elite units to supplement Soviet forces. In case of protracted war, the uncertain motivation and morale of the draft army and civilian population could well necessitate deployment in the potentially unreliable Eastern European zone of far more Soviet troops than Eastern Europe provides for the front line. This assessment does not hold regarding the potential value of deploying select Eastern European military units in third-world countries to enhance Soviet influence and expansion, as the Cuban example shows.

Politics and Ideology

From the political point of view, the 'external empire' has probably become an embarrassment to the Soviet Union and a handicap in her pursuit of foreign political objectives. Soviet domination of Eastern Europe seriously inhibits renewal of the detente process with the United States. It cements the defensive military and political alliance of Western Europeans who daily witness its military-colonial dimension. It stands as the most significant obstacle to a cohesive international Communist movement under Soviet direction and a decisive reason for the spread of Euro-communism. The United States cannot accept detente with a power which every decade or so intervenes dramatically in Eastern Europe. As Europeans, America's NATO Allies are especially sensitive to this blatant expression of Soviet imperial appetites. Furthermore, there is little difference between the European right and left in condemning Communist repressive measures which are directed not only against dissidents and intellectuals but against workers and free trade unions. Indeed the enduring Soviet detente with Western Europe will lapse only on the day Soviet troops invade an Eastern European country.

From the ideological point of view, Eastern European countries represent far less a showcase for Soviet ideology and the Soviet model of 'socialism' than a prime example of their failure. For decades Soviet leaders and ideologues have accounted for political repression, intellectual intolerance, economic backwardness and social inequality in their own country by reference to the isolation of Russia's Revolution in conditions of Tsarist under-development and capitalist encirclement, by reference, that is, to a state of perpetual emergency. Yet these basic features of Soviet power have not essentially altered despite the added security of westward expansion. And now they characterize countries which enjoyed, prior to the Soviet takeover, in some cases more democratic traditions, in other cases higher levels of industrialization.

The deepest source of the inevitable and irreversible decline of the Eastern European Empire is common to almost all component states. They lack legitimacy. Soviet and satellite leaders hoped and expected that the governments imposed on the area in 1944–8 by Soviet force behind narrow native Communist bridgeheads would, over time, mute if not erase the popular memory of their violent origins. Almost forty years later, these governments have failed to do so.

The legitimacy of regimes spawned by revolution, whether 'authentic' or 'inauthentic', may derive from popular support expressed in traditional or legal forms, from elite support reflecting the cohesion and interlocking strength of key power centres, and from performance. Legitimacy grounded in popular support did not obtain because patent Soviet controls and interventionism denied native governments their traditional source, nationalism, and their legal source, free elections at all levels. Legitimacy grounded in elite support did obtain under ordinary circumstances, but the cohesiveness of the power structure and the reliability of support from other power centres (the security and armed forces, the communications networks, the official trade unions, etc.) weakened in times of crisis (1953, 1956, 1968, 1980–81). This form of legitimacy ultimately depends less on internal structures than on external coercion. It is only through performance that certain Eastern European Governments (East Germany and Hungary) gained a limited and grudging acceptance among the population. Yet legitimacy grounded in performance is the most fragile and least dependable form of all.

The real test of a regime's legitimacy occurs at times of crisis when rulers attempt to mobilize reserves of support. The paucity of such reserves in Eastern Europe reveals that satellite governments rest finally on Soviet power and determination to sustain them and on popular fears of the danger from the East. Especially disquieting for Soviet leaders is the report of both research and observation: the younger generations of East European countries exhibit an equal if not higher level of dissatisfaction with Communist regimes than do older generations

The dilemma of native power elites is insoluble. On the one hand they will gain strong popular support only by advocating the anti-Soviet cause of national independence with the accompanying risks of Soviet military intervention. On the other hand they will retain power only by ensuring unqualified Soviet support and, if need be, Soviet military intervention. Communism was victorious in the twentieth century primarily because the regimes which were forged in 'authentic' Communist revolutions identified themselves with national interests, nationalism and independence. It is the crucial flaw of Communist regimes in Soviet-controlled Eastern Europe that they cannot do so.

Yet other circumstances work to thwart acceptance of these regimes as legitimate. First, in contrast to experience in the Soviet Union, Eastern Europe has failed to produce professional classes that identify more than superficially with the regime. If persons with higher education in the Soviet Union do not exhibit the hallmark of an 'intelligentsia,' that is, a critical political attitude, Eastern Europe boasts a genuine intelligentsia, created under Communist rule, that is potentially or actually hostile to Communist leadership. Second, Eastern Europe remains immune to Soviet Russian cultural influence. The contempt for Soviet Russian culture, the shallow acceptance of dogmatic Marxism–Leninism even in the Party, the deep attachment to religion and church, the affinity for Western values and traditions – all combine to reduce the Communist leadership to an alien and shallow stratum markedly different in stability and effectiveness from its counterpart in the Soviet Union. Third, virtually unique among historical empires, the Soviet dominator surpasses the dominated in only one attribute: absolute military power. It lags behind in standard of living, economic development, educational levels, and cultural richness.

However, this single superiority, absolute military power, has so far sufficed and in all likelihood will continue to suffice as the means to forestall defection, not to say disintegration. After all, historically, empires do not disintegrate when the metropolitan power is at the peak of military strength. If apocalypse does not threaten the Eastern European Empire in the next decade, serious instability surely does.

The Prospect for Destabilization in Eastern Europe

In the 1980s, legitimacy in performance may be wrecked on the shoals of economic distress. Just because the key basis of the legitimacy of East European regimes rests with economic performance, there has emerged a pronounced pattern according to which economic discontent translates into social instability and political unrest. Virtually the same serious economic problems confront Soviet and Eastern European leaders. Much-needed improvements in economic performance for both will depend essentially on a successful shift from extensive to intensive sources of growth. But it is in Eastern Europe that the difficulties are more profound economically, more dangerous politically, and more unpredictable in their likely outcome. Let us sketch some eight circumstances that aggravate the situation for East Europeans and herald an even greater general destablization there in this decade than in the USSR.

- First, because Eastern European economies have already utilized intensive sources of growth to a much greater extent than the Soviet Union, there exist fewer reserves for correcting the irrational organization of production, incentives, and diffusion of high technology than in the Soviet Union. To counter the decline in growth over recent years and the prospects of further decline in the mid and late 1980s will require a degree of improvement in intensive methods that only Hungary has achieved.
- Second, if the direct and indirect military burden of Eastern Europe falls far below the Soviet contribution, both in absolute terms and in share of GNP, it has tended to rise at approximately the same rate. For the Eastern European economies, which are so much smaller and more developed than that of the Soviet Union, the ratio of growth of military expenditures is even more burdensome than in the Soviet Union. The general international situation scarcely promises relief.
- Third, it is highly likely that economic difficulties will force the Soviet Union to reduce or eliminate subsidies which take the form of selling energy and other raw materials below world prices and of buying inferior goods that would not find other markets. Moreover, forced Eastern European investments in Soviet development may soon exceed Soviet credits to Eastern Europe.
- Fourth, even more pressed than the Soviet Union to earn hard currency in Western and Third-world markets for technological imports, the East Europeans will find it increasingly difficult to compete with Western goods in Third-world markets and to enter Western markets where near-term recovery will proceed mainly from utilizing existing industrial capacity. An inevitable curtailment of technological imports will in all likelihood be accompanied by continued imports of grain and foodstuffs from the West, thus exacerbating an already unfavourable balance of trade.
- Fifth, all Eastern European countries contend with problems of servicing foreign debts which are sizeable and, in the case of Poland, catastrophic. At a time when their ability to earn foreign exchange is eroding, they must nevertheless press for export production that will further constrict domestic consumption. Moreover, after the experience of the early 1980s, they can scarcely expect generosity from the international banking community.
- Sixth, Poland's insolvency sorely disturbs regional economic development. Not only has Poland failed to deliver goods and credit repayments to her Eastern neighbours, but the latter must commit substantial resources to alleviate Poland's difficulties. Even Polish sources confess that the next two or three years will bring no significant change.
- Seventh, given the present situation, all Eastern European countries have undertaken (and will have to sustain well into the decade) austerity programmes that strike the working class and undermine efforts to raise labour productivity.
- Eighth, in this decade Eastern European leaders will find it difficult to alleviate their economic difficulties by accelerating the implementation of existing reforms or initiating new ones. The managerial reform

in East Germany as well as the market-orientated reform in Hungary have probably exceeded the point of greatest effectiveness. To achieve better results, the Hungarian leaders would have to violate the political taboo of every Communist government, job security for the working class. Other satellite countries would find it economically difficult and politically dangerous even to attempt the Hungarian type of reform for just the same reasons as the Soviet Union, with the additional difficulties imposed by an unfavourable international market and credit situation.

That the commonly-shared economic dilemmas of the 1980s will in all probability have a greater destabilizing impact on the Eastern European society and polity than on the Soviet goes beyond those aggravating factors in the 'external empire'. The expectations of Eastern European populations far exceed those of the Soviet working class, and the gap between what is and what should be will certainly intensify their dissatisfaction. Moreover, should the austerity programmes place disproportionately high burdens on Eastern European working classes, as seems probable, the disparity in living standards among diverse groups will reinforce the sense of injustice which was the single most important impulse in the Polish eruption of 1980. Paradoxically, it may well be that this cause of discontent will erupt more dramatically in Hungary where the differentiation of personal income and standard of living is more visible if not much greater than in neighbouring Eastern states. Dissatisfaction of the Eastern European working classes will also feed on the consequences of reduced educational expenditures in a time of budgetary constraints. Education has been the most important avenue of intergenerational mobility and a major guarantor of relative stability.

Do Soviet leaders apprehend the systemic nature of crisis in Eastern Europe with its promise of imperial decline? Only the prolonged and unsolved Polish crisis began to drive home to the Soviet political elite and their advisers the profound dangers. The Polish case at once demonstrates the dire disruptive potential of these complex underlying problems common to all Eastern Europe and the unswerving Soviet determination to secure its dominion whatever the cost. In addition, the Polish case exhibits elements unique in Eastern European experience. For leaders as well as analysts the key question is whether the Polish case will remain unique or whether it forebodes the fate of the 'external empire'.

The Case of Poland

Unique was the role of the Polish working class, major groups of which, in contrast to Poland and Hungary in 1956 and Czechoslovakia in1968, initiated, sustained, participated, and provided leaders for the organized defence of their rights. Unique too was the rapid merger of the workers' movement with a majority of the intelligentsia and later with part of the peasantry – in effect the expression of a unified Polish nation against Communism. And unique was the dual power which endured about a year and a half. Security and elite military forces neither disintegrated nor betrayed the formal government in Poland as they did in Russia's revolutionary year of 1917. If in both historic situations the minority emerged victorious over the majority, Poland's fate, unlike Russia's, was decided by overwhelming external force.

Unique were the depth and coherence of the proposed economic and political socialist alternative to orthodox Communism. Unique was the extent of disintegration in the Party and State apparatus which ceased only with the forced installation of a military-security government. And even after the imposition of martial law and the crushing of Solidarity, unique was the persistence of non-violent active resistance by the Polish nation to military rule and Soviet Communism. Finally, unique was the elimination for all intents and purposes of Poland's military contribution to the Warsaw Pact, an alarming turn which obliges the Soviet Union to redesign contingency plans for a war in Europe.

The installation of a military-security government represented for Polish Communists and their Soviet mentors is an act of desperation, not of long-range planning. It achieved the purpose of avoiding the more costly and unpredictable alternative, direct Soviet armed intervention. But from the Soviet perspective, nothing is solved. The Pope's visit in June 1983 exposed to the world the vast gulf between a hybrid government without subjects and a disaffected population without influence. Solidarity was defeated as an organization and representative of dual power, but the 'other' power, the Catholic Church, not only survived the experience but emerged stronger in authority and more radical in aspirations. At the same time the Communist establishment has been fractured dangerously along two axes: the Party versus the military; and the moderates versus the hardliners. From its very inception, military rule with the attendant military infiltration of the weakened party apparatus at all levels appears as the only alternative to greater chaos.

Tsarist and Soviet tradition firmly upholds the principle and practice of civilian and Party ascendancy over the military. Today, Soviet leaders are paralyzed on the one hand by fear of prolonging a military regime in Poland and the fear of abolishing it in favour of civilian Party rule on the other. To avert a popular explosion, to prevent a recrudescence of Solidarity, to ensure a minimum of political stability in Poland – these are the immediate Soviet objectives. Only a military-security government would appear capable of achieving them.

Neither Polish citizens, Polish Communists, nor Soviet leaders can find comfort in prospects for the future. A violent outbreak remains possible, with its inevitable armed response from the East. Should this not occur, there is excluded for the next three to five years the restoration of an orthodox Communist regime, whether in civilian or military garb, for it could provoke civil war. Excluded also is the restoration of a competing political organization modelled after Solidarity by workers and their allies, for it would surely provoke Soviet invasion.

The sole feasible short-term solution would involve a political compromise mediated by the Church which would gradually reorganize the Communist regime and return its overall political monopoly and at the same time permit the constitution of officially-sanctioned trade unions which on the micro-level would realize certain of the demands of the defunct Solidarity. The restored regime would recognize the Church's place in Poland's spiritual and, to some extent, secular life. It would redirect its economic planning to modest satisfaction of the consumer. A number of years will be required to stabilize the economic and political situation, to achieve pre-Solidarity levels of production, and to commence planning for major change in the Polish economic system. It seems safe to predict that the level of political, social and economic stability in Poland will remain low through the 1980s and that changes in policies and structures will be introduced very gradually and with only partial effect.

The Challenge for Soviet Policy

The new Soviet leadership clearly appreciates the potential for serious instability in Eastern Europe during the remainder of this decade. It has yet to formulate any realistic long- or even intermediate-term plan for ensuring and strengthening the viability of the Eastern European holdings. The main lines of Soviet policy toward Eastern Europe are now taking shape. They proceed from a broad analysis that draws conclusions not only from the perceived lessons of Poland but places these conclusions in the larger context of Soviet economic difficulties and the state of relations with the West.

Soviet leaders are now persuaded that they committed a number of mistakes in Poland. Impressed in the early and mid-1970s by the satellite drive to build a 'second industrial Poland', fueled largely by Western credits, the Soviet Union failed to press for alterations in goals and means when, after 1976, the bloody unrest in Gdansk, Gierek's manifest difficulties, and the well-founded criticism by some Polish and most Western economists exposed the chaos of overambitious and poorly-executed plans. Surprised by the extent of the labour unrest in the summer of 1980, the Soviet Union failed to intervene decisively in internal Polish Party matters or in relations between the Party and Solidarity. The Polish case illustrates how independent was the native Communist leadership in

Eastern Europe with regard to domestic and especially economic questions, how slack was Soviet monitoring of internal developments, and how unsatisfactory was the initial Soviet response to the Polish turbulence.

Soviet economic difficulties in this decade, which have been exacerbated by the state of the international money and commodity markets, seriously impair the Soviet ability to bear the burden of substantial subsidies to Eastern Europe (as well as Cuba and Vietnam). Given the lower rates of Soviet growth, this burden increases and now absorbs between a quarter and a third of the increments of Soviet investment growth. At the same time the Soviet leaders are becoming increasingly impatient with the modest level of Eastern European participation in Soviet economic development.

The actual and potential vulnerability of Eastern Europe to social unrest significantly complicates Soviet relations with the West and presents irreconcilable contradictions to Soviet policy-makers. On the economic side, the Soviet Union has come to fear Eastern European economic dependence on the West (what the Soviet press calls 'the imperialist trap'), while acknowledging that Western European support of Eastern European economic development might ease pressure on Soviet resources. On the political side, social peace and a degree of cultural liberalism in Eastern Europe cements the Soviet detente with Western Europe and underpins any hope for restoration of detente with the United States. Improved relations with the West, and especially with the US, however, encourage liberal forces in Eastern Europe and impede Soviet efforts to contain them.

In the context of this analysis, the main outline of Soviet policy towards Eastern Europe includes much closer supervision of political orthodoxy (particularly in Poland and Hungary), pre-emptive crackdowns on dissent, encouragement of siege mentality and crude anti-Western propaganda, greater pressure against experimentation, and rapid reaction to signs of social and political unrest. It includes also the sharp reduction of Soviet subsidies on oil and other raw materials to Eastern Europe (and Cuba) and the warning of their possible elimination. Finally it includes the more energetic pursuit of an old and long-resisted goal of greater integration through COMECON (CMEA) of the Eastern European and Soviet economies with regard to division of labour, co-ordination of investments, technological exchange, and collective projects. If the political direction of Andropov's policy (orthodoxy over liberalism) was clear, the economic direction was less so.

Written and spoken evidence suggests that Andropov would soon have taken steps toward serious middle-of-the-road economic reforms in the Soviet Union. When he became General Secretary in December 1982, the specialized and general Soviet press featured lengthy discussions of Eastern European innnovations in planning, management and incentives. Often expressed was the need for the Soviet Union to adopt creatively the experience of Eastern Europe, especially Hungary and East Germany. In Eastern Europe, however, the evidence is more ambiguous. Soviet leaders are not pressing to introduce economic reforms where they do not already exist – in Czechoslovakia, for example. Nor, on the other hand, are they pressing for a return to orthodoxy in countries where reforms are well advanced. At the root of the inconsistency lies the primacy of political over economic considerations. The Soviet Union apparently accepts established reforms and their economic consequences while fearing the political consequences of new or bolder reforms. Thus the major influence on Soviet attitudes comes from Poland not Hungary.

Soviet policy in Eastern Europe during this decade will stress political stability over economic development. That stability ultimately depends on improved economic performance and improved economic performance depends ultimately on potentially destabilizing economic reform. This dilemma mirrors the contradiction between the two key Soviet goals in Eastern Europe – to preserve Soviet dominion and to ensure domestic stability. The first requires orthodoxy; the second requires innovation.

Eastern Europe and Soviet Domestic Policy
No survey of the situation in the Soviet Union's 'second arc' would be complete

without exploring its significance for the domestic and foreign policies of the imperial power herself. Most commonly, Eastern Europe is regarded as a bridge between Western countries and the Soviet Union. Surely this image holds for technological transfer and economic experimentation. However, the far greater significance of the Eastern European Empire is its very existence and its endemic instability. For Soviet domestic policy the effect is to inhibit political and economic liberalization at home. Soviet leaders fear the consequences across borders in either direction of any departure from a sterile orthodoxy. For Soviet foreign policy the effect is even more complex and contradictory.

First, the commitment to hold the Eastern European Empire is far more important for Soviet leaders than the commitment either to secure a durable *rapprochement* with the West or to expand their power in the Third World. Second, with regard to the Third World, Eastern Europe, especially East Germany and Czechoslovakia, significantly contributes to the extension of Soviet influence – through military and security advice and training, weapons delivery, and economic exchange and aid. Third, given the fact that priorities in Soviet policy are directly correlated with distance from centre, difficulties in Eastern Europe tend to reinforce retrenchment in foreign policy, as the Polish case shows.

Fourth, the situation in Eastern Europe bears heavily on the policy of detente with Western Europe and the United States. Given the importance of the European detente to Soviet interests, Western Europe has the leverage to moderate Soviet policies in Eastern Europe. Less discussed and more important is the leverage that dominion over Eastern Europe affords the Soviets Union *vis-à-vis* Western Europe. Twenty-two million East German hostages serve as a powerful restraint on West German policy towards the Soviet Union and on West German willingness to support American post-detente policy towards the Soviet Union. Moreover, the rebirth of strong German nationalism, this time on the left of German politics, has raised again the question of German reunifi-

cation, not as a long-range historical prospect but as a question to be resolved in this century. Such illusions give the Soviet Union room for the manipulation of German politics. As for the United States, Soviet leaders must decide whether the advantages of a renewed detente, hitherto the central and seemingly irreplaceable focus of Soviet foreign policy, outweigh the disadvantages in the form of inevitable pressures for liberalization and independence in Eastern Europe.

If successive explosions fail to rock Eastern Europe during the remainder of this decade, serious tensions will surely persist within client states and between them and the imperial centre. Poland will remain for years to come the focus of Soviet attention and fear in the area. It remains to be seen whether Western Europe will exercise its virtually unused leverage to affect Soviet imperial policy and the direction of Eastern European development. (Without some semblance of detente with the Soviet Union, the United States enjoys virtually no such leverage.) The situation in the 'second arc' during the 1980s will act as a restraint on vigorous Soviet policies toward the outside world, but it is no doubt futile to anticipate that Soviet foreign policy will abandon global objectives to concentrate on either imperial or domestic problems.

For forty years the Soviet Union has had the good luck to confront crisis in only one Eastern European country at a time. Even if this good luck holds in the 1980s, Eastern Europe will spotlight Soviet weakness and failure. Even more important, it may generate the sparks that could ignite a large-scale military conflict. It will impede the conduct of East–West relations at a lower temperature and at a higher level of co-operation, especially in that area which affects all mankind – the control and reduction of nuclear weapons.

The Third Arc: The People's Republic of China

For over two decades after Khrushchev discredited Stalin's legacy in 1956, Soviet leaders encountered the greatest risks and costs of Communist encirclement in the third arc. Along thousands of miles of eastern and

122,997

25

LIBRARY
College of St. Francis
JOLIET, ILLINOIS

south-eastern borders, vast quantities of men and materiel were fixed in varying degrees of readiness against the once loyal Communist ally, while military planners were obliged to make complex preparations for war on two fronts. Since 1979, however, the virulence of the conflict between the Soviet Union and the People's Republic of China (PRC) has been abating. Both sides have quietly, cautiously and slowly moved toward normalization of state relations. Before long, if nothing like the shock of another Afghanistan intervenes, they will probably achieve a degree of *rapprochement* that would have appeared highly unlikely to most informed observers just a few years ago.

The Prospects for Sino-Soviet Rapprochement

Signs of Sino-Soviet *rapprochement* proliferate. They recall the initial steps taken towards Sino-American reconciliation early in the 1970s. There are conversations among diplomats and exchanges of journalists, scholars and athletes. There are the adjustments on both sides in ideological formulations of their respective interests. There is the scaling down of the propaganda war with attendant alterations in the scope and focus of accusation. There are re-evaluations of Western policies and restatements of the pre-conditions for serious negotiations. Some limited negotiations have started. If these signs have yet to produce striking results, the mood on both sides heralds major improvements in bilateral relations.

Soviet policies were decisive in creating the conflict, but Chinese intransigence during the Cultural Revolution and through the 1970s was decisive in bringing the relationship to a boiling point. Repeated Soviet overtures for improving relations were rebuffed before and after Mao's death. That the process of normalization has begun owes its primary stimulus to shifts in Chinese attitudes and policy orientations. The Chinese have publicly revised their ideological formulations. The United States has lately joined the excoriated Soviet Union as a 'hegemonic' super-power. The Soviet Party–State is characterized and criticized with less vituperation than before. Most important, the

Chinese have gradually moderated their position on the three preconditions essential for serious negotiations and improved relations.

For some time China had insisted on Vietnamese withdrawal from Kampuchea, Soviet withdrawal from Afghanistan, and Soviet reduction of forces on the Chinese border together with total withdrawal from Mongolia. Following two years of cautious modification, the Chinese position now appears to state that serious negotiations can begin if only the Soviet Union shows willingness to embark on the road to partial fulfilment of any of the preconditions. (Incidentally, extensive conversations with Chinese and Soviet officials suggest that the former place greater stress and expect greater success with regard to the first precondition while the latter are more sanguine of some movement with regard to the third.)

Why has the People's Republic of China shifted her policy so considerably, especially in the last three years? The answers lie in the Chinese evaluation of their domestic situation, the balance within the Sino-Soviet-American triangle, and the changing international environment. President Reagan's policy towards China has clearly damaged Sino-American relations and accelerated the process of Sino-Soviet *rapprochement*. Chinese leaders were embarrassed and affronted by America's handling of the Taiwan issue and especially by continued deliveries of advanced military equipment. They deplore the symbolic rather than the actual effect of Reagan's actions, however, since they realize that the United States has not fundamentally altered its China policy.

In addition, the Chinese are fearful of association with President Reagan's policies in the Third World. These policies can elicit only dismay from a power that applauds third-world aspirations and seeks to lead their struggle.

Ironically, the consistent hard line maintained in American relations with the Soviet Union – a posture urged by the PRC in the past – now works to distance the Chinese from the United States. Reassured by Reagan's strong line against the USSR the PRC can relax her vigilant warnings about Soviet 'hegemonism'. Indeed, one can argue,

26

it is an axiom that poor Soviet–American relations draw the Chinese toward the Soviet Union, while good Soviet–American relations, on the other hand, draw them closer to the United States.

The Chinese softening of preconditions for normalization with the Soviet Union stems less from specific American policies, however, than from the need for stabilized relations with a less threatening neighbour in order to pursue internal modernization. Chinese leaders perceive less danger from a Soviet union beset by domestic and especially economic difficulties. They expect the phase of retrenchment to persist in Soviet foreign policy. All these considerations strengthen the position of those in the Chinese elite and especially the Chinese Armed Forces who counsel more independence in China's position within the strategic triangle and criticize excessive leaning towards the United States.

Developments in China

Difficulties encountered in implementing the ambitious programme of reforms in China demand a greater concentration on domestic affairs and a greater need to minimize the danger from the Soviet Union. Of the 'four modernizations', it should not be forgotten that the Chinese place the military modernization last. The process of de-Maoization in China, the opening of contacts with the West, the difficulties in the industrial sector (especially the high level of unemployed youth), and the continued success with experimental economic policies (reminiscent of the 1920s in Russia) have visited on the Chinese with a vengeance the dilemma of trade-offs between political interest and economic effectiveness so well-known from the history of other revolutionary regimes.

Abandonment of old slogans, devolution of economic power, re-evaluation of the past, and uncertain plans for the future all heighten the anxiety among leaders and bureaucracies that control will be lost over the population and particularly over the youth and intelligentsia. They seek more strenuously a new ideological compass by which to indoctrinate the population and strengthen authoritarian control. In this regard the West constitutes a greater danger than the Soviet Union, as the leadership acknowledged by terminating the short-lived 'democracy' campaign. As a matter of fact, China is becoming more interested in certain phases of Soviet historical development. The process of post-Mao evolution has many elements in common with both the Soviet period of the New Economic Plan (NEP) and with the post-Stalin experience.

If in the autumn of 1982 Soviet specialists were stressing the slowness of the reconciliation process and the unlikelihood that it would alter the basic shape of the strategic Soviet–Chinese–American triangle, in the spring of 1983 they were arguing that the process would be quicker and broader than earlier anticipated. Some even spoke of improved relations at the Party as well as state level. Chinese specialists have consistently cautioned Westerners from underestimating the difficulties of the process and overestimating its likely extent. If the Chinese wished not to endanger their American connection, the Soviet Union wished to bring home the dangers of Reagan's policy towards the Soviet Union by flaunting the likely pay-off of speedy and successful negotiations with the PRC. In fact, however, the movement toward normalization is taking place neither as fast as the Soviet Union would have us believe nor as slowly as the Chinese would have us believe.

The Consequences of Sino-Soviet Reconciliation

Just as Western policy-makers and analysts several years ago were prone to exaggerate the unalterability of Sino-Soviet tensions, now they are prone to exaggerate the likely consequences of the process of reconciliation and its susceptability to Western and especially American influence. If one cannot predict the detailed progression of the Sino-Soviet *rapprochement*, one can be quite certain about its limits. Normalization will certainly end the reciprocal vilification in the press; stimulate scientific, educational, cultural and athletic exchange; increase the communication of unclassified materials; facilitate the visits of journalists and economic experts; reduce the isolation of accredited diplomats; reinstate Chinese relations with pro-Moscow Communist Parties; and, more important, expand trade, perhaps even substantially. Quite possibly, the Sino-Soviet border dispute will be resolved by compromise. (The Soviet Union has, after all, vacated all islands in the Ussuri River with the exception of one opposite Khabarovsk.) Eventually, a Sino-Soviet agreement could produce mutual troop reductions along the border and possibly, if not probably, a non-aggression treaty might be signed.

The consequences of the normalization process should not be exaggerated, however. Normalization will bring no Sino-Soviet political or military alliance, not even detente. Nor will it bring restoration of friendly relations between the two Communist Parties. Normalization will lessen tensions, but it will not erase Chinese suspicions of Soviet hostiity to Chinese ambitions. It will not deter Chinese efforts to reach agreement with Japan on issues of defence and trade. Finally, the PRC will perpetuate Sino-Soviet tensions in the Third World by opposing Soviet 'hegemonist' expansion there.

Normalization of Sino-Soviet relations, however far and fast it develops, will thus not alter certain cardinal facts of the Chinese-Soviet-American triangle. The USSR and the PRC remain potential enemies whose security is measured only in relation to the adversary's weakness. The Soviet Union remains a present and future danger to China, while the Chinese will continue to fear little and gain much from a United States that remains hostile to the Soviet Union. Regardless of normalization, the Soviet Union aims to prevent or delay China's attainment of genuine great-power status. Prejudice and fear govern Soviet relations with a country which shares a border of 6,000 km, contains the largest population in the World, and possesses the will and resources to reclaim its historical greatness. As long as the Soviet threat persists, the US has no reason to oppose the growth of Chinese power and international stature, even if she has no enthusiasm for underwriting the Chinese process of modernization.

Normalization will not obviate the need to keep one-third of Soviet armed forces and one-quarter of her rocket forces opposite China. Nor will it relieve Soviet military planners of the necessity to plan for two-and-a-half wars and economic planners of the necessity to finance them. Nor will it facilitate the more central Soviet goals of destroying the Western Alliance or restoring a semblance of detente with the United States.

Normalization will strengthen China's position in the strategic triangle, but it will not secure China a place equidistant from both partners. Given Chinese fears, needs and interests, her position in the triangle will remain skewed in favour of the United States. Sino-American relations will remain closer than either Sino-Soviet or Soviet–American relations. The United States remains the pivotal country in the strategic triangle and derives more advantage therefrom than either of the other two powers. What China is now doing is simply trying to improve her position in the triangle without at the same time strengthening the Soviet position *vis-à-vis* the United States.

The 'China Card'

The content of Andropov's policy towards China in no way differed from that of his predecessor in his last years. Current policy, however, exhibits a new urgency and flexibility that is rooted in the disintegration of the Soviet–American detente, the threatening American military build-up, and the potentially greater Japanese military presence. If Soviet fears of encirclement subsided somewhat during the early 1970s, they surfaced again by the end of the decade. The Soviet Union began to see herself not only as the object of an unfriendly encirclement, both 'capitalist' and 'Communist', but also began to exaggerate the growth of both the Western and Eastern components of the encirclement. Andropov's energetic effort to accelerate the *rapprochement* with the PRC was as much an effort to break out of this acutely felt encirclement as was his policy to divide the United States from her Western European Allies.

As for China, the pursuit of this new direction in foreign policy represents merely another, if significant, expression of how China's leaders regard their national interests. The process of normalization has an internal and profound dynamic, neither sparked nor guided to any real degree by the conduct of the United States. If President Reagan's policies toward the PRC have had an impact on the direction of Sino-Soviet *rapprochment*, they certainly do not explain it. Former officials of the Carter Administration accuse Reagan of losing 'our China card'. They thereby perpetuate vain illusions and a shortsighted manipulative approach to relations with China. The United States would be well advised to forget about the 'China card'. It is of interest here to include the private observations recently expressed to me by a high-level Soviet sinologist:

It may be that American analysts, when delving into Chinese policy changes, may be making the same mistake we made in the 1940s when the Chinese revolution triumphed. We expected that China for many years would become a strategic ally of the Soviet Union in matters of foreign policy. We paid rather dearly for these hopes. They cost us a lot. Now, on another level, the United States has done more or less the same thing. I remember how after Nixon's trip to China, especially in the mid-1970s, the American press and American official circles took quite a favourable view of the high level of animosity against the Soviet Union in China. Everyone was saying these anti-Soviet feelings must be fostered and fanned. Peking must be helped, strengthened, this anti-Soviet animus must continue to be fostered in order to change the strategic balance on the planet. I think it was also a mistake for the United States to believe that China could become a long-term ally of the United States. I think a more realistic view on either side must convince us of one very important element: that on this globe a great power has appeared, with its own interests, with its own strategic considerations, which do not jibe with the national interests of either the United States or the USSR. At present we have a sort of bi-polar idea that two great powers more or less guide the destiny of the world. This is true if you think of the balance of forces, but we should not forget that soon the Chinese leaders will burst upon the world arena as a third super-power. We may disagree as to whether that is possible soon or not. Whether China will achieve such power or not is another question. We may see it in our own way, but the fact that China wishes it is something else. This is the motive force of Chinese policy. This is why it has distanced itself from the US and comes closer to us.

The United States should be satisfied that there exists an independent China which by her very existence, her geographical location, her historical attitude towards Russia, her military power, and her experience with the Soviet leadership provides an important obstacle to the expansionist plan of America's main adversary, the Soviet Union. Surely US policies towards China should embody this fact with greater comprehension, subtlety and consistency than the Reagan Administration has demonstrated so far. But the US should be aware that she can influence China's attitudes and actions only in a very limited way. The truth of the matter is that the United States never had a 'China card' to lose.

Conclusion
From the midpoint of the last decade the Soviet Union has been expanding externally while declining internally. At this juncture of history, contradictory pressures vastly complicate the policy choices of Soviet leaders. On the one hand the magnitude of domestic difficulties demands urgent and concentrated attention. On the other hand the international environment offers sterling opportunities for the expansion of Soviet power and influence, especially in the Third World. Internal decline will surely continue or even accelerate during the remainder of the 1980s. The desire to translate newly-achieved Soviet global military power into international influence will perhaps heighten the risk of active Soviet intervention in the world's most troubled regions. The key question of the Soviet succession remains as yet unanswered. What will be the major direction of Soviet efforts? Towards the alleviation

and resolution of problems within the Soviet Union and its empire? Or the energetic pursuit of external advantage?

The United States and her Western Allies have opportunities in this decade much greater than those in the last to influence Soviet international behaviour. The combination of circumstances within and outside the Soviet Union encourages prospects for reducing the virulence of the inevitable conflict between East and West by devising acceptable rules of international conduct on both sides and by achieving agreement on limiting, reducing and stabilizing the arms competition. The Soviet Union will be more amenable to serious negotiations at a time when she is preoccupied with domestic and imperial problems, when she contemplates the escalating costs of a new cycle of military competition, when Kremlin succession has interrupted the inertial drift of Soviet policies, and when Soviet leaders are learning that there is no substitute for better relations with the United States and for a controlled management of the East–West conflict. The principal question for this decade is not what the Soviet leaders will do. It is what the United States and the Western Alliance will do, for on their choices will largely depend the policies of any new Soviet leader.

The Challenge to the West: Problems, Objectives and Policy Options

DR THEO SOMMER

Thirty-six years ago George F. Kennan wrote his famous 'Mr X' essay which has since become a classic: 'The Sources of Soviet Conduct'. His basic point was that Kremlin policy is the product of ideology and circumstances. Kennan regarded the structure of Soviet power as 'committed to the perfection of the dictatorship and the maintenance of the concept of Russia in a state of siege', and he foresaw for the future 'a duel of infinite duration' between East and West. But he also suggested that the West, while containing Soviet expansion, could 'force upon the Kremlin a far greater degree of moderation and circumspection . . . and in this way promote tendencies which must eventually find their outlet in either the break-up or the gradual mellowing of Soviet power'.

It is quite remarkable that, a generation after Kennan put down his observations, his general analysis still holds. The interaction of ideology and power in both internal and external Communist politics continues to puzzle the West. The Soviet Union is still torn between her traditional siege mentality and a growing awareness that she cannot escape the need for at least limited co-operation with the West – an awareness, at any rate, that in the age of nuclear weapons and economic interdependence there must be limits to confrontation. And now, as then, Western statesmen find themselves at odds over the question of whether in the 'duel of infinite duration' relentless anti-Communist crusading or rather a judicious detente policy is the best way of promoting either the break-up or – more realistically nowadays – the mellowing of Soviet power.

The answer to this question depends to a large extent on how one views Soviet behaviour in the recent past; how one evaluates the posture and the purposes of the new Kremlin leadership; and how one projects current attitudes and announcements into the future. Is the Soviet Union hopelessly riveted to a policy of expansionism? Is she unswervingly committed to an unending arms build-up? Could she be tempted to write off detente in Europe? Will the need for reforming the creaking economic system induce peacefulness and caution or will successful reform only give a fresh impetus to adventurism abroad?

The Brezhnev Years

For the Soviet Union the eighteen years of the Brezhnev era were a period of both remarkable achievements and deep frustrations.

Under Brezhnev's rule, the Soviet Union became a truly global power. She achieved strategic parity with the United States. During the first half of the 1970s, detente yielded the formal recognition of the *status quo* in Europe as well as the implicit legitimization of Soviet predominance in Eastern Europe. The Soviet Union projected her power deep into the Third World, sweeping up, in the process, Angola and Mozambique, gaining a strategic foothold in the Horn of Africa, notably in Yemen and Ethiopia, and invaded Afghanistan. At the same time she witnessed the decline of American power and assertiveness after the Vietnam debacle, the submergence of China in the anarchy of the Cultural Revolution, and the impotence of dissent within the Soviet Empire. Economic growth was intensive enough to support a policy of both guns *and* butter; the prospects for closer economic co-operation with the West and a steady influx of technology and credits from the capitalist countries were bright; and a fair number of openings elsewhere promised further gains at low risk and low cost.

By the mid-1970s this favourable situation began to change.

Strategic parity with the United States remained a fact, yet even under President Carter the trend in the balance of military spending was reversed; SALT II, signed in June 1979, was never ratified; and, after the Soviet invasion of Afghanistan, the spirit of accommodation gave way to a new truculence in Washington.

Detente soured after Afghanistan and became a dirty word after the suppression of the Polish reform movement. Co-operation slackened again – for political and for economic reasons. The basic balance in Europe remained intact but, as it turned out, the Helsinki process had more of a 'Finlandizing' effect on Eastern Europe than on Western Europe.

Soviet involvement in far-away places proved costly and inconclusive; Ethiopia and Afghanistan are cases in point. The Soviet position in the Middle East – already badly shaken when President Sadat evicted his Soviet advisers from Egypt in 1972 – all but collapsed ten years later. The Soviet Union did not manage to wring any profit from the Iranian Revolution; during the Lebanese War of 1982 the USSR revealed herself as politically powerless to influence the course of events, while Soviet military equipment was widely seen as inferior when compared with Israel's American-supplied weapons. The stock of the USSR in the Third World has never been lower.

The United States is in a much more assertive, even confrontational spirit. President Reagan's policies vis-à-vis Central America convey the message to the Kremlin that the risks and costs of Soviet entanglements abroad have risen. A deep strain of conservatism running through the Western democracies spoils the Soviet Union's flirtation with the American and West European peace movements. The attempt to normalize relations with China after the death of Mao Zedong has so far yielded only limited results.

The most important change, however, concerns the Soviet economy. It is no longer a high-growth economy. The growth rate during the current (eleventh) Five Year Plan has dropped to 2.5%. The leadership knows that the infra-structure of the Soviet economy are as deficient as its innovative powers, that its inflexible management system is incapable of meeting the needs of a modern industrial society, and that only decentralization, material incentives and the introduction of at least some market elements can overcome the present stagnation. A declining labour force, diminishing resources and the vagaries of agricultural production compound the problem. Reform is inevitable. But to be effective reform would have to cut deep into the established privileges of the *nomenclatura*. It will most certainly meet with fierce resistance – reason enough for Andropov to have made haste slowly.

Prospects for Change

How is this change of circumstances going to affect Soviet politics and Soviet policies? There is, of course, no certainty. Yet it is perhaps useful to remember that great nations, like super-tankers, change direction only slowly. Their interests tend to endure, and so do their practical inclinations, regardless of the ideological fashion of the moment. The next question to ask is, therefore, what are the basic and presumably enduring interests of the Soviet Union?

The primary interest of the Soviet leadership is undoubtedly the consolidation of Soviet power in Eurasia. For Europe this means that they will continue to maintain Soviet control over Eastern Europe. History has taught them the lesson that the access routes to the Russian heartland must be denied to any potential aggressor, that at least a *cordon sanitaire* of friendly states should provide protection to them. Better yet, that an area of undisputed Soviet paramountcy should cover the Empire's wide-open Western flank. For Siberia – the growth area of the future – it signifies a redoubled effort to secure it against Chinese designs.

No less important is another interest: that of maintaining strategic parity with the United States, or, as the Soviet leadership prefers to put it more generally, 'equal security' for the USSR. In this regard, I am on the side of those who argue that the Soviet Union – no matter how hard-pressed she might be economically – will never allow the US to recapture military superiority. She will make every effort to keep up or catch up with the United States. Short of a major breakthrough in disarmament talks, there is nothing that could induce her to slow down the growth of her defence expenditures, let alone cut her arms spending. We may take Andropov's words at face value: 'Any policy directed towards military superiority over the Soviet Union has no future and will only heighten the threat of war'. The USSR will remain a super-power second to none – this is the inevitable Soviet response to the 'second to none' philosophy of the Reagan Administration.

Another interest, though not negligible, is certainly subordinate to the first two: exploiting targets of opportunity in the developing world. The thesis that the Soviet Union had embarked on a relentless geopolitical advance across the Southern half of the globe, pursuing a grand strategy to subvert and engulf the Third World, has always been open to doubt. Her interventions resulted more often than not from a combination of suddenly emerging local opportunities and Western miscalculation or weakness. The hallmark of her actions was caution rather than recklessness. While it is reasonable to assume that she will not forego any future opportunities opening up in the Third World, her recent experience is bound to make her even more circumspect. Meanwhile she has most certainly realized that there are no easy solutions for the turmoil in the world's geopolitical fault lines, but only protracted commitments which are a drain on her resources, that her Third-world allies tend to be unreliable, incompetent and ungrateful, and that the firmer posture adopted by the West towards Soviet intervention has drastically raised the costs and the risks of activism in the Third-world.

While these three interests – in securing the Soviet Empire, maintaining military parity with the United States and trying to spread Soviet influence – may be taken as permanent, the way they are going to be pursued is not immutable or preordained. Soviet policies will be influenced by two significant factors. One is the impact of the Soviet economic crisis on the Soviet system. The other is the choice offered to the Soviet leadership by the West.

Soviet Economic Problems

The grave economic problems facing the Soviet Union will no doubt give rise to bitter disputes, even conflicts, within a leadership which is already beset with the difficulties of a large-scale generational change. In the West there is considerable contention about the bearing these disputes and conflicts may have on Soviet foreign policy. Are they going to favour the 'hawks' – or will they provide grist to the mill of the 'doves'? Are there 'hawks' and 'doves'?

Eastern Europe

For three decades after the war, Soviet economic power provided some of the vital underpinnings of Russian paramountcy in Eastern Europe. Of course, in the last analysis Soviet domination of her Western *glacis* has always rested on her military strength (and the threat to use it) in order to subdue any would-be reformer or defector. Yet the Warsaw Pact countries certainly drew some profit from their economic connection with the Soviet Union. This situation has clearly changed, especially in the field of energy and raw material supplies. Eastern Europe has very little to gain from the Soviet Union during the years ahead. Seweryn Bialer ventures the guess that it will remain *politically* dependent on Moscow but will become *economically* more dependent on Western Europe.

The USSR, Professor Bialer suggests also, will increasingly be 'forced, owing to economic difficulties, to maintain her domination by intimidation and the threat to use force'. In particular, Professor Bialer expects no Soviet tolerance for bold Polish reform experiments: 'Should new troubles explode in Poland, direct or indirect Soviet reaction will likely be swift and harsh'. This is most certainly so. On the other hand, it could be argued that precisely the loss of economic muscle might induce the Soviets to grant the countries of Eastern Europe more leeway in conducting their economies – reform substituting, as it were, for Soviet aid – so long as reform does not touch upon basic Soviet security interests. Even timid steps towards updating the Soviet system might embolden reformers all over Eastern Europe – and the USSR might actually permit them to go ahead. This is what a more 'organic relationship', as once postulated by Helmut Sonnenfeldt, could amount to.

It is hard to say which school of thought is going to win out in the end. The leaders of the USSR have to make up their minds about what is more important to them in Eastern Europe: cohesion on the basis of a rigorously imposed Soviet model, or viability on the basis of more diversity? It is a difficult choice, for imposed cohesion carries the risk of being punctuated ever more frequently by violent explosions, whereas diversity might ultimately break the mould not only of Communist uniformity but of Communist unity.

Military Parity

The Soviet Union is spending between 12 and 15% of her gross national product (GNP) for military purposes. As a share of her entire economic effort, this is from two to four times that invested in defence by most NATO countries. However, there is no reason for the West to panic. For one thing, translating defence rubles into defence dollars is so haphazard an exercise as to be virtually meaningless. Second, even on that dubious basis of calculation, NATO spent $286 billion on defence in 1981, the Warsaw Pact only $196 billion. Third, the CIA has recently acknowledged that, during the 1970s, the average annual increase of Soviet defence expenditures amounted to 2% rather than to the 4% previously claimed (which means, in effect, that throughout the decade NATO Europe increased its defence budgets more than did the Soviet Union). Fourth, it is worth underlining that the Soviet GNP is only about half that of the United States, and the Soviet growth rate is slowing down.

The real point in our context is a different one. The Soviet Union is putting a far larger share of her national income into the military sector than the industrial democracies for roughly the same result. In other words, she produces security in a highly uneconomical fashion. The question is: will she be forced to cut back investment in the defence sector by the worsening economic situation?

Again, there are different views about this in the West. Pessimists argue that any Soviet leadership will have to pay a price for the support of the Army and the security forces. That price will include: a reassertion of discipline; a soft-pedalling on reform to guarantee to the marshals that the best resources will continue to be channelled their way; and a pledge not to touch the defence sector in the unavoidable fight over resource allocations. Seweryn Bialer has summarized the case of the sceptics quite effectively:

Certain pressures will work to continue expanding Soviet military might regardless of cost. As achievement in other fields declines, the military might could well become to an even greater extent the showcase of the state's success and glory. Moreover, military power will remain for a long time to come the dominant foreign-policy resource of the Soviet Union. High military spending will in all likelihood be assured both by the momentum of the already planned military build-up and by the greater political weight of the military establishment as the potential ally of contending groups in periods of succession and interim leadership.

Given the enhanced role of the Red Army in the coalition of forces on which Andropov's rule rested, there are hardly any optimists around who expect the Soviet military to be cut along with their budget. William Hyland's question is still valid: 'What new leader would try to consolidate a bid for power on a platform of reducing defence?' A quarrel with the marshals is the last thing any Soviet leader would wish for. Undoubtedly, there will be rising pressures to limit military growth as resources are shrinking and the burden of keeping the Soviet military juggernaut in shape will be felt much more harshly than at any time during the Brezhnev era. But, as long as the 'duel of infinite duration' between the super-powers goes on, it would be quite unrealistic to expect to see any significant slackening of the Soviet Union's defence effort.

The best one can realistically hope for is that competing elite groups will create enough pressure to prevent the automatic allocation of constantly growing funds to the military, and that realistic Western proposals for arms limitation and disarmament might help to reverse the previous trend.

Soviet Expansionism

The political costs of Soviet adventures in the Third World have been high, particularly in Afghanistan. In other places, – such as Cuba and Ethiopia – the financial costs of Soviet involvement have placed a heavy burden on the Soviet treasury. This burden seems bound to increase as economic problems in the USSR multiply. What effect is this going to have on the Soviet Union's global behaviour? Again, different answers are being given in the West.

The pessimistic answer is that formulated, for instance, by William Hyland. A new leadership, he argues, might be tempted to make up for its domestic problems with foreign successes: 'A new leader may conclude that the Soviet Union should indeed claim its place in the sun . . . A new generation might be willing to press its claims with much less regard for risks, with greater persistence and determination but resting its policy on a solid foundation of military power'. NATO's military improvement programmes and China's modernization plans, Hyland suggests, might, rather than inhibiting Soviet expansionism, encourage the Soviet leadership to act if they concluded 'that time was running out, and that the optimal moment for a geopolitical breakthrough had arrived'.

The opposite view – that the Soviet Union would pursue a line of pragmatic moderation and peaceful competition in the Third World – is vented only with a great deal of caution. Earlier predictions to that effect by Soviet-ologists like Robert Legvold or Morton Schwartz at the beginning of the 1970s are still remembered with some embarrassment by Western analysts. But Neil MacFarlane, to quote only one scholar, argues quite convincingly that:

The benefits of Soviet interventionist behaviour in the 1970s have been lower and the costs higher than foreseen. Growing internal problems favour great moderation in the conduct of Soviet foreign policy . . . It is clear that the Soviet Union will for the rest of this decade evince far less activism in her military policy in Third-world conflicts.

MacFarlane also reminds us that historically the Soviet Union has have always avoided seriously provocative behaviour in the international arena during periods of internal crisis. One might add that Soviet restraint was very noticeable both in the Lebanese crisis of 1982 and (at least so far) in the Chad crisis which began in 1983.

The safest guess is that the Soviet Union, while not necessarily straining for further geopolitical advance, will probably want to protect her standing, that she will take a wary view of costly new commitments but is unlikely to refuse the promise of easy gain, and that she will certainly rise to any US challenge posed in the Third World.

On all three counts – Eastern Europe, the arms race and policy with respect to the Third World – the new Soviet leadership is presumably still undecided. As Dmitri Simes has noted: 'Soviet leaders themselves probably do not now know the answers, especially since they do not like to focus on hypothetical situations'. The economy will be only one factor in their assessment. Another is of at least equal importance: the policies pursued by the West *vis-à-vis* the Soviet Union.

Eastern Europe

Eastern Europe poses a perennial problem to the West. Imposing the Soviet pattern uniformly on the satellites may have seemed the best course of action for the USSR after World War II. Over the long haul, however, it carried great risks and penalties. It grated against deep-seated national traditions; it ignored cultural differences, and it roused psychological aversion. Reaction was inevitable. Indeed, spontaneous uprisings against Soviet overlordship have become a regular feature on the East European scene. East Germany 1953, Poland and Hungary 1956, Czechoslovakia 1968, again Poland in 1970,

1976, 1980–83; the list is formidable, and it does not even include the breakaway of Yugoslavia in 1949 and the desertion of Albania in 1960, nor the minor Bulgarian upheavals in 1965. Today, these spontaneous eruptions probably pose the greatest danger to European peace. At the least, they are a permanent source of instability and concern. It is deeply ironic that the very insistence on the part of the Soviet Union that Eastern Europe be moulded in her own image creates the most serious threat to her own security. Greater tolerance of diversity could serve her security interests much better.

The West has at times pursued different policies towards Eastern Europe, verbally as well as practically. First, there was much talk and no action about 'rollback' or 'liberation' of the captive nations – but the 'balance of terror' put paid to that in the 1950s. Then there were feeble attempts to drive a wedge between the Soviet Union and her satellites by building bridges to the countries between the Elbe and Bug rivers but turning a cold shoulder to the Soviet Union and to East Germany. This was advocated by Zbigniew Brzezinski and put into practice by West Germany's Foreign Minister, Gerhard Schroeder, during the 1960s. It soon became clear, however, that it was impossible for the West to establish good relations with Eastern Europe while continuing to wage Cold War against the Soviet Union. Detente, to have a fair chance of success, must be conducted towards the entire Warsaw Pact, including the Soviet Union and the GDR. This was the concept underlying the Nixon/Kissinger approach and Chancellor Brandt's *Ostpolitik* during the early 1970s.

We have since shed a few illusions about the speed and the sweep of change detente might bring about in the East, but it seems that the basic tenets of the 1970s still hold true. We cannot hope to improve relations with the Communist countries of Eastern Europe if this endeavour is conceived or perceived primarily as an effort to incite them against Soviet overlordship. We cannot expect a stable relationship if destabilization of the Soviet sphere of paramountcy appears to be the West's avowed aim. It would be wanton, even in terms of a purely Machiavel-lian definition of Western interests, to aim at the break-up of the Soviet Empire. The dissolution of the Ottoman Empire between 1815 and 1914 should warn every would-be wrecker of the Soviet Empire that such processes carry enormous risks of great-power conflict and global conflagration.

It follows that, each time a spontaneous uprising in Eastern Europe against Soviet domination and Communist oppression occurs, the West finds itself confronted with an excruciating moral dilemma. We sympathize with the rebels; we protest against their brutal suppression; and we usually impose some kind of sanctions such as travel restrictions, interruption of diplomatic dialogue, or punitive economic measures. But we realize full well that expressions of sympathy calm our own injured consciences more than they benefit those with whom we agonize. We realize too that our protests are impotent and that not even sanctions can influence the course of events. Many outraged Westerners call for 'deeds', yet deep down we know that in the nuclear age interventions, which would have been considered normal in former times, are no longer permissible. The nuclear weapon subjects all of us to the harsh maxim that peace serves justice better than justice serves peace. It is our political duty and our moral responsibility to uphold the Eastern peoples' right to freedom and self-determination. On the other hand we have no choice but to renounce immediate punitive action and rely instead on long-term societal processes in the East to resolve the dilemma of the present. I would add that we must judiciously, unflaggingly and with great patience do everything within our power to help those mellowing processes along.

After each uprising in the Soviet orbit, East–West relations have taken a turn for the worse, for a long while after 1956, for a shorter span after 1968, and for an as yet undetermined duration after the imposition of martial law in Poland. Inevitably, however, the 'decent intervals' ended. At least once – after the suppression of Dubcek's reform movement in Prague – *rapprochement* grew directly from crisis and five years of detente followed five months of bitterness. Many feel compunction about such apparent callousness. Against them I would strongly argue that we simply do not have any alternative.

It would be criminal to encourage a heroism of despair in Eastern Europe for we would be unable to lend it any support. It would be folly to pursue a policy of sanctions that could only hurt those whom we are trying to help. And it would be immoral to forego a dialogue that might both mitigate the methods of the oppressors and the lot of those under their yoke. However awful this basic truth may sound to us, we have no choice but to return to detente after each case of suppression, resuming the effort to limber up, to humanize or, as it were, to 'Finlandize' Eastern Europe, or, as Lord Carrington put it, to 'subvert by example' the Eastern system, thus trying to heal the fissure that divides Europe into two. If the USSR challenges us to another Cold War, we must not flinch, but we should not be the ones to start it. If there is any prospect of accommodation, it does not lie in a return to unmitigated confrontation, which would only strengthen the hand of the hardliners. Rather it lies in a return to policies of detente which, over the long haul, are going to favour the reformers in Eastern Europe. We must hope that their reforms – measured and carried out so as not to menace fundamental Soviet security interests – will stick next time. They might be permitted to stick because the Soviet leaders themselves embark on a policy of reform, or because they grow tolerant enough to permit developments in Eastern Europe which they deny to their own people, or because they might be too weak to prevent such deviations from the Soviet model.

This amounts to a policy of controlled, peaceful and piecemeal change – one that would ultimately alter the face of Eastern Europe without triggering off the defence mechanisms arising from the age-old Russian security complex. It does not promise any certainty, but at least some realistic likelihood of success. In contrast, a Western policy aiming at the outright destabilization of the Soviet Empire would produce the very opposite: retrenchment rather than alleviation; glacial stagnation rather than change; Communist uniformity instead of Communist pluralism; and the East–West confrontation instead of *rapprochement*.

The Impact of Western Policies

In the same vein, Soviet views of the 'arms race' are, to a large extent, contingent upon Western, especially US arms policies. There are, no doubt, inertial forces built into the Soviet system which make for a continuous growth of military spending. It is also true that the momentum of the Soviet armaments programme is hard to explain in rational terms of defensive needs – witness the enormous increase of intermediate range and ICBM missile forces. The Soviet military machine is formidable, it is being constantly modernized and the Soviet leaders have shown that they are prepared to use it.

It goes without saying, then, that the West must look to its defences. Detente has never yet reached the point where the iron necessity of securing our existence has relaxed. We must be ready to deter attack, and we must be able to defend ourselves in the event that deterrence fails. This requires, first of all, that a balance of forces is maintained between East and West – a rough equilibrium which would signal to any potential aggressor that aggression will not pay. Secondly, it requires the participation of the United States in the provision of both deterrence and defence for Western Europe. Thirdly, it requires a cohesion of political will without which the impressive panoply of Western military strength would be worthless.

It is, however, quite a different matter for the West to strive for military superiority, let alone to crank up the 'arms race' primarily in order to 'spend the Russians underneath the waves'. It is not only wrong in substance but also counter-productive to spread the message that the United States is today inferior to the Soviet Union by every measure of military power. The Russians are not ten feet tall, and the West is by no means dwarfed by them. This goes for the strategic nuclear balance: deterrence still works and the Americans have not become 'Number 2' in the world. For this reason Soviet superiority in the Euro-strategic field, albeit pronounced, is not the tragedy it is often made out to be. The whole INF issue has more to do with the balance of determination than with the balance of forces. Nor is there any reason to panic over the conventional balance. There are certainly problems with Western conventional defences, but no-one in his right mind would want to trade them for the shortcomings, weaknesses and problems that beset the USSR. The allies of the Soviet Union are highly unreliable. Besides, NATO has been making considerable efforts to improve its military posture since 1978. There is no justification for belittling NATO's capabilities or exaggerating those of the Warsaw Pact.

A number of factors argue against the kind of massive arms programme launched by the Reagan Administration.

First, it is based on faulty analysis, if not on a dangerous inferiority complex. It aims at over-insurance. It proceeds not from a cool assessment of how much is enough but rather from an attempt to amass as much as possible. And it evokes in the USSR the same sort of dire apprehension about first-strike strategies and pre-emptive war designs which are adduced in the US to rationalize US programmes.

Second, defence has become too expensive to make 'the sky the limit'. Not many European NATO members are in a position to fulfil their pledge to increase defence outlays by 3% annually. They all face severe unemployment, sizeable budget deficits and painful financial constraints. No-one can lavish limitless resources on the military as our societies are ailing. Western Europeans favour a *sound* defence effort. At the same time they feel strongly about three things: money is not the whole answer to military problems; no-one nowadays can have all the guns and all the butter they want; and, in this day and age, social stability is an important element of security. One cannot motivate soldiers to fight for poorhouses. Apart from that, the US budget deficit – so far the chief result of Reagan's weapons programmes – threatens in a very real sense her economic recovery because of the pernicious effect it has on interest rates and on the dollar exchange rate. But as Michel Tatu has pointed out: 'No foreign policy is valid, no matter how well-founded its intentions, unless the economy of the country is strong enough to provide the means with which to implement it on the one hand, and unless it is supported by domestic and allied public opinion on the other'.

Third, most experts agree that it is quite fallacious to expect that imposing extreme economic choices on the Soviet Union would bring down the system. It is equally fallacious to assume that putting military pressure on the Soviet leadership would cause them to reconcile themselves to a position of inferiority. To quote Seweryn Bialer once again:

One should not doubt that a military build-up regardless of cost and sacrifice will meet any perceived danger to the basic security interests of the Soviet Union or to the hard-won parity with the West. This is why those American politicians and analysts who promote regained military superiority over the Soviet Union cannot hope to see their goal realized.

Fourth, a pronounced American appetite for weapons will engender a pronounced Soviet appetite for weapons. Many serious people in the West are convinced today that the 'arms race' is at worst a recipe for disaster, at best a grievous waste of resources and talent. Both sides are spending more and more money on arms yet, for all this tremendous effort, no-one has gained in security. In fact, both East and West feel probably less secure today than at anytime in the past. The 'arms race' is no longer self-explanatory. Only an honest and purposeful attempt to make arms control work and bring about disarmament can provide a moral justification and a political legitimization for such new arms programmes as may be inevitable. Only realistic Western proposals – not propaganda exercises like 'zero options' or 'deep cuts' – can convince the USSR that the West is not 'out to get them'. Without restraint in the West, there will be no restraint in the East. The MX will beget the counter-MX, as the SS-20 begat the counter-SS-20, and so on. If the arms spiral is ever to be broken, a 'focus of evil' or 'we will bury you' attitude is the wrong approach. The pursuit of strategic superiority by the

West will most certainly only motivate the Soviet leaders 'to arm and arm, regardles of the cost' (Bialer).

The Third World

The Third World will remain the cockpit of conflict, unrest and tension for some decades to come. This will create countless temptations for the super-powers to intervene. Again, Soviet behaviour will, to a considerable extent, depend on Western attitudes and policies.

If the United States appears willing to frustrate those Soviet global ambitions which threaten central Western interests, that is bound to make the Soviet leadership think twice before embarking on foreign adventures; already the risks and costs of exploiting opportunities in the Third World dictate retrenchment. If, on the other hand, the United States conveys the impression that it is committed to a strategy of world-wide 'roll-back' or seems to be yearning for East–West 'Fashodas', as once favoured by Zbigniew Brzezinski, the Soviet Union, for reasons of ideology and prestige, will certainly shed her fear of overextension, throw caution to the winds and intensify her involvement in more distant areas.

Prudence would argue in favour of discrimination. Not every turbulence in the Third World is due to Soviet machinations, although the Soviet Union may try to profit from it. It is useless, even self-defeating, to superimpose the pattern of East–West conflict on the North-South relationship, and wrong to turn every Southern problem into an issue between Washington and Moscow. Global competition between the United States and the Soviet Union will no doubt continue. It is in the Western interest to limit the conflict potential of this great power rivalry rather than increase it, to dampen Soviet aggressiveness rather than whet it, and to reduce the intensity of the conflict rather than maximize the risks of confrontation.

Both sides should shun 'Fashoda-type' collisions. They should learn to look the other way instead of using every local or regional disorder as an incentive or a pretext for intervention. Because the super-powers kept out, the Biafra conflict remained a West African civil war. Had they intervened, it would have become the centre of a world crisis. Once the Soviet Union fails to raise regional issues to the level of super-power conflict, there is no reason why the United States and her allies should press her into the East–West conflict. Firmness *vis-à-vis* Soviet encroachments should not preclude an open-minded search for areas in which agreement might be possible on the basis of mutual interest. Such areas might include enforcing nuclear proliferation; limiting conventional arms transfers; sponsoring negotiations for resolving regional conflicts; and mutual undertakings not to intervene in specific conflicts.

Conclusion

What does all this add up to? It is clear that the West must be able to hold its own when challenged. The objectives of Western policy are also obvious: to avoid war; to contain Communist expansion; to domesticate and ultimately change the Soviet–Marxist system; and to steer its evolution in a direction more favourable to Western interests. As to the methods to be pursued in this endeavour there is contention amongst Western statesmen. My own view is very close to that propounded by Lord Carrington in the 1983 Alastair Buchan Memorial Lecture. We need a positive political strategy for dealing with the Soviet Union. We should realize that Moscow is already, 'a decaying Byzantium' but we should not rejoice too much – or too soon. We cannot significantly accelerate the process of decay; decaying empires have a way of eluding collapse for a long time, nor can there be any question of taking a bulldozer to the Soviet Empire either. We must talk to the Russians, because 'talking to an equally heavily armed but far less scrupulous adversary is not a concession: it is common prudence'. Arms control is in everyone's self-interest, not only economically but in terms of real security. The democracies have a duty to themselves to be true to their own first principles: dialogue; openness; sanity; and a non-ideological approach to the dangerous business of international affairs. We must not resort to crude, one-dimensional moralism. We should realize that indiscriminate economic sanctions are neither feasible nor desirable. The Soviet leaders must face disincentives against continued obstreperousness and be offered incentives for a more positive relationship. Recently there has been too much stick and too little carrot. We should not over-react. We should not shun personal contacts between top statesmen. 'We must deal with the Russians simply because they are there.'[1]

The West must not panic in the face of an ailing and aging Soviet Union. It must not succumb to the temptation to slide back into Cold War; it must be prudent and prepare for the possibility that the Soviet Union might in fact use its military power inside and outside Europe; it must deter or counter such use; but it must not depict the Russians as giants. Their weaknesses are glaring, and we can take advantage of these weaknesses to interest them in selective co-operation, to enmesh them in a web of interdependence and mutual interest, and thus to induce, in the fullness of time, moderation in Soviet leaders rather than pushing them into a corner from which they might blindly strike out.

NOTES

[1] *Survival*, vol. XXV, no. 4, July/August 1983, pp. 146–53.

The Problems of the Western Alliance in the 1980s

HENRI SIMONET

For some time now any description of the state of the Atlantic Alliance and any attempt to predict its future has had to confront one simple common assumption, namely that the Alliance is passing through a serious and lasting crisis.

Moreover, a subsidiary assumption is that this crisis could deliver a mortal blow to the Alliance. The pessimistic description that appeared in the IISS *Strategic Survey 1982–1983* which provoked such a commotion was in line with these assumptions.

However, despite these now ritual assumptions, it is still exceptional to find many people making the deduction that the Alliance is becoming useless or that one can allow it to disappear without too much anxiety.

This refusal to draw the logical conclusion from a permanent state of crisis is easy to understand. The Alliance is part of the East–West balance of forces. It is a symbol of that balance and it is a major factor in the relationship between two antagonistic systems – built around the two super-powers – that have been opposed to each other since the end of World War II. Deliberately to question the Alliance's role would be equivalent to attempting to overthrow the whole structure of politico-strategic relations that has received much (perhaps undue) credit for averting a major and probably suicidal conflict within the industrialized world.

Where is the sensible man, the sincere democrat either of conservative or progressive, liberal or Christian conviction who dares to proclaim frankly that the Alliance is dead or dying and thus becoming unnecessary?

Perhaps a few do believe this, but the majority of our fellow countrymen, interested in the problems of Western security, are unwilling to admit it. This is true even for some segments of responsible opinion that could be considered to be in favour of the dismemberment of the Atlantic Alliance. Fear of the decease of the Alliance has even been suggested on occasion by a prominent leader of one of the principal European Communist Parties. Such a fear certainly still prevails in Europe, for which any irreparable weakening of the Alliance will mean a revolution concerning Europe's relations with the continental super-power. A set of sophisticated and complex balances would be put into question, beginning with the European *status quo* itself. On the other hand, even if such a possibility does not necessarily imply a total withdrawal of the US to 'Fortress America' (one might imagine that bilateral linkages between the US and various European countries could to an extent, whatever they may involve, compensate for the disappearance of the integrated military organization of the Alliance), it would nevertheless imply a radical strategic and geopolitical change with incalculable consequences.

It is generally accepted by the experts that the public debt of a country is not paid off by the depreciation of its currency but that its financial burden is lightened by this depreciation. One might transpose this situation to international relations. International treaties are rarely denounced. They lose their '*raison d'être*' under the impact of concealment, suspicion, illwill and passivity from the countries which once subscribed to these treaties. Then the day arrives when it is realised that they no longer have any utility; one perceives only the disadvantages of the treaty.

If – God forbid – such an appraisal should ever have to be made of the state of the Alliance, it will certainly provoke huge movements, if not among public opinion then surely in political circles. One can reasonably anticipate that these movements will be preceded by flying sparks, confrontations and attempts at reconciliation.

But the process of unravelling is difficult to stop once it has reached a certain degree of automaticity and inevitability. Then it would probably be impossible to try to reverse this trend. Perhaps also, amongst those who have emphasized the Atlantic crisis, some might hope to avert the process by exorcizing it with a description of its effects. It is to be feared however that this magical cure can prove its value only after inter-atlantic crises become recurrent and then it would be too late.

These remarks are not aimed – like the writers of science fiction or political fiction – at formulating scenarios to explain the collapse of the Alliance. I am convinced that, even if one recognizes the seriousness of present tensions and crises within the Alliance, they may not lead inevitably to its paralysis and disintegration. I hasten to say that my own convictions do not rest on confidence in the wisdom of nations or their leaders. History counsels us to be on our guard against such acts of faith. Nor are my convictions based on a reassuring certainty that an end to the Alliance is unthinkable. Too often have men – without knowing it – been taken in by one of le Rochefoucauld's maxims '*même le pire n'est jamais certain*' (the idea that the worst may never happen). Tension and misunderstanding become the rule; convergence of policies becomes reserved for those rare and exquisite moments when weariness and necessity are helpful and allies come to an agreement on the text of an ambiguous communiqué, conciliatory and deceptively unanimous. I am aware of all this and I keep myself from these illusions. My firm belief is that, even while threatened by drift, the Alliance remains founded in vitality and hope.

I will attempt to draw up a reasonable and realistic characterization of my position. This report is meant to be a message of hope without complacency, one which points out the difficulties and risks that lie before a recovery that is both indispensable and possible.

Analysis of the various ups and downs of the Alliance over the last 30 years and the ways in which they were resolved to avoid irreparable breaks should restore confidence in the Alliance's future. Moreover, when some of these vicissitudes occurred nobody foresaw then that, paradoxically, they could contribute to the strengthening of the whole Alliance. Thus one cannot in retrospect consider the decision made by the French Government in 1966 to sever its links with the NATO integrated military command to have weakened the Alliance. However, the consequences of this decision leaves a margin of autonomy for the French – and sometimes their criticisms of US Alliance initiatives provoke irritation in Washington. This irritation tends to dampen the enthusiastic reappraisal recently made in Washington concerning the consistent rhetoric used by the French Government *vis-à-vis* the Soviet Union and the various anxious analyses made by the French authorities on the hegemonial tendencies and expansionism shown by the Soviet Union. In the present neutralist and pacifist cacophony, it even appears that France may receive the label of 'best ally'. Such a certificate of good Atlanticist behaviour is now rarely awarded even to countries whose fidelity and solidarity have never been in question.

Another example lies in the fact that, while the Graeco–Turkish dispute has certainly not contributed to reinforcing the Southern flank of NATO, Italy has barely wavered in doing her share to implement the two-track decision of 1979. I do not mention these two examples in order to shrug aside the real disquiet that should be inspired by the present challenges which confront the NATO Alliance. However, these two examples show the ability to sort out these challenges in a rather less absolute perspective and in a more relative way than in the pessimistic descriptions found here or there when some analysts examine the question of Alliance survival.

In reading about or listening to gloomy assumptions on the fate of NATO, one sometimes gets the impression concerning the Alliance that the question, asked in a famous book written in the early 1970s by a Soviet dissident, Andrei Amalrik, 'Will the USSR survive in 1984?', is being asked about NATO. My objective is not to ask that question for NATO. However, we cannot have any guarantee that it will never be asked. One might keep in mind that even if '*le pire n'est jamais* certain', it still remains a possibility; therefore one warns against it.

I am convinced that, if there is at present a crisis in the Alliance, it remains controllable by those who have the capacity to analyse the crisis correctly, the will to draw lessons, and the political courage to implement solutions. With this report I wish to contribute modestly to an analytical search for the prerequisites of recovery.

We must also remember that we must explain the Alliance and its policies to our fellow countrymen, especially when fundamental issues for the Alliance are becoming part of the internal debate in many of our countries. This will not be the least important task of those who have to deal with disoriented public opinion, torn between the economic, social and political difficulties facing us today and likely to face us tomorrow.

The Elements of the Problem

The objective is to place the Alliance firmly in a proper perspective in order to fulfil its original aims, while at the same time dealing with challenges stemming from a strategic, political, economic and social international environment radically different from that which prevailed when NATO was created.

The problem of the future of the Alliance suggests a need to answer a set of questions, including:

- What is the nature of the Alliance? Does it still correspond to what was expected of it by those who created it in 1949–52?
- How does it perceive its identity? Especially how is this identity perceived by the populations of the various countries constituting the NATO Alliance?
- What is the nature of the crisis? And, if there is a crisis, how to cure it?

The Nature of the Alliance

When it was established, the NATO Alliance was conceived as a reaction to the threat posed by the Soviet Union to Western European countries. The fear of the Soviet Union led them to search – almost in panic – for the security and protection that *only* the US could provide. Thus two components

were essential from the start: the military dimension of the Alliance; and the American involvement in it (it was a unilateral commitment since no-one considered at that time the need for any reciprocity).

The political dimension of the Alliance was asserted later because of the end of the Korean War and the first steps toward what would later become detent. These did much to make the European Allies less keen to rearm. Furthermore, the reduced perception of a direct military threat made it less urgent for European governments and public opinion to implement a massive and lasting rearmament effort.

In any case, it soon became clear that rearmament of the West was feasible and tolerable only with German participation. This brought a new political problem and, moreover, the question of inserting the Federal Republic of Germany into an organization that would definitively anchor her among the Western countries. Thus one can see that Western anxiety about the siren song from the East toward the FRG is not new.

The US, confident – and perhaps over-confident – in both her military supremacy and in her ability to take on a global and world-wide role (exemplified by President Kennedy in his inaugural speech) worked toward a grand design for the Alliance under American leadership. Paradoxically, during the whole of this period what later became a major political problem, that is to say the first use of nuclear weapons, did not create major turmoil at all either in the US or in Western Europe. In addition, despite the discordant assertions made by General de Gaulle, who openly questioned US determination ultimately to escalate to the strategic level for the sake of the Alliance, political debate within NATO never at this time over-emphasized the question of the use of nuclear weapons as it has since the end of the 1970s.

How is the Alliance Perceived?

Ever since the centre of gravity of the Alliance moved toward strategic and military issues, it has come to be perceived differently than it was at its inception – by both governments and especially by the people. For European governments, the Alliance is becoming a source of internal difficulty: in their allocation of public resources, Alliance requirements needed more and more to be managed in the context of a severe economic crisis; and in their public consensus about the Alliance itself. Since its political objective appeared blurred, it became more difficult to mobilize people behind it.

The emphasis put on strategic and military matters, plus the Soviet-American controversy in which American rhetoric and phraseology sometimes gave the USSR an easy alibi to justify her expansionism, gradually shifted Western Europe's perception of the role of the NATO Alliance.

In contrast, American opinion tended to assume that NATO was a partnership in which the US carried the main part of the common burden. One might think, moreover, that it is dangerous, for a Nation–Continent – even if the Vietnam syndrome begins to be overcome – to be so suspicious of any foreign military involvement that could degenerate into military intervention in a remote theatre of operations. This is why implementation of the two-track decision of 1979 has taken on such a decisive significance, as we will see later.

As a result the Alliance has encountered difficulty in recent years in finding its identity as a *political* organization. This has produced a shift in its centre of gravity towards the military dimension. Even discretion by responsible politicians in their efforts to use military concepts to address the political challenges of the pacifist message in Europe does not prevent confirmation of the Alliance's exclusively military character for those who ignore or pretend to ignore the decisive role of the NATO Alliance in maintaining peace and security in Europe.

In a phrase, NATO suffers today – at least among its Northern European members – from an identity crisis. It no longer seems to present a clear image of a partnership for countries deeply bound to peace, animated by a political vision of their future, and for whom military investment is not an end but only a means for obtaining peace and security.

The Nature of the Crisis

The history of the Atlantic Alliance is sprinkled with crises. How could it have been

otherwise if one considers its exceptional duration? The Alliance has always overcome each crisis but without finding a way to cure the fundamental causes. If it remains true that each crisis has had its particular characteristics, analysis of them could perhaps provide the basis for assertion about what kinds of similarities or differences the present crisis has in comparison with its predecessors.

If one looks at those times of confrontation or tension which one might call 'crises', one is led to conclude that both in 1956 and in 1973 the disagreements concerned conflicts arising outside the areas covered by NATO. This is the only common ground between these two crises which placed the US on the one hand, and some of their Western European Allies on the other, in a totally opposed position. The fact that the area which provoked such turmoil within the Alliance was the Middle East naturally leads to the conclusion that tensions and conflicts arising periodically in this area are one of the permanent factors of division.

In 1956 two European Allies jeopardized US global interests by their military actions in the Middle East. In 1973, on the other hand, the European Allies judged that the NATO Alliance should remain neutral *vis-à-vis* the Israeli–Arab conflict.

The 1966 crisis, following French withdrawal from the integrated military command of NATO, certainly shook the Alliance, but it appeared in the long run simply to be an expression of a desire for more independence by a major member of the Alliance. Contrary to what might have been feared when France withdrew from the integrated military command, this decision did not seriously endanger the overall military potential of NATO.

As far as the Multilateral Force (MLF) is concerned, this episode hardly revealed a crisis within NATO. It was rather an ill-conceived, unprepared and poorly implemented attempt to bring the European Allies into the management of the nuclear deterrent designed for their protection.

Finally, the Graeco-Turkish conflict is both too peripheral and too specific to be considered as a crisis liable to shake the

Alliance deeply. This does not mean that the fissures it creates in the Southern flank of NATO should be ignored or even minimized but the background to the confrontation is so deeply rooted historically that there could be no possibility that NATO could be insulated from it when the Alliance includes Turkey and Greece amongst its ranks.

However, the crisis initiated by the Soviet invasion of Afghanistan and prolonged by the clash in Poland between the Party and the vast majority of the Polish population are of a different nature for NATO.

Four years of suspicion, recrimination, misunderstandings, and quarrels broken by intermittent harmony and co-operation, is a more than ordinary crisis. An 'ordinary' crisis is a temporary state when the balance of forces and common interests are disturbed for a short period of time before moving towards a new balance and a new convergence of interests. But in this recent crisis the opposite seems to have happened. Disturbances of the social and political equilibrium and national disagreement have become the norm. Solid consensus and the sharing of common interests appear to be of short duration and even unusual.

Practically no major political, economic and social interests of the various Alliance countries are immune either alternately or simultaneously to a clash of interests and to differences of opinion. The disagreement on economic and monetary policy, and suspicion about strategic aims and long-term policy towards the potential menace that still cements the Alliance together have all been present on a permanent basis within NATO for a number of years.

Finally, there is a kind of fatalism which is new and which leads some analysts to see these recurrent disagreements and confrontations as inevitable, until culminating in the twilight of the Alliance. The IISS report already mentioned is an example of such an assessment.

What is the Cure?

To remedy a crisis which may be structural in nature implies by definition the identification of the factors that are at its origin and cause its continuation. It is probably illusory to think that once these factors have been identified it will then be easy to eradicate them completely. Perhaps the best one might hope for would be the containment of the effects of crisis so that the overall cohesion of NATO will not be too greatly affected.

In the following section I shall attempt to identify those unfavourable factors which are acting against the strength and the dynamism of the Alliance. At this point, I believe it would be useful to begin by describing quickly the best way *not* to find a cure.

A first precept – often ignored within the Alliance – is to not give in to temptation to resort to a facade of rhetoric. One often gets the feeling that, each time the Alliance is confronted with a difficulty or a disagreement, stirring proclamations about cohesion and unity substitute for the absence of a common will.

This tendency amongst NATO countries periodically comes together with what I call 'a globalist temptation' which consists of seeking to subordinate the various difficulties sometimes dividing the Alliance to a common Atlantic denominator. In this respect, the Williamsburg communiqué – like most of the communiqués which have ended such meetings or the longer conferences which join the Atlantic community as a whole – demonstrates the limits on the will to display collective cohesion in every field of interest to the Alliance.

Challenges of the 1980s for the Alliance

We recognize clearly that the Alliance has been confronted in the course of its existence by international events that have provoked successive crises among the Allies. On the other hand, it has rarely been Soviet activism that was the direct cause of a crisis among the Allies. But, since the invasion of Afghanistan, Soviet expansionism has led to frustrations on both sides of the Atlantic which could be considered to be a 'windfall profit' for Soviet leaders pursuing a policy of power and intimidation. The next decade may bring further added benefits to the USSR due to the increasing difficulties that have arisen in the last few years. Various transformations have occurred in the antagonistic systems of both West and East and the subsequent problems thus created have multiplied since the end of the 1970s. The NATO Alliance will now have to cope with many areas of tension within its ambit. One can summarize the four challenges that NATO will either have to overcome or at least to manage in the sense of limiting to ensuing damage to tolerable levels:

- the political challenge;
- the economic challenge;
- the strategic challenge;
- the international challenge, primarily from third-world instability.

The Political Challenge
It is the political challenge that appears to be the most global and the most fundamental. All these challenges are, in a sense, political. Moreover, if any one of them reaches a particular intensity, however confined initially to a particular field or particular aspect of the Alliance relationship, it risks becoming a political struggle.

The political challenge is also the most fundamental. The Alliance – because it is defensive – must be able to rely on a single strategic vision of the world. It will only be able to resist the peacetime tensions and conflicts of interest if it can rely on a political concept which is not grounded on insuperable divergences amongst the Allies.

The achievement of a prevailing consensus about the many issues confronting the Alliance and its members concerning both the relationship between them and their political opinions, is the substance of the political challenge. This suggests that the political challenge has two dimensions:

External, for the Alliance must redefine its role *vis-à-vis* the threat which is its *raison-d'être*, and also *vis-à-vis* the new manifestations of this threat in our international environment that is both unstable and interdependent.

Internal, to the extent that the Alliance must retain public support in the member countries.

First, concerning the external dimension of the political challenge, one obviously looks to the Soviet threat to Western Europe, a Western Europe which was exhausted at the end of World War II. As the Soviet military threat gradually became less pressing and as the Western Europeans adjusted psychologically to the existence of a non-democratic part of Europe integrated willy-nilly within the Soviet Empire, the purpose of the Western Alliance was no longer so obvious.

In parallel, Western Europe has become an economic entity whose economic weight in world affairs is greater than the sum of all the individual economies that make up the European Economic Community (EEC). Finally, if it is going too to adopt without qualification the assumption put forward by some American analysts that the 'American Century' has reached its end, the US has certainly realized that her economic strength relative to Europe – not to mention Japan – has been reduced. The recrudescence of US dynamism *vis-à-vis* Western Europe, which is barely emerging from the economic stagnation resulting from the worst economic crisis since World War II, ought not to lead us hastily to conclude that we have returned to the world economic relationship that prevailed until about the end of the 1960s.

It is also worth recalling briefly the vicissitudes of detente. Detente for the majority of the Europeans represents, beyond political differences, something very important. This is not generally the case in the US. Yet the question of discord among the Western Allies cannot be reduced simply to a difference in the perception and understanding of detente. Moreover there were times when detente had the same meaning for both the Western Europeans and the Americans. Both held to the illusion in the 1970s that the USSR would abandon her natural character. We should also recognize that the USSR was really interested in detente between 1965 and 1975. She subscribed to important agreements such as SALT I and the Four-Power Agreement on Berlin. The USSR certainly helped – within the limits of her influence – to promote a settlement of the Vietnam War. She had had to accept her exclusion from participation in the Middle East even though she never renounced a desire to play a role in maintaining special links with Syria.

Thus in Soviet terms detente never implied either an end to ideological and political struggle, or the exercise of restraint in her quest for military superiority, in matters that were not covered by international agreements. In contrast, detente implied the right to maintain, by any means, Soviet control over Eastern Europe.

The Soviet Union took advantage of internal events in the US (especially Watergate and the War Powers Act) to exploit her opportunities. This applied particularly to the military penetration of Africa (with the Cuban proxy in Angola, and Soviet, East German and Cuban troops in Ethiopia), to the excessive armament of Soviet forces in every military field (including the SS-20) and to Soviet intervention in Alliance policy, particularly at a time when NATO was confronted with difficult military decisions such as those on neutron weapons and theatre nuclear weapons.

As one looks at Soviet international policy, the impression remains that, since the light of detente has been turned low – often as a result, of Soviet activity, Soviet leaders appear both surprised and disappointed. When President Carter dramatically changed the direction of US policy after the Soviet invasion of Afghanistan (a change amply confirmed with the election of President Reagan), the Soviet leadership appeared frustrated and even disturbed by the absence of a privileged dialogue with the United States.

The non-ratification of SALT II, even if it had no real consequences (since the provisions of the agreement are being followed more or less by both parties), symbolized an American refusal to continue a special relationship with the USSR according to the rules that had once been defined.

The Soviet reaction to America's breaking off the dialogue has been to promote a systematic anti-American campaign in Western Europe and in the rest of the world. The Soviet Union indicts the United States with total responsibility for the increase of tensions in the world.

The new US Administration of Mr Reagan is firmly dedicated to demonstrating to the USSR (and also to the Atlantic Alliance) that the Administration knows perfectly well what its objectives are and what programmes it intends to implement, whatever the costs.

This resolution inspired American foreign policy to take a more militant course.

Decisions taken by the US in the field of rearmament have certainly impressed the Soviet Union and the way in which policy toward the USSR has been implemented and the tone of the declarations by which this policy was revealed to both adversary and allies have certainly made a real impact on America's Allies. Moreover the Allies have had no difficulty in admitting the necessity, emphasized in US policy, of establishing a real balance of forces with the Warsaw Pact.

Rather it has been the *tone* of various official US statements that has made the Allies upset or anxious. On the whole, the basic aim of US policy, re-establishing US defence against the huge Soviet military potential, is accepted. Yet doubts remain as to whether the US has the will seriously to negotiate arms-control agreements. One cannot exclude the possibility that certain segments of the US Administration do indeed hold sceptical views about the future results of arms-control negotiations. This attitude certainly worries the Western Europeans.

However, it would be unfair not to recognize that the Reagan Administration has modified its position, precisely in order to alleviate Western European anxieties and to dissipate Western European scepticism about US willingness to reach an agreement with the Soviet Union.

In the US, detente has come to be, associated with feelings of guilt and especially guilty naïveté because it led to unrestrained Soviet expansionism. Furthermore, a firm belief has spread amongst some of the US leadership that the USSR is dishonest. It would therefore be immoral to develop a genuine dialogue with the Soviet leadership.

This does not mean that the Reagan Administration considers it impossible to reach an agreement with the USSR on arms control. It is beyond all question that the United States has since 1981 tabled serious and comprehensive proposals for the START and INF talks. However, US approaches to arms control seem still to be conceived within a framework of mutual antagonism: the aim is to reach only limited and verifiable agreements.

It would appear that the US leadership is not yet ready publicly to modify their opinions about Western European attitudes to the division of labour within the Alliance, to the defence burdens falling on the US, and European detente, opinions widely expressed after the Soviet invasion of Afghanistan. Even if this formulation is critical of the way in which Western Europeans view their relationship with the USSR, it is far from being false considering the fact that it highlights the continued attraction of detente for the Europeans despite its troubled passage since 1975.

The vagaries of detente and the reactions to it on both sides of the Atlantic underline the point that the Alliance is bound to be in permanent crisis if it does not collectively define an 'Ostpolitik'.

In other words, the NATO Alliance must establish a consensus about what the rules should be and how they should be applied in the relationship with the USSR and the other Warsaw Pact countries. Particularly how should the Alliance define its objectives and the limits it intends to place on Soviet international activism and ascendancy over Eastern Europe.

Enduring disagreement on these subjects will undermine the NATO Alliance. In fact, during the disagreements within the Alliance over economic sanctions in 1982, which centred around the gas pipeline question and the accompanying US embargo, one finds the main characteristics of the two antagonistic theories of 'roll-back' and 'containment', which defined the options available to the US vis-à-vis the USSR at the start of the Cold War. One sometimes gets the feeling that some segments of the American leadership are indeed tempted to update some version of the 'roll-back' theory, looking towards the collapse of the Soviet Empire from both economic difficulties within the USSR and centrifugal forces in the satellite countries.

Stemming from this assumption is the idea – totally unacceptable for the West Europeans – of taking a term from the Marxist lexicon, and exploiting the 'internal contradiction within the Communist system'.

The debate about which precise economic sanctions to apply to the USSR and Poland after the Polish government decreed martial law demonstrated clearly the extent to which the Alliance can be damaged as a result of legitimate differences of opinion about the effectiveness of sanctions against a country violating the international order respected by other countries.

It appears almost certain that, if the US wished to persuade her Allies systematically to develop a policy of restricting trade with Eastern countries, a policy aimed at jeopardizing the vested interests created by detente, or a policy of economic sanctions in order to bend Soviet foreign policy or even to facilitate a redistribution of political and economic power within the USSR, there will certainly be a clash of interests among the Western Allies.

Considering the tendencies present in US foreign policy, the Western Europeans have reason to become worried about what they consider to be a dangerous mixture of intellectual single-mindedness and Manichaeism. They will be close to thinking, as André Gide once said: 'it is with good intentions that bad literature is written'. They will add: 'and it is with noble and dignified principles that bad politics is performed'.

Many Europeans are so passionately committed to detente – perceived as a kind of life insurance premium for peace in Europe – that they are ready to avoid taking any initiatives on their own, or encouraging any changes by the peoples of Eastern Europe in their submission to Communist regimes and integration into the Warsaw Pact. Otherwise, how can one explain the speed with which high level statements were issued to indicate that, since Poland was integrated into the Russian *imperium*, nothing will be done by the West to interfere in upheavals in their sphere of influence? It is worth reflecting that the most likely cause of war could be Soviet failure in their efforts to create a political-economic system that would prevent any disturbance within the Soviet sphere of influence.

To summarize, it would appear impossible for the Alliance to overcome the political challenge that confronts it, if it is unable to define a comprehensive doctrine for its relationship with the East. To a certain extent it is essentially a question of how to extend, deepen and update the Harmel Report. Nevertheless even though such an intellectual effort appears essential if difficult, it will not be enough. There is also an internal dimension to the political challenge facing NATO. Since this dimension is incomparably broader than it was ten years ago, it now deserves the utmost attention. The internal political and moral debate spreading throughout the Alliance spares few countries even if it is still limited to specific segments of our populations: the churches; youth (whether organized or not); political organizations of the left; some trade unions; and the ecological movement.

The Internal Political Challenge
If one looks to the present situation in Western European countries – where the debate appears to be more strident – and if one compares this with trends in certain segments of US society and US political leadership, one finds both a common theme and totally opposed ideas. The common theme relates to hostility towards nuclear weapons ('no first use') or to a total rejection of nuclear weapons ('better red than dead'). The problem is not so much to rebuff such ideas, but to maintain the credibility of both the Alliance and its strategy in the face of a reluctant and worried public opinion.

In Western Europe this frame of mind carries with it a tendency to accuse the US rather than the USSR of responsibility for allegedly increasing the risk of confrontation and even war.

One is thus led to the paradox – hardly credible to many Americans – that some Europeans aim all their criticisms at their ally, guilty (in their minds) of trying to restore for the benefit of Europe the Euro-strategic balance overturned when the USSR began to deploy SS-20s – and doing it, in what is a second paradox, at the request of one of the then most important of European leaders – himself a social democrat.

Of course the USSR has tried hard to take advantage of this situation. It now seems certain that, if the present debate within the Alliance ends with a deferral of the two-track decision of December 1979, this would have extremely serious consequences for both Alliance strategy and its political base. Without political vision the Alliance will not be able to withstand the damaging effects of struggles for influence, conflicts of interests, national or continental selfishness, and Soviet policy.

This nation, the Soviet Union, strives with impressive steadfastness to realize her pan-European ambition, which is to find herself alone with a Western Europe from which the US has withdrawn. Sometimes Europeans forget that the US is a European power. Not because of geography – unlike the USSR – but because of the Alliance. Therefore it remains of the utmost importance that the countries of the Alliance reach agreement on the subjects mentioned above or, at least, that they limit the scope and violence of their disagreements.

The political vision should be based on the one fundamental shared interest, which is to avoid war in Europe and to guarantee mutual security with an appropriate, coherent and credible strategy relying on effective means of defence. This leads to the development of ideas about what I call the strategic challenge.

The Strategic Challenge
Without a strategy for deterrence and defence, the Alliance no longer has a centre of gravity. For some years, Alliance strategy has been reminiscent of those elegant and fragile antique chairs which one can admire from a distance but dare not sit on for fear of collapse.

In an era of strategic nuclear parity, a strategy for deterrence is bound to be ambiguous. Its deterrent effect relies first on the total uncertainty remaining in any opponent's mind about the probability of answering an aggression with nuclear weapons. However, ambiguity should be confined only to that and should not relate to the physical capability to retaliate if necessary.

The problem for the strategic doctrine of the Alliance is not to be found in this element of uncertainty – rather it is to be found in the confusion created in Western Europe by the multiplication of ideas and declarations by the US since the end of the 1970s.

Through constant reiteration that the Soviet military build-up has created a quantitative and qualitative gap to the detriment of the US, Americans have themselves encouraged doubts about the effectiveness of deterrence. If one constantly asserts that one is weaker, one runs the risk of convincing one's friends.

Debate on how to put an end to the 'window of vulnerability' has been temporarily closed with the report of the Scowcroft Commission and with the approval by Congress of the solutions proposed by the Administration. But this is only one phase in a long quest by the US to maintain – or, for some, to re-establish – a credible deterrent.

The present debate has had tremendous consequences for Western European public opinion since it places the strategic doctrine of the Alliance under strain. Most of the countries of Europe have accepted, and even wished, that nuclear deterrence should remain in place and stable because it seems to be the only way of making war impossible.

It has taken part of a generation, roughly between 1964 and 1982, for public opinion in Europe to recognize that a nuclear war could be more than a war between the superpowers. The philosophy underlying flexible response implies that Europe would be deeply involved in the second echelon of escalation in a nuclear war.

Unfortunately, nuclear deterrence implies too that some consideration be given to the eventual implementation of nuclear strikes. Nuclear deterrence prevents war breaking out only if its credibility is assumed. And this credibility exists only if one plans for the possibility that deterrence could break down and so thinks about how to run that war. It is hard to imagine a country playing a game for its survival when the probability is that the holocaust will render that search futile. 'Mutual Assured Destruction' can, if need be, be considered as a strategy; but this is impossible if suicide is certain.

The agitation provoked in certain countries of the Alliance by the deployment of INF at the end of 1983, and the possibility of further violent reactions, find their origin in the anxiety stemming from the realization that once deterrence has failed, conventional and nuclear war could finally become a reality.

The various challenges, which now and for the future will constitute the test for Alliance cohesiveness and viability, do not all seem equally acute or pressing but it will be difficult to cope with the strategic challenge.

This is so, first of all because US strategy for intercontinental strategic weapons is entering a phase of revision. Until the next decade this will give a transitory character to the choices now being made. It would be surprising if the internal debate which has opened up in the US did not have political consequences within the Alliance.

Secondly, it is because uncertainty and confusion are more dangerous for the credibility of deterrence than is precise definition of its nature and its political and military implications. The Alliance must integrate the following into a global strategic framework:

– The structure of the American deterrent, whose main features do not yet clearly emerge from the debate about the MX.
– The continuation of the strategic dialogue with the USSR, in order to obtain limits on the development of intercontinental weapons such that quantitative levels are reduced step-by-step. The political adhesion of public opinion in most Alliance countries raises risks in accepting a strategic dialogue which amounts to no more than the codification of the arms race.
– The reaffirmation and preservation of the solidarity of the strategic security of the two pillars of the Alliance – which after all constitute its very essence.

One cannot ignore the stimulating ideas that General Rogers has advanced in the debate, but for a reason different from those usually given to justify them. They do not offer an alternative to nuclear weapons, for it is almost certain that the use of highly accurate weapons with great destructive power against the second echelon of Soviet forces will rather be a factor accelerating a Soviet decision to employ short, and medium-range nuclear tactical weapons. Now it is precisely this that frightens people who are not generally preoccupied with the devastation that nuclear weapons could cause in the USSR. To repeat, this is why the solution advocated by General Rogers is not really an answer to the anguish of public opinion, nor, therefore, to public questioning about eventual recourse to nuclear weapons.

On the other hand, these ideas do raise questions, as do those of the advocates of 'no first use', about a postulate of NATO's defensive strategy, that there is a threshold beyond which war enters a nuclear phase. This threshold is a function of the relative inferiority in conventional weapons, an inferiority due to the budgetary and economic constraints imposed by the politico-social system on Western States. As in the controversy surrounding 'no first use', or the propositions concerning a 'nuclear freeze', it is assumed that the imbalance in non-nuclear forces and the asymmetry in capacity to maintain a significant military apparatus in peacetime are diminished. The question nevertheless remains whether the ideas of General Rogers might become an issue to be addressed if, in a hypothetical case, US strategy were one day to lead to a redeployment of conventional forces in favour of theatres other than Europe.

The Economic Challenge
The relationship between the EEC and the US has never been easy. It has comprised successive confrontations defused in the end by laborious compromises. This can be attributed partly to the ambivalent American attitudes towards the policies of the Community and partly because the EEC appears to have difficulty in adjusting its policy to rather erratic US economic and financial policies.

This ambivalent attitude results from the mixture of success and self-deception of the US in her European policies. Soon after the last war she fostered the idea of establishing institutions for promoting joint economic co-operation between the Western European countries and she worked towards the gradual integration of the European economies. The US succeeded in that aim without finding satisfaction for her expectations. Instead of an understanding and co-operative partner ready to back the US in her assumption of world-wide responsibilities, the US found instead what she sometimes perceives as an intractable partner and an inconsiderate competitor.

The US periodically wavers between irritation (and even, sometimes, exasperation) brought about by the Western European will for autonomy, and realism deriving from the belief that a divided Europe caught again by its particularist demons – a temptation to which Europeans are still inclined – will certainly be more easy to control, even if it is not necessarily more reliable. For their part, Western Europeans have a tendency to expect everything and nothing from the US. One can easily find an American leader who will diagnose the schizoid nature of Western European policy towards the US. Difficulties surrounding the present economic crisis have stirred up characteristic tensions in the commercial and monetary relationship between Europe and the US. Of course, there have always been problems between the 'partners', either through competition for gaining contracts in outside markets or because of their conflicting interests in monetary matters. The present difficulties are not new; complaints being made by the present French President about the American benign neglect of the volatility of the dollar are quite similar to the complaints made by General de Gaulle when he ordered the *Banque de France* to convert the French national monetary reserve from dollars to gold.

What *is* new stems from the magnitude of the risk embodied in the breadth and number of the present conflicts, and also from the dangers presented by the inability to find solutions to these conflicts of interest. They could seriously affect the understanding which remains indispensable to the functioning of the Alliance.

There is also competition with Japan and this is probably more destructive for some sectors of the US economy than competition with Western Europe. However, both the US and Western European economies are going through analogous problems of obsolescence and retrenchment in those economic sectors whose origins go back to the first age of the Industrial Revolution. Competition is here more harsh and selfishness more uncompromising. Moreover, Western Europe is becoming an agricultural power whose capacity to export outside EEC territory is backed by a policy of subsidy, less and less tolerable for some in politics and in the agricultural sector. In this matter, the US tends to believe that Western Europeans are trespassing on a domain reserved for American producers. Agriculture has always been a potential area of conflict. Nowadays clashes go beyond particular problems, such as the 'Chicken War'.

The US bitterly reproaches the Community for its policy of subsidy which allows Western European farmers to (unfairly) compete with American farmers in foreign markets. The Western Europeans reply that financial support to agriculture in Western Europe is lower than it is in the US, that the community remains a net importer of agricultural goods of which a large share comes from the US, and that openings to the Mediterranean producers (such as Spain and the Maghreb) are part of a policy aimed at the political stabilization of this area. Moreover, the Western Europeans argue that it is unfair to criticize their export of agricultural products, since the US sells wheat to Egypt and other countries at a price well below that obtaining in the world market without considering how this could affect the interests of her Allies.

Concerning steel, it is only because Europeans accepted costly and difficult self-restraint on exports that a clash was averted after the US threatened to raise new duties on steel imports into the US. This battle is not yet over. American industrialists have launched a new offensive against European exports of special steels which are not included in the agreement.

The low price of oil in the US allows it to gain price advantages in American exports of synthetic fibres. The growing protectionism in some industrial sectors (cars, textiles, shoes) and hidden subsidies to export through the DISC (Domestic International Sales Corporation) system are other examples of the many commercial quarrels which divide Western Europeans and Americans.

But two other questions have taken on a particular political prominence: the gas pipeline; and monetary policy. Concerning the pipeline, the Europeans have been infuriated that – under the pretext of the embargo of American licensed items for export to the East – brutal intrusion by their American partners has interfered with the Western European strategy of diversifying sources of energy supplies, without taking European interests into account. In monetary matters, beyond the problems introduced by the erratic fluctuations of the dollar on the international exchange markets, it is also the absence of any concern for other countries in Federal Reserve policy and US interest rates which provokes bitterness among Western Europeans, particularly now in France.

When one considers the various grievances of this side or that, one cannot help but be struck by its familiar character. Fundamentally, *plus ça change, plus c'est le même chose*, as the popular wisdom would have it. Western Europeans have the feeling that the US intends to make them bear some of the consequences of the US Administration's economic and monetary policies. They also get the impression that the US considers 'burden shifting' to be a legitimate exchange for the protection that the super-power provides for her Allies.

As for the Americans, they have also experienced feelings of injustice, and note that Western European grousing has never ceased; the only change is in the subject of their bad temper and recrimination. Whatever the Americans do, they are criticized. If the dollar falls, Europeans complain about the artifical advantage this gives for American competitiveness. If the dollar rises, Europeans complain about the American leaders' lack of interest in the effects of the status of the dollar on the state of their economies. One certain fact is that the US accepts only with great reluctance the implications that stem from the international economic interdependence that she advocates.

The Western Europeans, on the other hand, have the feeling that rigid US adherence to the principle of interdependence wobbles somewhat when her status of military super-power and dominant economy allows her to evade certain constraints which could otherwise limit her political autonomy.

During the Vietnam War, as today, the Western Europeans perceived that the US was managing a purely American budgetary and monetary policy without consideration for the consequences that this might have for various Western European economies.

This is a debate whose end is not in sight, because it is inherent in the fragmentation and instability of the international economic and monetary system.

The creation in 1979 of the 'European Monetary System' (EMS) was intended to remedy the instability of the dollar-standard and the erratic fluctuations it imposed upon European currencies. Four years later, Western countries are still in search of an orderly monetary system in which the key currency – the US dollar – will recover a relative degree of stability. The idea of 'stability zones' (ECU, yen and US dollar) responds to this preoccupation. So far, the idea has been pushed aside, on the grounds that the basic conditions of the market are determining and that intervention by Central Banks – particularly to stabilize the US dollar – will not have a decisive effect upon them. This reasoning – sensible in itself – feigns to ignore the fact that among the factors which determine 'the basic conditions of the market', there is the financial and monetary policy of the United States, and beyond that the policy of a super-power and all the weight of her dominant economy.

Finally, one might hope that the Alliance and its members have drawn some lessons from the painful dispute of the gas pipeline issue. The crisis triggered by the pipeline can be seen as a case study of what should not be done (on both sides) if one wants to prevent differences in conception and interests – differences which constitute the daily bread of an Alliance – from degenerating into confrontation, in large part unprovoked and certainly harmful to the cohesion of the Alliance.

This does not mean that one should underestimate the importance of strict control on transfers of technology. Nor should the possibility of economic sanctions against the USSR be excluded. In certain cases, a violation of unwritten rules of good international behaviour – this deliberately vague formulation is the consequence of the highly contingent and blurred policies of democratic states in this area – requires that the community of democratic nations demonstrate its disapproval by economic and political sanctions. Still, it is necessary to see that, in the final analysis, the sanctions do not cause more damage to the cohesion of the Alliance than they inflict in penalties upon the offender state.

The Challenge of an Unstable Third World
The international environment of the Alliance, and especially the Third World, will not remain unchanged. The instability of the Third World will not lack for sources of potentially damaging debates within the Alliance. In a more and more interdependent world, the alteration of the international environment cannot be ignored by the Alliance. Tensions and conflicts in some areas of strategic importance, either for the Alliance or for some of its members, could have an effect on its cohesion. Yet there are no precise guidelines which, formulated in advance, will protect the Alliance against unfavourable repercussions from the transformation of the international environment and from conflicts that could arise in the Third World.

If there is an area where consultations will be essential, it is this one. To repeat, no precise rule can be determined in advance. However, there are more lessons that have emerged from the recent past. The Allies would do well to keep them in mind, so that they do not find themselves again in the middle of a crisis which seemed totally unforeseen when its threads were apparent for a long time.

This concerns the Western Europeans first of all. They cannot ignore the slowly shifting centre of US economic and political interests. If the twenty-first century is to be – as is often said – the century of the 'Pacific Basin', this means that Western Europe will no longer necessarily have first place in America's geopolitical perspective. The frame of mind that prevailed in the Congress some years ago, when Senator Mansfield wished to bring his famous amendment to a vote, could arise again. A renewal of 'neo-Mansfieldism' would, for example, be perfectly conceivable if further cruise missile and *Pershing* II deployment were postponed by the European governments.

This does not mean that Western Europe will cease to represent a dominant strategic interest for the US but one cannot exclude the possibility that the super-power might be led, one day, to reconsider the distribution of her conventional forces, either temporarily (e.g. a reduction in US forces in Western Europe for the sake of the Rapid Deployment Force (RDF) called to another theatre) or on a permanent basis.

Western Europeans attribute to their ally a tendency – not to say an obsession – to assign to each area of tension in the Third World a high degree of interventionism by the USSR and her allies or clients. In return this tendency – according to Western Europeans – has distorted analysis of the objective situation and of the remedy to cure it. This, too, has led Western Europeans to be extremely reserved about possible military solutions. There is no doubt that this is an area of conflict between American unilateralism – that is, the tendency to press ahead so long as the strategic interests of the United States require it, brushing aside the objections and inclinations of the Allies – and the more nuanced view that Western Europeans often have of the factors of instability and the sources of conflict.

The adherence of the Japanese Prime Minister to the Williamsburg communiqué might be favourable to Western Europe. Western Europe would be wrong not to take into consideration that for her American ally security remains a global issue, not limited to the defence of the Western European redoubt. Western security has a more interdependent character since the Soviet threat – in particular her deployments in Europe as well as in Asia – spares no-one.

On the other hand, American vigilance about political developments in Central America should suggest to Western Europeans how carefully they should behave in this particular area of the world. Little by little the United States is moving away from the abstention, if not the reservations, imposed by events in the early 1970s.

The Allies will not escape from formulating principles destined to guide the Alliance's reaction in case of conflict outside of NATO's own security area. This should be done with the utmost circumspection and with the minimum of formality compatible with an effective response. But this should be done, for otherwise the Alliance will be externally paralyzed and internally divided if such events ever occur.

Relations Between Eastern and Western Europe: Prospects for Change: I

DR HANNES ADOMEIT

The Shrinking Margin of Manoeuvre

The early 1980s have again brought into sharp focus the question of whether the two halves of Europe have a significant agenda of business to explore with each other or whether Western European relations with the Soviet Union and Eastern Europe are merely a factor of Soviet–American relations. The answer to this question provided by Alastair Buchan in the early 1970s was that there *is* a legitimate agenda for Europeans to take care of and that Western European relations with the Soviet Union and Eastern Europe *are* to some extent capable of autonomous development.[1] This answer was probably uncontroversial considering the international conditions obtaining at the time: the temporary shelving of Soviet policies of selective detente *vis-à-vis* the West; the pursuit of common interests in Soviet–American relations; excellent prospects of East–West trade expansion; reasonably good chances of significant arms-control agreements; broad consensus in the Western Alliance concerning conceptual and practical approaches to the USSR; and relative stability and tranquility in Eastern Europe. Today, however, not a single one of these conditions continues to apply. It may be necessary, therefore, to supply new answers to the opening question.

Ever since the deterioration in Soviet–American relations began in the 1970s the margin of acceptable deviation by the European countries from the policies of the super-powers has been shrinking. This is due to a number of factors of which two stand out as particularly important. First, although the Soviet leadership is intent on conveying the impression of 'business as usual' in East–West relations in Europe, not least so as to blunt the edge of American hard-line ('anti-Soviet') policies and draw the Reagan Administration into a Soviet-defined process of 'normalization', the degree of flexibility – both internal and external – permitted to the Eastern European countries has always been rather narrowly circumscribed and this is especially so in the wake of the Polish Crisis. Moreover, Andropov's predilection for restoring discipline at home and in the Bloc further circumscribed Eastern European flexibility. Secondly, although the degree of foreign policy autonomy enjoyed by the Western European countries is much greater than that of the Warsaw Pact members, any major initiatives taken by the former in the direction of broadening East–West political and economic co-operation contain the risk of further enhancing divisive tendencies in the Western Alliance and they are thus likely to be diluted in effectiveness or avoided.

As these two constraining factors show, prospects for change in the relations between the two halves of Europe crucially depend on the interaction of developments in the Soviet Union, Eastern Europe, and the Western Alliance.[2] More specifically, concerning the *Soviet Union*, they are a function of:

- The internal stability of the country, and the strength and composition of its leadership.
- The degree of success or failure experienced by the present or subsequent leaderships in making the necessary transition from extensive to intensive economic growth and thus improving the overall performance of the Soviet economy.
- The priority given by the Soviet leadership to the military as against the civilian sector of production and, by extension, to military versus ideological, political and economic forms of competition between the two opposed world systems.

- The assessments made by the Soviet leadership as to the relative importance of Eastern Europe, the cost effectiveness of Soviet control of this area and the possible repercussions of East European deviation from the Soviet model on the USSR herself.

As for *Eastern Europe* as an agent of change in the relations between the countries across the political and socio-economic divide in Europe, the following factors are of particular significance:

- The political stability and economic viability of the individual Eastern European regimes.
- The degree of success or failure encountered by the Eastern European leaderships in enhancing political legitimacy, alleviating popular discontent, stimulating voluntary co-operation and initiative, and bridging the gap between the Party and society.
- The ability of the Eastern European regimes to embark on successful economic reform, increase economic efficiency and prevent the recurrence of serious economic and, of necessity, political crises.

As regards the *Western Alliance*, attention needs to be paid to the following problems:

- The extent to which the Alliance adopts a strategy of punitive sanctions or a policy of peaceful engagement. More specifically, change depends on how far the Alliance aims at enhancing Soviet weaknesses, accelerating the 'decline of the Soviet empire' and using Eastern Europe in this context as a lever of 'destabilization' *or*, conversely, whether it is prepared to accept reasonable (i.e. not unlimited) Soviet security concerns in Eastern Europe and work for an improved *modus vivendi*.
- The scale of Western economic engagement in the USSR and Eastern Europe, the predictability or unpredictability of the Western involvement, and the degree to which Eastern access to Western technology, expertise and credit is made dependent on political criteria.

It is obvious that the interaction of all of these factors makes prediction about the prospects for change in East–West relations in Europe a hazardous endeavour. However, the direction of change will probably occur within the boundaries set by past experience. In particular, it is very doubtful whether the detente of the 1970s (just as with the Cold War preceding it) can and will be replayed in the 1980s. All the major actors previously participating in the process of detente are acutely aware of its fate. Yet perceptions differ as to the origins, evolution and demise of detente in the 1970s, and it is these perceptions which will largely shape the policies in the 1980s. A closer look at the legacy of the past is therefore warranted.

The Legacy of Detente: Promise and Progress

From the viewpoint of all three major protagonists (the Soviet Union, Eastern Europe and the Western Alliance) the first half of the 1970s may well appear in retrospect as a golden era. The USSR had successfully liquidated the 'revisionist' experiment in Czechoslovakia by her military intervention in August 1968: after the Spring of 1969, 'normalization' proceeded under Husak without any major challenge from within or outside the Party. In Poland, the workers' riots of December 1970 had produced a new leadership under Gierek regarded in both East and West as determined and capable of turning the country into a modern industrial state. In East Germany, too, the leadership of Honecker promised to be more pragmatic and 'technocratic' (though most likely not more liberal) than that of his predecessor who had outlived his political usefulness for the USSR because of an increasing lack of precisely these qualities. Hungary under Kadar, notwithstanding her reluctant participation in the termination of the Prague Spring and a partial retreat from the principles of economic reform in 1972–3, continued to implement her New Economic Mechanism – the most far-reaching and successful of all the reforms attempted in the CMEA until today. Bulgaria under Zhivkov, which had formerly (in 1966) envisaged even more fundamental economic reforms, was deterred from implementing them after 1968 but remained committed nevertheless to an increase in economic exchanges with the West and also began to improve her agricultural system. Finally, Romania under Ceausescu was becoming less of a nuisance for the Soviet Union while retaining in Western eyes a useful function in preventing *Gleichschaltung* (unification) within the Bloc and enhancing foreign policy differentiation towards the outside world.

These developments in Eastern Europe were both facilitated by and, at the same time, they reinforced shifts which were taking place in the policies of the Soviet Union and the Western Alliance. In particular, the following new conditions affected East–West relations:

– After the Soviet leadership had again demonstrated its resolve in 1968 to prevent sweeping socio-economic reform forced, in its view, upon a weak Party leadership 'from below', the Soviet Union was – perhaps paradoxically but, in essence, prudently – showing interest in such *limited* reformist schemes as promised to improve economic efficiency without threatening the primacy of the Party.

– In line with this new sense of prudence and realism, the Soviet leadership was aiming at a more flexible management of the Warsaw Pact (the reforms of 1969) and CMEA (the comprehensive programme of 1971), both providing for improved participation of, and perhaps a greater sense of popular identification among, the Eastern European members of these two organizations.

– As economic reformism had been at the root of much of the political 'revisionism' in Czechoslovakia, reform as a means of enhancing economic performance in the Soviet Union had been much discredited. As a consequence, large-scale import of Western technology and access to expertise and credit began to look like an attractive alternative. Whereas the Soviet Union in the 1960s had for various political reasons been reluctant to consent to an expansion of the East Europeans' trade links with the West, she no longer objected to such expansion in the early 1970s.

– In the 1960s, credit relations between Western banks and Eastern European banking and trading organizations had been at a very low level. This changed dramatically in the early 1970s. Faced with a glut of petrodollars, and acting on the assumption that central planning in the CMEA countries guaranteed strict financial discipline, that the Soviet Union would assist the smaller members if they were to run into liquidity problems (the 'umbrella theory') and that, therefore, all of CMEA could be regarded as one single area of low financial risk, Western banks began to extend credit liberally.[3] As a consequence, the net debt of the Eastern European countries rose from $6 billion at the end of 1970 to $21.2 billion at the end of 1975. Western credit, both commercial and governmental, thus began to play a major role in the economies of the Eastern European countries and provided a major stimulus for East–West trade.

– An even more important – perhaps decisive – stimulus was provided by the improvement in East–West political relations. More specifically, the Soviet acceptance of the inclusion of the United States in the Conference on Security and Co-operation in Europe (CSCE) in 1970 laid the basis for a broad process of expanding political and economic relations. Concurrently, the evolution of West Germany's *Ostpolitik* deprived the orthodox forces in the Soviet Union and Eastern Europe of a powerful device with which to exclude that country from involvement in the area.

To summarize, the first half of the 1970s brought a considerable increase in economic, financial, scientific and cultural relations between the two parts of Europe. Personal contacts between members of governmental and non-governmental elites multiplied, and lasting trust (some of which persists until now) resulted. As for Western Europe, it was perhaps West Germany which benefited most. Not only did her trade with Eastern Europe increase by a considerable margin but she also gained in political status and influence. The quadripartite and intra-German Treaties had improved the status and viability of Berlin. It was becoming easier for West Berliners and West Germans to visit East Germany. Conversely, the Eastern European countries were also benefiting from detente. In 1971–5, the growth rates of their economies easily surpassed those of the USSR and the OECD countries (Bulgaria: 7.8%; Czechoslovakia: 5.6%; East Germany: 5.4%; Hungary: 6.2%; Poland: 9.8%; Romania: 11.3%). Since economic developments brought tangible improvements in the standards of living and met rising popular expectations, Eastern Europe enjoyed a period of unprecedented stability and tranquility and the Communist regimes gained greater legitimacy. This idyllic state of affairs was not to last.

The Legacy of Detente: Disappointment and Decline

In the second half of the 1970s a number of factors combined to lead to deterioration of internal conditions in Eastern Europe and in the relationship between East and West in Europe. These factors, furthermore, were of such a scale and importance that their impact extended into the early 1980s and is likely to persist for the foreseeable future.

What accounted primarily for the downturn in the political and economic fortunes of Eastern Europe (and for much subsequent domestic and international disillusionment) was the significant imbalance between massive Western involvement and meagre efforts at reform. Economic co-operation with the West *could* have served as a useful basis for economic reform and for increased market-oriented integration in CMEA (as advocated by Hungary and as contained, in part, in the 1971 comprehensive programme). However this opportunity for significant internal reform was – with the exception of Hungary – not taken. The significant volume of Western technology imported for the most part did not fall on the fertile ground of efficient economic organization. It fell instead on the waste land of ideological inflexibility and bureaucratic procrastination. As a result Western technology essentially formed a separate part of the economy, generating its own requirements for further increases in imports of Western semi-manufactures and spare parts, as well as raw materials, thereby increasing demands for scarce hard currency.[4]

The import-led growth strategy adopted by the Eastern European countries foundered upon a second major rock: the fourfold rise in the world market price of oil. For the West this rise began in 1973 in the wake of the War in the Middle East and, in conjunction with structural deficiencies of the Western economies, led almost immediately to deep recession. This, in turn, led to a reduction in demand for Eastern European primary and manufactured products, and to a reinforcement of protectionist tendencies in the West with the aim of safeguarding domestic production from cheap Eastern European products and services. It also raised the difficult (and still acute) problem for Eastern Europe of how to repay mounting debts to Western banks and governments and forced Eastern Europe to cut back drastically the volume of Western machinery imports (a trend clearly discernible by 1977–8).

Contributing to the onset of serious economic crisis in Eastern Europe were the intra-CMEA adjustments to the increase in the world market price for oil. For the most part, Eastern Europe was protected from the main impact of the increase until 1975. Only then did the USSR revise the intra-CMEA pricing mechanism with prices from then on to be changed annually on the basis of a five-year moving average of world market prices. As a result, the Soviet Union more than doubled the price of her oil exports to Eastern Europe in that year.[5] In conjunction with rises in the price of other fuels and raw materials, the terms of trade were thus sharply turning against the Eastern European countries in relation to the USSR, necessitating increased exports of machinery to compensate for this trend. However, the Soviet Union did not extort a corresponding increase in products demanded from Eastern Europe; instead she ameliorated the harshness of the terms-of-trade shift by, in effect, extending credit. As Phil Hanson has written, the Soviet leadership behaved like the better sort of landlord, 'raising the rent belatedly and by rather less than the general rate of inflation, and allowing more time to pay'.[6]

Once the sharp deterioration in Eastern European economic conditions had become clearly visible in 1978–80 – after the cushioning effects of socialist planning had begun to wear off and Soviet subsidies and credits had started to flow more thinly – a third main blow was dealt to the political and economic conditions in Eastern Europe and to the relationship between the two halves of Europe. This was the drastic curtailment of Western credit. Only rather belatedly were the Western banks begining to realize that the indiscriminate lending race to the East had been unwise. Their risk assessment had to be revised; the 'umbrella theory' was unfounded. This realization resulted not in cautious adjustment but in overreaction. Between the end of 1980 and September 1982 the Western banks recalled considerable amounts of capital from Eastern Europe (estimated at $6 billion). Coupled with a widespread reluctance to 'throw good money after bad', new loans to the area declined to a trickle. Poland in 1980 was the only major exception; it did receive a major loan from West German banks as a result of government pressure and backed by guarantees. The declaration of martial law in December 1981, however, put an end to politically-supported loans to Poland. Debt rescheduling – and not only for Poland – became the main order of business.[7]

A fourth main factor contributing to the decline in the fortunes of the Eastern European countries and their relations with Western Europe emanated from the deterioration of the Soviet–American relationship. For a time, until about the Autumn of 1980, it appeared as if detente were indeed divisible and that Europe could remain an island of calm in the rough seas of global super-power rivalry. This impression was fostered by the fact that much of the super-power conflict – from the Middle East in 1973 to Afghanistan in 1979–80 – occurred in areas from which Western European powers had withdrawn their forces or where they had at least significantly reduced their military presence and profile so as to avoid overcommitment and overextension of limited resources (e.g. Britain in the Persian Gulf, France in Indochina, Italy in East Africa, and Portugal in Angola and Mozambique) or where the

Western European powers had never played a security role. In view of the long history of Western European disengagement or traditional lack of presence, US attempts at short notice to persuade the Western European States to recommit themselves or to involve themselves where they had never been involved before were sure to meet with an ambiguous response. This could easily be construed as a policy of equidistance from the super-powers (a policy which some vociferous sections of Western European opinion would indeed like to see adopted).

The impression of Europe as an island of detente was nourished also by fundamental conceptual differences in the Western Alliance concerning Soviet power and how to cope with it. These differences coalesced most conspicuously on the issue of sanctions and economic leverage, or the lack thereof, *vis-à-vis* the Soviet Union. The Western European stance on this issue (refusal by and large to participate in across-the-board sanctions against the Soviet Union and Eastern Europe) could easily – although wrongly – be interpreted as an indication of normality ('business as usual') or, what was worse in US eyes, as a form of appeasement and accommodation to Soviet power masquerading as normality.

Finally, Soviet political leaders and propagandists did their best to reinforce the idea that, as N. Portugalov put it, the 'concept of the divisibility of detente' was indeed valid and that 'to a certain extent it does correspond to political reality'.[8] Giscard d'Estaing and Helmut Schmidt were graciously received by Brezhnev. There was no overt pressure on Berlin. Until Autumn 1980 intra-German relations remained untouched. Indeed the number of visits by West Germans and West Berliners to East Germany grew and telephone, telegram and telex facilities between the two halves of Germany increased.

The German problem thus came to play again a significant role in East–West relations. This role, however, did not and does not flow from any expectation of the West German government that the Soviet leaders are about to make some grand offer for German reunification (even though Soviet diplomats have been known to drop meaningful hints about such an offer at late evening cocktail parties in Bonn). Nor is it connected with a strong nationalist current inside and outside the Peace Movement willing to put NATO at risk in exchange for reunification. On this issue realism abounds in all sections of the public. The GDR is correctly considered by them a cornerstone of the Soviet Union's Empire in Eastern Europe, and thus as too important for the USSR to let go.

The role of the German problem in East–West relations, therefore, hinges on West German objectives less ambitious than reunification. These include the viability of West Berlin, making life more bearable for the East Germans, maintaining as much contact as possible so as to prevent the two halves of Germany from further drifting apart and facilitating change in East Germany and Eastern Europe (*Wandel durch Annäherung*).

These objectives obviously put a brake on potential 'hardline' policies towards the East and provide Soviet diplomacy with, from its point of view, useful openings. But at the same time they are a significant challenge: the Soviet leaders can no longer hope to use effectively the traditional bogeyman of West German '*revanchisme*' and 'militarism' to enforce bloc discipline. They find themselves confronted instead with West Germany as a significant pole of attraction and competing for a share of influence in Eastern Europe.

Despite all the superficial indications of normality and the pretence of 'business as usual', however, objective conditions were inexorably and negatively affecting European affairs and constraining the European countries' freedom of manoeuvre. Foremost among these conditions was and still is the Soviet arms build-up. Its massive scale since the mid-1960s has necessitated Western responses which have in turn had disadvantageous repercussions in Eastern and Western Europe, and on the relations between the two. Thus, as early as November 1978, at the meeting of the highest political body of the Warsaw Pact in Moscow, the Soviet Union was demanding greater military integration in the Pact and (ostensibly as a reaction to NATO's commitment to raise defence spending by 3% annually in real terms) exerting pressure on the smaller members of the Eastern Alliance to increase their military expenditures by 5%.

Similarly, the widening margin of Soviet superiority in medium-range nuclear systems in Europe, which led to a response by NATO in the form of the 1979 dual-track decision, evoked in turn strong Soviet and East European opposition and vigorous Soviet support for the Western European Peace Movement to undermine NATO's response. It also had the effect of putting further strains on East–West political relations in Europe.

These strains were increased by the events in Poland after the summer of 1980. Serious domestic political crisis coupled with a catastrophic economic decline put an end to Poland's important role of bridge-building between East and West.[9] It also tended to increase the perpetual anxiety of the East German leaders concerning political instability in the GDR and elsewhere in the socialist community and raised their concern about possible economic repercussions. Therefore it also affected intra-German relations. In the autumn of 1980 Chancellor Schmidt's planned visit to the East Germany was postponed and the East German government unilaterally increased the minimum exchangerequirements for visitors.

As it turned out 'business as usual' did not obtain even in business. In fact, East–West economic relations, including those between the two halves of Europe, reacted very sensitively to the changes in the East–West political climate, despite the absence of substantial sanctions embarked upon by the Western European countries, despite all the credits, and despite the 'pipes-for-gas' deal with the USSR. This tacit or automatic linkage is indicated by the steady *decline* of the share of the CMEA countries in overall OECD trade since the mid-1970s (if trade between the countries of Western and Eastern Europe is looked at separately the result is the same) rather than increase in that trade as public perceptions would seem to have it.[10]

The Prospects for Change
The legacy of detente and its demise will be difficult to cope with. Most of the trends in

objective conditions and policies adopted in the latter half of the 1970s and the early 1980s are of considerable force and cannot easily be arrested or reversed.

This applies, first of all (to return to the analytical framework constructed above), to *Soviet policy*. Regrettably but undeniably, one of the most pronounced trends in Soviet policy during the Brezhnev era, and also under Andropov was the emphasis on military as against civilian values in society – on military production ('guns') instead of consumer goods production and agriculture ('butter'); and on military power rather than ideological, political, economic and cultural penetration to expand Soviet influence. Given the tremendous Soviet investment in arms production since the mid-1960s, the achievement of strategic parity, the improvement of conventional and theatre nuclear advantages in relation to NATO and the apparent strength of opposition in Western Europe to the deployment of *Pershing* II and cruise missiles, there is evidently a strong temptation for the Soviet leadership to 'cash in' on its investment. This could mean, in practice, more threats of new deployments, intransigence in arms-control negotiations (further fuelling divergencies between the United States and Western Europe) and continued reliance on domestic pressures in NATO countries to erode Western security policy.

Yet increasing emphasis on military power does nothing to alleviate the Soviet Union's pressing social and economic problems. Indeed this emphasis is probably one of the more important causes of these problems. Moreover, military occupation or the threat of military intervention as the primary form of exerting influence must be considered inherently unstable and distinctly costly. This is true, in particular, for the Soviet Union's relationship with Eastern Europe where the Soviet leaders are facing acute dilemmas.

On the one hand, Eastern Europe – for ideological and military-strategic reasons – remains of central interest to the Soviet leadership. Its stability and integration in the Soviet sphere of influence and security will remain top of their foreign policy priorities.

Yet Soviet–East European relations are still as 'unorganic' as they were in 1976 when Helmut Sonnenfeldt warned about the dangers of crises in Eastern Europe leading repeatedly to Soviet military intervention which might, possibly, spill over into an East–West military conflict. Furthermore, from the second half of the 1970s until 1981 the economic costs for maintaining the Soviet empire in Eastern Europe were steadily rising; Western estimates conclude that the Soviet Union has granted Eastern Europe large trade subsidies, averaging $5.8 billion per year during 1974–8, increasing to $10.4 billion in 1979, $17.5 billion in 1980 and peaking at $18.6 billion in 1981. Subsidies declined to $15.1 billion in 1982.[11]

Although the sums involved in these opportunity costs are by no means negligible (they amount to about 1% of Soviet GNP), they seem bound to continue to decline since the world market price of oil has been falling (from $34 to $29 per barrel for OPEC oil in March 1983 alone). Cash flows could even be *reversed* if world market prices for oil stayed very low and if the USSR chose to adhere strictly to the 1975 CMEA pricing mechanism. If one assumes in addition that the Soviet economy continues to grow at the rather slow pace of 2% per annum in the foreseeable future, the problem of Eastern Europe as an economic 'basket-case' requiring fundamental change in Soviet–East European relations should not be overdrawn. Moreover, the record of Soviet relations with other countries (notably Cuba, Vietnam and Afghanistan) shows that the Soviet cost/benefit analysis is *not* determined primarily by criteria of economic efficiency.

Rather than economic opportunity cost, the main problems in Soviet–East European relations centre around ideological commitment and cohesion, military power and influence, and political legitimacy and stability. These conditions are in turn crucially dependent on the economic state of affairs in Eastern Europe. In fact, every major political crisis in this area can be said to have been triggered by economic factors.

As events in Poland in 1980–81 demonstrated so dramatically, the nexus of economic crisis and erosion or even loss of political control by the local Party leadership poses tremendous security risks to the Soviet Union. This nexus reduces the reliability of the allied country's armed forces and erodes the effectiveness of the Soviet military posture towards Western Europe. Hence, even though – according to an East European source – the USSR is carrying 'over 80% of the *defence* burden within the framework of the Warsaw Pact',[12] the Soviet leadership may still consider it expedient to grant the Eastern European countries further exemptions from big increases in military spending.

A similar reasoning applies when examining a second dilemma. Instinctively, after their experience with the Jackson–Vanik and Stevenson Amendments linking human rights to trade concessions, the Western emphasis on human rights in the context of the CSCE as well as the proliferation of human rights groups in the Soviet Union and in Eastern Europe, and the rise of *Solidarność* in Poland in conditions of, by and large, continuing detente in Europe, the Soviet leaders are clearly inclined to tighten the screws in Eastern Europe. This is in order to restore ideological orthodoxy, to spur economic integration in CMEA, to improve military co-operation in the Warsaw Pact, to clamp down on economic reform efforts, and to impose severe restrictions on economic and financial links with the West.

Yet such remedies could either be wholly ineffective or they could even worsen the disease they are intended to cure. In some instances too, they are quite unnecessary. East Germany is ideologically orthodox and relatively stable politically but it is also actively engaged in East–West trade, notably with West Germany. Czechoslovakia has for the most part made the acceptance of current Soviet inclinations the basis for her domestic and foreign policy. In other instances, as in Hungary, such remedies would severely weaken the economy and the body politic. In Poland, rather than strengthening the system's immunity, they could cause her collapse.

If the Soviet leaders were to refrain from pursuing their inclination to crack the whip, it would be due to their increasing awareness that the cost of maintaining tight control in Eastern Europe has gone up and the effectiveness down. After all, in an ever more complex socio-economic organism simple solutions – repression and mobilization – will no longer suffice. What is needed to raise economic performance and to make the transition from extensive to intensive growth is to increase labour productivity. This, in turn, can only be achieved (as Andropov has several times stated in relation to the Soviet domestic scene) by improvements in morale, in voluntary co-operation, in individual responsibility and in personal initiative.[13] In other words, making the transition from extensive to intensive growth, and from quantity to quality, requires a change from coercion to persuasion. This, too, gives the East European leaderships some leeway. They can legitimately claim that they are the competent authorities for judging of how best to achieve this change.

An indication of both the Soviet tendency to want to tighten the reins and a measure of the success achieved by the Eastern European countries in asserting some autonomy is provided by the postponement yet again (in April 1983) of the much delayed summit meeting of the Eastern economic alliance. The Soviet Union is known to want such a meeting to endorse closer co-ordination of planning, production specialization and participation by the Eastern Europeans in the development of Soviet natural resources – in short, a much closer interlocking of the Soviet and East European economies. Owing to the principle of unanimity in decision-making in CMEA, however, the Soviet Union is reported not to have succeeded in structuring the agenda in accordance with her stated preferences.

This raises the question of whether the Eastern European *countries* may be able in the future not only to maintain the *status quo* but to *expand* their freedom of manoeuvre within the Bloc and towards Western Europe.

For the most part, the answer to this question must be negative for a number of reasons. Foremost among them are the bleak prospects of economic recovery. In the next few years, the state of the economies of the Eastern European countries and their bargaining power *vis-à-vis* the Soviet Union and the West are both likely to decline – and perhaps decline dramatically. Whereas the Western industrialized countries are already gaining a respite from steep rises in the price of energy and have adjusted reasonably well to the high price levels of energy, the Eastern European countries are still paying somewhat less than the world market price for Soviet imports of raw materials, oil and gas (although, as noted, this gap is narrowing and could even open in the opposite direction) and they have still to make significant structural changes to save energy. They continue to receive above-average payments from the Soviet Union for their industrial products even though, more often than not, these products would be difficult to sell on the world market. Finally they have run up very large trade deficits with the USSR (about six billion roubles in the period 1975–80, and over three billion roubles in 1981 alone, over half of which is accounted for by Poland).[14]

All this makes their negotiating position in relation to the Soviet Union quite weak. It would weaken even more if the Soviet Union's exchange earnings were to decline due to further deterioration of her terms of trade with the non-Communist world or because of delays in the construction of the Yamal (Urengoy) Pipeline to the West. This would increase the pressure in Moscow to curtail energy and raw materials deliveries to the CMEA countries and to rechannel them to hard-currency areas.

Economic weakness, of course, is bound to have political consequences. Eastern European dissent or deviation from the Soviet foreign policy line and Warsaw Pact policy toward the West (e.g. on security and arms-control questions) will tend to become increasingly rare.

Similar weakness of bargaining power characterizes Eastern European relations with the West. The recession, though slowing, means that in the years to come there will be only a very limited demand for Eastern European goods; any significant improvement of the OECD economies would have noticeable effects on East–West European trade only after some delay. Most importantly, however, after the large increase in borrowing from Western banks and governments prior to 1980–81, the Eastern European countries will be plagued by debt servicing problems and, simultaneously, by the difficulty of obtaining new credit. Indeed, recent data show that international bank lending appears to be contracting much more sharply than expected. Since the end of 1981 outstanding loans to Eastern Europe have, as noted earlier, declined by about $6 billion with the sharpest decline ($1.4 billion) taking place in the first three months of 1983.[15]

Domestic conditions, too, are likely to deteriorate. Having, with the exception of Hungary, squandered the opportunity of embarking on far-reaching economic reform with the aid of massive Western involvement, the Eastern European leaderships are still facing the problem of having to make major structural changes – but now in an adverse international context. Not being able any longer to draw on liberal Western credit for the purchase of consumer goods and foodstuffs, living standards are very likely to slide – in some countries, like Poland and Romania, probably more than in others. Upward social mobility of the working class has slowed down too. Furthermore, having been insensitive to environmental concerns and bent on maximizing production, often using outdated plant, the countries of the 'iron triangle' (East Germany, Poland and Czechoslovakia) are incurring large-scale ecological damage to densely forested areas amounting perhaps even to a major ecological catastrophe.

All these developments will do nothing to improve regime legitimacy and political stability. General apathy, resignation and frustration may alternate with violent upheaval.

Considering the current Soviet tendency to discourage market-oriented reform along Hungarian lines, to tighten CMEA and Warsaw Pact integration and to reduce East European trade dependence on the West, and taking into account the likely deterioration in socio-economic and political conditions in Eastern Europe as well as its shrinking bargaining power in foreign affairs, the Western Alliance is called upon to show initiative in overcoming the current stalemate. Given the circumstances, such initiative can only be concerned with damage limitation in the first instance. Prospects for more far-reaching change are likely to arise only after slow progress and as the general state of East–West relations, notably Soviet–American relations, improves. Change thus requires, if not a comprehensive approach or grand design by the Alliance, then at least policies which do not run at cross purposes.

Outlines of a Future Policy

Such policies must proceed from the following premises. First, since it proved an unattainable objective to 'roll back' or otherwise force the Soviet Union to relinquish control over Eastern Europe in a period of US nuclear monopoly or, in the 1950s and 1960s, strategic superiority, it is highly unlikely that the USSR could be compelled now to accept major changes against her will in the current era of strategic parity and Soviet preponderance in several categories of the East–West military balance in Europe.

On the other hand, both the ability and the will of the Soviet leadership to change the system and policy are quite limited. Such change as has occurred in Eastern Europe in the direction of greater internal liberalization and resistance to participation in the expansionist, hardline policies of the Warsaw Pact has, of course, not been due to Soviet initiative and good will but to popular pressures in Eastern Europe filtering upward and acting in conjunction with more realistic, and reformist elements in the local Party leaderships.

Thus, while change in Eastern Europe cannot be achieved from the outside and *against* the wishes of the Soviet Union, it is equally unwise to work *through* the Soviet Union. Western policies must manoeuvre carefully between the Scylla of provoking Soviet intervention and the Charybdis of accepting the socioeconomic division of Europe as final.

Second, as the preceding point suggests, the Eastern European countries should not be measured with the same yardstick as the Soviet Union. This applies not only to the prospects of reform. It also pertains to the impact of contact with the West. Western trade – or trade sanctions – have a proportionally greater effect on the economies and societies of these smaller countries than on that of the allied super-power. In principle, therefore, wherever structures are being developed in Eastern Europe facilitating East–West economic, scientific and cultural exchanges, the opportunity should be taken by Western Governments, banks, enterprises, trade unions, and scientific and cultural institutions to help in their evolution.

Third, in each and every case of such evolution its premises, scope and direction should carefully be examined. Each country in Eastern Europe is different. Western policies must therefore be based on a country-by-country approach. As the experience of the 1970s has shown, Western involvement will largely be wasted if it is not met by flexible, market-oriented structures and the will to reform on the other side. Countries having such structures or being in the process of developing them should receive preferential treatment.

Fourth, special attention in this context should be paid to the problem of debt. The private market has been reacting to the increase in Eastern European indebtedness in such a way as to discourage any increase in financial ties. This is unfortunate. Bankers should not be allowed to swing from one extreme (overextension of credit) to the other (withdrawal of funds to the maximum possible extent) and without regard for differences from country to country. The arrangement of a DM 1 billion loan to East Germany by the Bavarian Prime Minister, Franz Josef Strauss, in co-operation with the Federal Government in Bonn is a step in precisely this direction. Additionally, in order to counteract the contraction of East–West European financial (and economic) ties, the intercession of international organizations such as the IMF (International Monetary Fund) and BIS (Bank of International Settlement) would be desirable. That such intervention in a favourable direction is in fact possible was evident in the Hungarian loan syndication in the summer of 1982 when the BIS joined in sharing some of the credit risk until the IMF formally entered the scene on a long-term basis.[16]

Fifth, as the history of violent repression in Eastern Europe from June 1953 in East

Germany to December 1981 in Poland demonstrates *ad nauseam* change in Eastern European domestic and foreign policy can be terminated *despite* Western restraint and despite assurances by reformist local Party leaderships and non-Party societal movements that they intend to live up to their obligations within the CMEA and the Warsaw Pact. This was particularly true of Czechoslovak Party leadership in 1968 but was also true of the main body of *Solidarność* in Poland in 1980–81. However, the prospects for change are much more likely to come to an abrupt end (and perhaps even to be reversed) when Western policy-makers and public opinion enthusiastically jump on the bandwagon of intellectual dissent and popular discontent, and openly advocate the 'exploitation of Soviet vulnerabilities', the 'finlandization of Eastern Europe' and the 'revision of Yalta'.

For change to evolve successfully – as witnessed by the Hungarian example – more than patience is required. It is also necessary to have in place a modest level of trade and other contacts with the reforming country as well as predictable, long-term criteria for the expansion of contacts. It is also advisable to establish a framework of East–West relations as suggested in the Harmel Report and adopted by NATO in December 1967 but never really given a fair test: to consider Western military security and co-operation with the East – deterrence and detente – not as contradictory but as *complementary* elements of one unified approach.

NOTES

[1] Alastair Buchan, *The End of the Postwar Era* (London: Weidenfeld & Nicolson, 1974), pp. 244–5.

[2] Ideas for the structure and analytical framework of this Paper are derived from the excellent discussion by J. F. Brown, '*The Future of Political Relations Within the Warsaw Pact*', unpublished paper, Radio Free Europe, May 1982.

[3] Klaus Schroder, 'Die RGW-Lander in schwieriger Schuldenkonsolidierung', *DDR-Report* (Bonn), no. 3, 1983, p. 144.

[4] Jan Vanous, 'East European Economic Slowdown', *Problems of Communism*, vol. XXXI, no. 4 (July/August 1982), pp. 1–19, *vide* p. 4.

[5] *Ibid*, p. 5.

[6] Philip Hanson, 'Soviet Trade with Eastern Europe', in Karen Dawisha and Philip Hanson, eds, *Soviet–East European Dilemmas: Coercion, Competition, and Consent*, Royal Institute of International Affairs (London: Heinemann, 1981), p. 99.

[7] Concerning Polish and other East European debts see Klaus Schroder, 'Die Verschuldung Polens im Westen', *Europa-Archiv*, no. 5, 1982, pp. 127–34.

[8] Commentary distributed by Tass, published in *Neues Deutschland*, 9–10 February 1980. N. Portugalov is a senior Soviet journalist who writes on West German and European security issues, and is apparently on the staff – or otherwise attached to – the Central Committee's Department of International Information.

[9] Christoph Royen, *Polens Lage und Zukunftsperspektiven nach der Suspendierung des 'Kriegsrechts'*, Research Paper, Stiftung Wissenschaft und Politik, Ebenhausen Munich, SWP–AP 2351, March 1983, p. 26.

[10] OECD Trade Statistics, Series A, as quoted by Friedemann Mäller *et al*, *Wirtschaftssanktionen im Ost-West-Verhaltnis* for (Baden-Baden: Nomos, Stiftung Wissenschaft und Politik, 1983), pp. 130–3.

[11] Vanous, 'East European Economic Slowdown' (*op. cit.* in note 4), p. 6. See also Michael Marrese and Jan Vanous, *Implicit Subsidies and Non-market Benefits in Soviet Trade with Eastern Europe*, Institute of International Studies, University of California, Berkeley, May 1982, and a short summary of this monograph in *The Wall Street Journal*, 15 January 1982. Similar estimates are provided by Elisabeth Goldstein, 'Soviet Economic Assistance to Poland, 1980–81', in US Congress, Joint Economic Committee, *Soviet Economy in the 1980s: Problems and Prospects* (Washington DC: USGPO, 1982). An interesting and, for the most part, convincing rebuttal of criticism concerning the methodological basis for the argument that Moscow has accorded preferential trade treatment to Eastern Europe in the 1970s and the first years of the 1980s is contained in 'Notes & Views: Correspondence', *Problems of Communism*, vol. XXXI, no. 6 (November/December 1982), pp. 85–6.

[12] Oldrich Behounek, 'RVHP a obranyschopnost Socialismu', *Historie a Vojenstvi* (Prague), No. 1 (1980), as quoted by John Erickson, 'The Warsaw Pact: The Shape of Things to Come?', in: Dawisha and Hanson, *op. cit.* in note 6, pp. 168–9.

[13] The most authoritative example is Andropov's first speech as Party Chief to the Central Committee in November 1982, *Pravda*, 23 November 1982, pp. 1-2.

[14] Marie Lavigne, 'The Soviet Union Inside COMECON', *Soviet Studies*, vol. XXXV, no. 2, April 1983, p. 140.

[15] 'BIS Data Raise Concern About Lag in Lending, *International Herald Tribune*, 19 July 1983, pp. 7 and 9.

[16] Thomas Krantz, *The Future Significance of American Banks in Euromarket Syndications to Eastern Europe*, Research Paper, Stiftung Wissenschaft und Politik, Ebenhausen, SWP–AP 2363, August 1983, p. 44.

Relations Between Eastern and Western Europe: Prospects for Change: II

PROFESSOR PAUL LENDVAI

There is already a vast literature on the various dimensions of East–West relations both in the 1970s and 1980s. A small Paper can only review some principal issues and tendencies which might be particularly relevant from a foreign-policy point of view. Even a brief discussion of the broadest questions and of possible future developments should be set in the wider context of some general observations. Though concentrating on Europe and excluding both the Sino–Soviet–US triangle and the global strategic balance, the questions considered here and the conclusions offered inevitably imply some overlap with other Papers.

The General Framework

A growing danger of a breakdown in communication and a mutual misreading of signals between the two world powers have stirred widespread fears in many European countries that the dynamics of confrontation in an increasingly disordered world might no longer be contained. The concern over the future is heightened by the fact that the continuing succession crisis in Moscow ('the second succession', i.e. that after Brezhnev *and* Andropov) coincides with the lack of foreign-policy consensus in the Western Alliance and what even many staunchly pro-American observers see as the dangerous over-reaction of the Reagan Administration to *any* challenge. A combination of these and related factors could create a situation in which a divided and seemingly prudent Soviet Politburo and, above all, its most influential advisers would, when faced with crucial policy choices, opt for the view that

they have nothing to hope for and nothing to fear from a West in disarray.

A regular visitor to East and South-east Europe is now struck by apparently parallel mixtures of fear and resentment in both East and West. On both sides the representatives of the political–managerial–intellectual elites are increasingly concerned about the *unpredictability* of the international behaviour of the respective super-powers. Conversely, public comments or inspired leaks from the political establishments in Washington and Moscow reflect complaints about the perceived or real *unreliability* of important allies (for example West Germany) or of satellites (of course Poland).

These impressions must not even for one second blur the basic difference between a voluntary alliance of sovereign and democratic states on the one hand and the last colonial empire, ruled by a bureaucratic dictatorship, on the other. Yet personal experiences as well as opinion surveys tend to confirm the validity of de Tocqueville's saying that 'in politics one must use the same type of reasoning as in war and never forget that the effects of events depend less on themselves than on the impression they give . . .' How else to explain that, at a time of an unprecedented increase in both Soviet military power and in the Soviet's boldness in using it as an instrument of world-wide political manipulation, wide segments of European public opinion see the Soviet Union as less of a danger than the prospect that reckless US policy under President Reagan may spark off a nuclear war? The primarily anti-American 'Peace Movements' in Britain or West Germany are not necessarily pro-Soviet as far as the masses are concerned, but 'objectively' they provide

---

This Paper was written before the shooting down of the Korean airliner in the summer of 1983.

much-needed ammunition for the Soviet propaganda apparatus at the very time when the so-called 'Soviet model' has become synonymous with ideological, political and economic decline throughout the East European empire.

At the same time setbacks to the West in politics or even in the domain of propaganda do not automatically mark gains for the Soviet side. Thus the television reports of genuine peace or anti-NATO demonstrations in the West are more often than not seen by viewers in Eastern Europe as a startling proof for the freedom of assembly in striking contrast to the crackdown on any kind of spontaneous movements from below in their own society rather than as evidence of yet another victory for Soviet peace-loving foreign policy.

At any rate, the advent of television dramatizes and magnifies the issues also in East–West relations, sometimes with unexpected repercussions. The fact that, apart from a handful of intellectuals, public opinion at large in Eastern Europe, even in traditionally friendly Hungary, has not been shaken by events in Poland has been at least partly due to the clever manipulation by controlled television and press coverage. It helped to reinforce a whispering campaign that 'reckless and lazy Poles do not work, they provoke the Russians and expect *us* to bail them out'.

A potentially important source of uncertainty concerning the future shape of East–West relations is the emergence of the successor generation everywhere with different political experiences, different values and different cultural choices, changing life styles and a heightening sense of social disorientation. This is a crucial factor shaping not only 'Peace Movements' and neutralistic tendencies in Germany as a whole, but also engendering nationalistic and religious revivals to a different degree from Poland to Soviet Lithuania, from Hungary to Yugoslavia (primarily Croats, Serbs, Albanians and Muslims in Bosnia).

The alienation of the youth and the growing disenchantment of the cultural elites are important sources of political instability in East and West. Yet it would be not only naïve but also politically dangerous to assume that generational changes must have a direct, let alone liberalizing, effect on policy-making in Eastern Europe. The higher degree of education and sophistication, of flexibility and even cynicism of the political elites should not be automatically identified (as is so often done in the media and even in specialist works) with a commitment to reformist and more liberal policies.

This is not to say that the role of personalities is negligible. On the contrary, the relative successes achieved by the Hungarian regime in gaining popular acceptance at home and a measure of international recognition, as well as the grave setbacks to Romania's external and domestic policies in the 1970s, have been in no small degree due to the startlingly different leadership abilities and styles of Janos Kadar and Nicolae Ceausescu. However, our perception of underlying political realities East of the Elbe should not be unduly influenced by the personalization of politics or by tactical shifts. A realistic Western policy always needs to pay atttention to what has *not* changed within the East Bloc, and within the systems, as well as to what has changed.

Take for example Hungary. Despite her bold economic experiments, moderate domestic politics and relative freedom of movement, her political mechanism is still essentially the same as in all other East Bloc countries. The Communist Party continues to claim a monopoly of power and truth. It still lacks legitimacy; its survival depends in the final analysis on fear of Soviet military intervention. Hungary still ranks as an occupied country with four Soviet divisions currently stationed (in official parlance, of course, only 'temporarily') on her territory.

It is something of a paradox that the very strength of Kadar, who since 1956 has dominated Hungarian politics, reflects the basic weakness of the system because there is no established mechanism for the succession. Ultimate control, though not on a day-to-day basis, remains with the USSR.

Leadership and Succession

This leads us to the problem of authoritative leadership and the succession at the very top which as always constitute a key source of instability for Communist regimes lacking legitimacy and subjected to Soviet domination. The examples of Poland (1953–6 and 1980–83), Hungary (1953–6 and 1972–6) and Czechoslovakia (1968–70) have provided ample proof that the question whether a given leader and his clique can ride out a factional battle depends on the degree of operational connections between the East European leaders and the Kremlin. Factional manoeuvring in Moscow with multiple contacts to rival contenders or 'informal groups' within such key institutions as the party apparatus, the military and secret service bureaucracy, etc., can emerge as a crucial factor in a crisis or even as the single most important source of instability.

This is the reason why the uncertainty concerning the line-up in the Kremlin or the very real issue of an earlier than expected 'second succession' affect, for example, not only the mechanism of crisis management in Poland. They are also directly related to the balance of power within the top leadership in each East Bloc state and thus also to the cohesion of the Soviet empire as a whole.

Neither the assumptions of a 'monolithic' system nor the deceptively simple 'interest group' theories have proved a reliable guide to the analysis of change and continuity in Soviet-type societies. The diffusion of power within the individual system and the high degree of operational control maintained by the Soviet Union over the army, security services and the key departments of the Central Committee apparatus in each Warsaw Pact country (except Romania) must be seen against the background of compartmentalization of decision-making. The control over and the co-ordination of Eastern Bloc policies is generally carried on in a bilateral and not a multilateral framework, that is between the Soviet hegemonial centre and each client state separately. This is one of the reasons why parallels drawn between the EEC and COMECON (CMEA), or between NATO and the Warsaw Pact summit meetings can be so misleading.

The scope of and limits to the external autonomy and internal diversity of the states belonging to the 'inner core' of the Soviet realm, that is East Germany, Czechoslovakia, Hungary, Poland and Bulgaria, both reflect and shape the given degree of stability or instability in a particular country. Yet ultimately it is the changing criteria in Moscow for what *is* essential to Soviet security interests that determines how far and how fast a ruling party within the Bloc can embark upon the road of economic or political experimentations, including openings towards the West.

Paradoxically, both extremes of Western and above all US policies towards the Soviet Bloc, swaying between almost total reliance on the 'carrot' of permissive trade and credit policies and on the 'stick' of threats and sanctions, stem from the same misunderstanding of the structure and workings of Soviet-type systems. Neither the Soviet Union nor the Communist client states can be treated as just another foreign state. The ideology of Marxism–Leninism remains as before the justification and the legitimacy principle for the Party bureaucracy, for the Soviet rule over historic nations in the guise of 'internationalism' and, last but not least, for the relentless expansion of her power sphere as the result 'of the laws of the class struggle on a global scale'.

Outlook for the Soviet Bloc

In assessing the extent to which positive contributions might be made in the 1980s to the East–West relationship, we must start therefore from the following assumptions:

– Despite the enormity of its economic problems and the combined burden of defence expenditures and foreign policy commitments, there is to date no real evidence of the Soviet leadership seeking (or being able) to slow down military spending and to prepare the ground for a major shift in resource allocations from the defence sector to the civilian economy. Quite apart from noting a shaky power base, Western observers often tend to dramatize the economic and consumer aspects and to underestimate the absolute primacy of ideological, political and strategic considerations uppermost in the mind of every Soviet leader who wants to retain or to gain supreme power. The talk

68

about the need for a break with Brezhnev's domestic policy immobilism has so far produced efforts to modernize the existing mechanism, to streamline and to purge bureaucracy and to tighten political-social controls, but these are not harbingers of a real economic reform.

- If this is the outlook for Soviet domestic policy and if we assume that, despite possible tactical shifts, the assertive global strategy of the USSR remains unchanged in the foreseeable future, the smaller client states must be prepared for a renewed Soviet drive in favour of more equitable burden-sharing. Whatever calculations we make, all agree on the point that the *per capita* defence spending by the smaller East European countries is five to ten times *less* than the corresponding figure for the Soviet Union. Andropov's speech at the June 1983 Plenum was a straw in the would that he would press for tighter control over Eastern Europe, not just militarily, but also in the political and economic sense. But Soviet pressures for greater co-ordination of foreign and economic policies will inevitably generate counter-pressures for greater freedom to follow national interests. This also means that the conflicts between external restraints and domestic aspirations, the manifold economic and political frictions within the Bloc as a whole (and particularly among the smaller member states) will become exacerbated rather than curbed.
- Despite the grave security and economic implications of the Polish crisis, one could argue that, at least in the short-term, the Soviet centre is better placed to deal with centrifugal tendencies within the Bloc than is anticipated in some Western scenarios. Here are some of the key positive factors from a Soviet point of view:
  - Military rule imposed by General Jaruzelski combined with the threat of the use of force from the outside staved off the collapse of the system in the heart of the East European empire without the use of force – the best possible outcome in a 'no-win' situation;
  - The reaction of the West Europeans after the crackdown in Poland and the split in

the Alliance over sanctions once again proved that West European desire for dialogue (and business) will always be stronger than the wish to punish aggression against countries already dominated by the Soviet Union;
  - The US posture of nearly total verbal animosity (while continuing to export growing amounts of American grain to the same 'evil empire') and the spectre of a nuclear holocaust have helped to re-create the corset of external threat so long used to hold the Bloc together;
  - In contrast to the early 1970s, the cohesion of the Soviet power sphere in Europe is no longer seriously threatened by the activist policy of Yugoslavia and Romania. For all their much publicized, occasionally hectic, diplomatic moves in European, Middle East and non-aligned politics, both countries for a variety of reasons (economic crisis, political and nationality tensions, human rights record etc.) have lost their appeal for the 'inner core' of the Bloc.

East–West Political Perspectives

The central focus for Soviet Bloc foreign policy *vis-à-vis* Western Europe has always been Germany. The maintenance of the division of the country is seen (not only in Moscow and in Warsaw) as the safest guarantee that Germany should never again become a military threat. The campaign against the deployment of intermediate nuclear missiles (INF) combined with psychologically reassuring hints of major economic joint ventures in case of good behaviour has been and is likely to be directed primarily at the Federal Republic, the crucial factor in the EEC and NATO, seen at the same time as what Lenin called the 'weak link' in imperialism.

Though the victory of the CDU/CSU under Chancellor Helmut Kohl at the Spring 1983 elections was – as was the Conservative success in Britain somewhat later – a setback to Soviet plans, West Germany remains the pivotal area both in terms of the military balance and the battle for the mind of Europe. Domestic polarization and the pacifist and anti-American tendencies in the ranks of the Social Democratic opposition in

West Germany provide ample scope for Soviet Bloc initiatives to drive wedges between the US and Western Europe, to whip up suspicions of intra-German neutralistic tendencies and to work towards the twin long-term objectives of splitting Western Europe from the US and of keeping the West fragmented politically, economically and militarily.

Despite Soviet assertiveness in playing a world role and embarking upon dangerous (and costly) ventures in other regions, there is no reason to doubt that Eastern Bloc external policies in Europe will continue to be characterized by a dualism seeking to combine limited accommodation with the West (pegged to access to advanced technology) and the tightening of Bloc discipline. The point of the matter is that the Soviet leadership has always aimed at a politically safe combination of the *appearance* of a genuine detente in the West with the *reality* of hegemony in the East. The basic dilemma of how to subvert Western unity without jeopardizing the cohesion of the Soviet power sphere, of how to strike a politically safe balance between the optimal degree of centralization of decision-making in Moscow and the optimal degree of domestic autonomy is bound to overshadow Soviet perceptions of East–West relationship in Europe.

What then is the real scope for Western initiatives in the political domain in the 1980s? The maximalist objectives propounded by some spokesmen of the Reagan Administration and based on the 'collapse theory' are not simply unrealistic; they are also counter-productive. Neither permissive trade and credit policies nor economic sanctions can be used as a means to achieve real internal changes in Soviet-type systems. What is urgently needed is a broad new consensus first among the experts and political advisers and subsequently at the level of the Secretaries of State on the realistic and attainable goals and on the possibilities for leverage to influence medium- and long-term international behaviour both of the Soviet Union and other European Communist states.

The West does not and cannot create situations nor initiate processes of emancipation or liberalization. From the Tito–Stalin break in 1948 to the Hungarian uprising in 1956, from the 'Prague Spring' and the subsequent Soviet intervention in 1968 to the emergence of the Polish Solidarity in 1980, the upheavals which shattered the Communist world were not engendered by Western policy-makers and in most cases were not even anticipated by the Kremlinologists. What the West can do is to reinforce positive processes and prudently to use bargaining linkages to discourage expansionist behaviour or to withhold economic benefits in pursuit of a concrete and limited goal.

For all the disappointments and the lack of public interest in endless diplomatic haggles over intricate and seemingly absurd details, the so-called follow-up mechanism of the 1975 Helsinki Conference on Security and Co-operation in Europe (CSCE) has proved to be an irreplaceable institutional mechanism for the easing of international communications and for an admittedly very limited, very selective but nevertheless definitely useful bargaining among 33 European states, Canada and the US. The agreements to hold not just another Review Conference in 1986 but also special experts' conferences on human rights in 1985 and on family reunification and emigration one year later are minor but helpful levers to reduce repression in Eastern Europe. As in the past, the intelligent combination of quiet diplomacy and public strictures at CSCE 'tribunals' could affect the fate of thousands of families.

Even modest trade-offs at linkage negotiations, if properly timed, can encourage co-operative behaviour or influence the choices of opponents. In view of the US–Soviet tensions of uncertainties about US intentions and of divergencies within NATO, it would be unwise to underestimate the importance of a differentiated approach towards the East European countries and to ridicule the potential role of small and medium-sized Western countries, including such neutrals as Switzerland, Austria and Sweden. A realistic goal should be the encouragement of diversity within the Soviet buffer zone through bilateral contacts.

As nationalism is bound to remain the most dangerous challenge to Soviet domination and as the very basis of this hegemony (the stationing of Soviet troops) is simultaneously the most powerful symbol of national resentment, moves strengthening the national identity of the elites and promoting cultural, economic and technological penetration from the West are intrinsically anti-Soviet in character and could contribute more to a constructive evolution than attempts at ostracizing 'the satrapies of Moscow'. A prudent, but consistent policy of small steps, distinguishing between the individual states and tying lines of credit and technological aid to the restructuring of economic policy as well as offering disincentives for breaking promises in the humanitarian domain could be a significant new departure without provoking instant Soviet retaliation.

Economic and Financial Links

Concrete policies for the East–West economic relationship in the 1980s cannot be even intelligently discussed, let alone some guidelines formulated as long as hypocritical rhetoric encourages the adversaries, confuses public opinion, and hides real and often conflicting economic and financial interests against the background of political and electoral opportunism in open societies. To put it bluntly, credits extended to East Bloc countries and Yugoslavia by private bankers and often guaranteed by governments have never been a kind of humanitarian aid nor parts of a 'grand design' to 'domesticate' the Soviets and to 'liberalize' or 'liberate' the client states in Eastern Europe. The West in the broadest sense – from Bonn to Paris, from London to Vienna – has financed and often subsidized trade with the East for such prosaic motives as profits, markets, contracts and job security.

In the 1980s the agenda of the West European states will be increasingly preoccupied with efforts to stabilize rather than to restrict an already shrinking East–West trade. The different degree of vulnerability of the Soviet Union and the smaller East European states requires differentiated policies, but also a steadier approach based at least on some common perception of mutual interest. It is important to regain a sense of proportion and to remember that the grand total of the Eastern Bloc debt is smaller than that of one single Latin American state. More important still, all the Eastern Bloc states achieved successes in 1980–82 in improving their external payments positions, partly through drastic import cuts and austerity measures, partly through rescheduling of their debts. The outlook is for further cut-backs in investments and for new rounds of belt-tightening.

A reassessment of East–West trade must start from the assumption that the COMECON (CMEA) states are faced with a choice between restructuring their economic system or returning willy-nilly to a greater degree of autarky coupled with the acceptance of what Andropov called 'a qualitatively new level of economic integration'. It is in the best interests of Western Europe (and the United States) to ensure that the clock is not turned back and that the progress towards greater autonomy and diversity in the East, however limited and tenuous, is not reversed. The security and strategic implications of trade (leakage of military technology, excessive dependence on energy imports etc.) have been very much in the foreground.

However, a critical review of past trade and credit practices indicates that more attention should be paid to the *qualitative* aspects of trade policy, that is the links between joint ventures and credit projects on the one hand and the encouragement of economic reform and decentralization, access to end-users and essential statistics on the other. Events in Poland and Romania should provide salutary lessons that contacts only with state bankers and planning bureaucrats are deceptive and that multiple and direct contacts at company level, including in the first place medium-sized and smaller firms, are essential to create incentives and to produce reliable information.

In different ways, recent developments in relations are important pointers to the future: with *Hungary* (IMF providing vital financial relief at a crucial juncture in 1982 for hard-pressed reformists); with *Romania* (the threat of the suspension of Most Favoured Nation (MFN) treatment for her exports to the US, forcing the withdrawal of an exorbitant tax on emigrants); with *East Germany* (the lightning trip of the Conservative Bavarian leader, Franz Josef Strauss, and the extension of a DM 1 bn credit line as an example for the

71

positive use of economic inducements to achieve limited humanitarian goals in intra-German relations); and with *Yugoslavia* (extension of credit and rescheduling of debt used as a lever to prod a weak central government to implement long-overdue squeeze measures).

If the West seeks to weaken and not to cement the Soviet hold over Eastern Europe in the long run, separate sets of rules should be applied in trade with the Soviet Union and in trade with the rest of the Bloc. Within a co-ordinated and mutually compatible Western policy, there should be widening scope for the prudent, limited and appropriately-timed use of financial and other inducements.

Hungary's membership of the IMF and the World Bank serves to underline the untapped possibilities in these and other international institutions (such as GATT, EEC and the Council of Europe). Only time will show how much what some call 'Kadarization' (inconclusive as it is) is applicable to other Communist countries. Today it is extremely difficult to imagine a solution along those lines to the continuing Polish crisis. Nevertheless the West should be prepared to move from the current posture of unremitting toughness to more flexible policies as soon as General Jaruzelski's Government takes credible steps towards liberalization and pluralism.

Arms-control Measures
The future stability of East–West relationship in Europe – still the decisive area in world politics – depends on the Soviet perception of a direct threat to her East European Empire and on the ability of the West to recognize common interests and common dangers and thus to make Soviet attempts at political intimidation unrewarding.

Without going into the intricate details of current negotiations (INF, START, MBFR, the 40-nation UN Committee on Disarmament (CD) in Geneva and the recently *de facto* concluded CSCE at Madrid leading to CDE in Stockholm) it is perhaps fair to say that for most European non-Warsaw Pact nations (including non-aligned Yugoslavia and tacitly also Romania, albeit nominally a full Pact member) confidence-building measures (CBM) rank as the most important potential contributions to enhancing a feeling of mutual security between East and West. Binding and verifiable agreements can constitute the only credible basis for disarmament.

Since World War II the threat of upheavals and war in Europe has come primarily as a result of Soviet use or threat of force in Central and Eastern Europe. The Helsinki Final Act requires all signatory states to give notification of major military manoeuvres, involving more than 25,000 troops, at least 21 days in advance of the start of the manoeuvre. Failure to give such notification of massive military exercises, involving Soviet, Polish and East German troops at the height of the Polish crisis, before the imposition of martial law, generated widespread fears of a possible invasion.

Limitations on military manoeuvres and large-scale military movements combined with the exchange of observers would complicate planning and preparations for a massive surprise attack. Exchange of information and advance notification of US and Soviet ballistic missile launches, precise verification provisions with regard to the reductions of conventional forces in Central Europe and an agreement at last over existing Warsaw Pact force levels, a ban on chemical weapons (including mandatory on-site inspections) and, above all, verifiable reductions in nuclear strength could be major contributions to the gradual reduction of tensions and mistrust in this decade.

However, it would be as unwise to exaggerate the importance of arms-control agreements as it would be to concentrate exclusively on the military aspects of the East–West relationship. The real challenge is political, moral and psychological. It is indeed profoundly paradoxical that, at a time when the Soviet model has lost validity, when the average unemployment benefit in West Germany is still one-third higher than the average East German *wage* (which is in turn by far the highest in the Soviet Bloc), when Western radio broadcasts and television news coverage create insurmountable problems of credibility for 'future-oriented'

Communist regimes, the political elite – or at any rate substantial segments of it in the Western Alliance – manifests a failure of nerve. In a very real sense, therefore, the greatest contribution to the stability of East–West relations should not be solely or perhaps not even primarily military preparedness, but should rather be the reconstruction of Western self-respect and self-confidence as a prerequisite for political will, social cohesion and moral resolution in the battle for public opinion.

The Strategic Implications of West–East Technology Transfer

RICHARD N. PERLE

For numerous reasons, some of which are not altogether clear, the Soviet Union, with her large population of mathematicians, engineers and highly trained technicians, has not developed efficient manufacturing production lines. The problem may, among other reasons, be rooted in the anomalies of central planning, insufficient (or wrong) incentives for Soviet managers and workers, failure to devise effective management techniques, and the politicization of the workplace.

The Soviet Union has sought to solve the problem through a systematic programme to acquire Western techniques and equipment. This approach is not new. Substantial Western technological aid preceded the Bolshevik Revolution by more than half a century.

Russia's coal, iron and steel-producing capability was originally developed with capital and technical assistance from British, French, Belgian, German and Dutch firms. Swedish expertise, in the persons of the Nobel brothers, developed the oil fields of Baku on the shores of the Caspian Sea. This crucial development made Russia the world's leading oil producer by 1901. As Carl Gershman explains in *Commentary* (April, 1979): 'The Trans-Siberian railway was built with Western (principally French) capital and technology, and the parallel telegraph line was built and operated by the Danes. Many American firms, too, participated in Russia's industrial development . . . International Harvester was the largest manufacturer of agricultural equipment in pre-war Russia and Singer Sewing Machine had holdings worth over $100 million and employed a sales force in Russia of over 27,000 people in 1914'.

When the Bolsheviks seized power in 1917 they appropriated all Western assets, but in three years, with the economy in a state of chaos, Lenin invited Western companies back under a system of concessions. By 1933 the concessions were eliminated, but this did not end Western financial and technical aid to the Soviet Union.

US companies built the steelworks at Magnitogorsk in the Ural Mountains, the largest steelworks in the world at the time (a copy of the Gary, Indiana plant of US Steel). The US built also the Dnepr River Dam in the Ukraine, critical to the development of Soviet hydroelectric power, the Gorki automobile plant east of Moscow, constructed by the builder of the Ford Motor Company's River Rouge Plant, and a series of major chemical installations.

Since those days, Lenin's quip that Western businessmen would sell him the rope he needed to hang them has become a cliché for capitalist greed. For many years the West has indeed sold the USSR much of what she has required to accomplish one of the most astonishing military build-ups ever. If Lenin were alive, he might well conclude with delight that the nature of the capitalist has not changed. Western countries have provided the military technology, equipment, and training that has enabled the USSR to convert her weak industrial base into a formidable military production complex.

In the 1920s, the Soviet Union obtained prototypes of numerous aircraft engines from Western manufacturers and built composite 'Soviet' models incorporating the best features of each. She also imported military aircraft from Britain, France, Holland, Italy, and Sweden, thereby gaining a design base for her own aircraft industry. During the 1920s and 1930s, she bought Western prototype tanks and based Soviet tank development on the best features of these foreign models.

The potential of dual-use technology was demonstrated early on. Western companies thought that they were only helping to mechanize Soviet agriculture when they provided assistance and equipment for construction of three great tractor factories – at Stalingrad, Kharkhov, and Chelyabinsk. The Stalingrad plant was in fact built in the United States and the components delivered to the Soviet Union. There, American and German technicians supervised its assembly on the lower Volga River. From the start the Soviet Union used the three plants for the production of tanks, armoured cars, and self-propelled guns. An American industrial engineer familiar with Soviet industrial practices noted that the Tractor Construction Trust emphasized 'production of tanks rather than tractors'. In 1932 an American engineer then working in the Kharkhov plant reported that tank production took precedence over tractor production and that the Soviet Union was training operators for tank production 'day and night'.

World War II and the Cold War
On 22 June 1941, the *Wehrmacht* surged into the Soviet Union from the Black Sea to the Baltic. Within weeks the Red Army teetered on the brink of collapse. The Soviet Union asked for and was given vast amounts of equipment from the West to support her war effort. At the end of the war, the Allies transferred radar equipment which, together with unclassified US publications on radar theory, were the basis of post-war Soviet radar developments.

After World War II, the Soviet Union pillaged what was left of German industry, moved thousands of scientists and engineers to the Soviet Union and acquired several thousand plants estimated to have equalled 41% of Germany's 1943 industrial capacity.

Also after World War II, the Soviet Union redoubled her efforts to increase her military strength and went shopping in other Western markets. One major purchase was the Rolls-Royce *Nene* jet engine, which powered the MiG-15, an aircraft that fought against United Nations forces during the Korean War. Germany had provided substantial help in designing the MiG-15 airframe.

However, Soviet military production often lagged in quality as it leapt ahead in quantity. For example, during the 1950s and 1960s, Soviet industry had difficulty producing the precision bearings required for missile guidance systems. In the 1970s, however, the Soviet Union legally purchased grinding machines from the United States that could produce such ball bearings. These machines aided development of the Soviet ballistic missile programme and freed financial and research resources for other purposes. Time and again over the last couple of decades, through legal purchases, use of open scientific sources, deceptive business practices and espionage, the Soviet Union has acquired US and other Western technology at a direct cost to the West of many billions of dollars and an indirect cost that is virtually incalculable.

All available evidence points to a Soviet decision, taken in the late 1950s or early 1960s, to invest heavily in the expansion of Soviet military power and the Soviet military-industrial base. One effect of this was to shift resources away from the civilian economy. At the same time it was decided that trade with the West could be helpful to both the civilian and the military sectors. Despite profound fears of liberalization, Soviet policy emphasized the ties between the Soviet system and Western capitalism. Westerners were encouraged – although they did not take encouraging – to believe that better over-all relations would result from increased trade. These links were then exploited, principally to develop the industrial base needed to permit the development of a modern military establishment. A collateral benefit for the Soviet Union has been the ability to play off Western European NATO members against the United States because of the Western Europeans' more immediate interest in detente and its accompanying commercial opportunities.

Detente is often dated from 1972, the year of the SALT I Treaty and the US–Soviet Agreement on Principles intended, by the West at least, to guide super-power relations. In the late 1960s and early 1970s American diplomatic and trade officials argued that increased commerce with the East would lessen tensions and open new markets. President Johnson spoke of 'expanding bridges' to the East. President Nixon foresaw a period of 'co-operation' replacing one of 'confrontation'.

The Export Administration Act of 1969 reversed previous policy and declared that the US would now 'encourage trade with all countries with which we have diplomatic or trading relations' and noted that trade restrictions harmed the US balance of payments. The Act authorized the Secretary of Commerce to revise regulations and to shorten lists of controlled commodities by removing items of non-military or marginal military use. That resulted in a less restrictive system of export controls, and it coincided with a Soviet judgment that high technology had become critical in the East–West military competition. The combination led to a qualitative improvement of Soviet strategic and conventional forces (based on Westen technology) in the midst of a massive quantitative build-up.

There are many elements that influence a country's ability to bring its military power to bear, in peace as well as in war. Geography and the ability to deploy troops are, of course, important, as are the quality and quantity of manpower. In such crucial parts of the world as the Eurasian land mass and its periphery the Soviet Union has an obvious geographic advantage that the US has sought to offset through alliances, the stationing of troops abroad, the pre-positioning of materiel and the development of efficient means of air and sea transport. The Soviet Union has an advantage in numbers that the United States cannot directly offset. Through superior training and motivation, it is possible for Western forces to outperform their Eastern counterparts, but we can only be certain of that by testing it in battle. Tactics and strategy are other crucial elements of warfare in which the West might well prove superior to its Soviet Bloc adversaries.

But the one area in which the competition is clearly defined is in weapons. Quantity is determined primarily by national priorities, reflected in levels of investment but quality is mostly a function of innovation, carefully designed and well-controlled manufacturing processes and a skilled and motivated work force. The Soviet Union has the advantage when it comes to quantity because her economy is centrally controlled and, as a totalitarian state in which the military establishment holds vast power, popular desires for butter rather than guns cannot be easily expressed. The Politburo sets the priorities and they are followed.

However, the West has the upper hand when it comes to innovation and manufacturing technique. In the Soviet command economy, individual initiative is discouraged and innovation languishes. The emphasis is on meeting quotas, which are based largely on what is possible with existing methods and machinery. Managers are disinclined to experiment, to take risks. There are few incentives for change, reform is sporadic and economic performance diminished.

In the West, however, innovation usually means increased profit and long-term gain. There is a vast market to be served, and service is well rewarded. The system is geared to change, with the attendant risks. As a result of that and other factors, Western manufacturing processes are more advanced than those in the Soviet Union. And, given the West's lamentable unwillingness to compete with the Soviet Union in quantity for social, economic and political reasons, the United States and her allies have sought to offset the Soviet quantitative advantage through the exploitation of advanced technology. Recognizing that it is not possible to protect technology forever, the wisest US policymakers concluded that it was both possible and necessary to protect lead times, the precious years it would take the Soviet Union to catch up. If the US is to have a margin of safety, it is embodied in those lead times.

When the Soviet Union substantially increased the pace of her military build-up more than a decade ago, Soviet leaders recognized that even vast quantities of relatively crude weapons would not accomplish their military purpose. They understood they would also have to substantially upgrade the quality of their weapons systems. This was necessary not only to arm Soviet forces, but also to be able to provide their surrogates with weapons comparable to those the West has supplied its allies and friends. The Soviet Union also understood that to meet her goal quickly she would have to gain access to more Western technology. To get what was needed, an elaborate collection effort was organized.

The KGB and the Intelligence Directorate of the Soviet General Staff (GRU) and Soviet and East European science and technology organizations play an important role in this well-co-ordinated effort to beg, borrow and steal Western technology. The Soviet State Committee for Science and Technology, for example, often takes the lead in negotiating government-to-government agreements to facilitate Soviet access to new and established Western technologies. Just one result of these relentless efforts is that the Soviet Union has succeeded over the last ten years in building her own microelectronics industry, almost entirely with design and production-line technology acquired in the West. This, more than anything else, is responsible for the quantum leap in sophistication in Soviet weapons systems. Through legal and illegal means in the last decade the Soviet Union has acquired defence-critical Western technology in the following fields: computers, radar, inertial guidance systems, lasers, metallurgy, machine tools, integrated circuits, robotics, superplastic materials and electronics-quality silicon. Technologies, acquired through acquisition methods ranging from fully licenced sales to illegal diversions and espionage, complement one another and allow the Soviet Union to turn seemingly innocuous purchases into weapons-system components.

The Soviet collection effort has been augmented by well-orchestrated disinformation. Partly as a result of its effectiveness, and partly because many in the West believed that expanded East–West trade and technology transfers would nourish a benign detente, the West failed to grasp fully Soviet objectives. Key Western organizations intended to control the flow of technology were allowed to atrophy. Soviet scientists and engineers are often able to reproduce advanced weapons in the NATO arsenal, largely because they can relatively easily

obtain the industrial techniques that makes manufacture possible. It is only now that the first tentative efforts to meet this continuing but recently stepped-up Soviet challenge are being replaced by more forceful measures.

Western Objectives
The Reagan Administration has no desire to conduct economic warfare against the Soviet Union or Warsaw Pact countries. However, the US government recognizes a critical need to overhaul and modernize the existing system of controlling militarily relevant Western technology.

Since just after World War II, the United States, Canada, and our Western European Allies (excluding Iceland and Spain) have been curtailing exports of equipment and technology to the Soviet Union and Warsaw Pact countries through an informal organization known as the Co-ordinating Committee (COCOM). In the early 1950s Japan joined COCOM. The common objective was to co-ordinate a Western effort to contain Soviet expansion.

COCOM's principal purpose has been to prevent the transfer of equipment and technology that contribute to Soviet military programmes or to the military programmes of other countries whose political and strategic goals threaten the United States and her allies. For a variety of reasons, including strong pressure to increase East–West trade, Western Governments have failed to make the COCOM case effectively.

The importance of both exploiting and protecting Western technology is now better understood. There is growing awareness that a superior technological base does not necessarily guarantee that the West will maintain its lead because some technical advantages, once lost, can never be fully regained. For example, the thrust-to-weight ratio of high-performance combat aircraft has long been an important Western advantage. It is made possible by advanced metallurgical processes developed in the United States. If the Soviet Union or the Warsaw Pact were able to copy or steal this capability, it is unlikely that we would ever be able fully to recover the lost advantage. Before making technology accessible to the Soviet Union, we need to ask whether we can afford the cost and the time as well as the risk.

Controls: A Balanced Approach

Although not everything can be protected – and protecting technology is not without cost – it is, in general, more cost effective to control technology that otherwise would contribute to the Soviet military build-up than *not* to control it. In many cases, significant defence-related resources such as microcircuits have been sold to the Soviet Union for a pittance. In the past, the West has gone through spasms of technology control followed by spasms of technology release.

A technology-control programme that is not consistently enforced is little better than no programme at all. A consistent programme is needed to help to create conditions for maintaining the balance of power and inducing genuine arms control. For example, if the Soviet Union had not used Western technology to improve her guidance systems, it might have been easier to convince her to accept reductions of strategic and intermediate-range nuclear missiles.

On the whole, the best way to prevent the Soviet Union from acquiring Western technology is by concentrating on protecting manufacturing techniques rather than products. By focusing on basic techniques we hope to slow the pace at which they can field new weapons. And it should be the 'state of the art' in the Eastern Bloc, not in the West, that should serve as a guideline for what may or may not be transferred.

The Controlling Mechanisms

Work has begun in the last two years on the overhauling of the international machinery for controlling technology. Perhaps the creakiest part of the control structure is COCOM itself, which has an annual operating budget of less than $500,000. COCOM lacks modern offices, adequate staff and even secure communications facilities and it has no capacity to carry out independent assessments. It is obvious that unless it is modernized and given additional staff and funds, there is no way it can effectively confront the extensive Soviet operation to exploit Western technology.

More significantly, COCOM has no systematic way of evaluating proposed transfers of technology in the light of the strategic criteria it is supposed to apply – the potential contribution to the Soviet military effort. This is because COCOM as an institution has no direct access to military experts from the participating nations. The United States has proposed that a military panel be created and that it become part of COCOM's regular organization.

Enforcement

Another area that requires attention is enforcement. This encompasses, among other things, the need for new national laws and close co-operation among law enforcement agencies, both nationally and internationally.

The United States has significantly enhanced her own enforcement. One programme, 'Project Exodus', deserves special praise. Exodus is a US Customs operation to monitor outbound cargo. Since it began in January, 1982, it has stopped a wide range of illegal transfers to the Soviet Bloc valued in the millions of dollars. Before January, 1982, virtually no cargo leaving the United States was inspected by Customs agents. Violators of US laws are now being indicated and those convicted are being sent to prison.

Non-COCOM Nations

Some progress has been made (but more is needed) in dealing with the advanced industrial nations outside COCOM. Most are intimately tied to the COCOM states and derive much of their industrial knowledge and technology from them. Many benefit from defence co-operation with the NATO Alliance while trading with the East. Often the transfer of Western militarily relevant technology is part of the bargain. Usually, contracts prohibit transfer of that technology to proscribed destinations, but only companies are obligated by such contracts, not countries. This makes enforcement complicated and sometimes contentious. On occasion, the terms of the contract may even conflict with national laws.

The system is clearly in need of change. The United States is developing technology-sharing arrangements that involve concrete, enforceable obligations on the part of the beneficiary states but the United States cannot do this effectively on her own. Similar efforts have to be made by the other COCOM nations. It is encouraging that some first steps in that direction are now being taken.

For numerous reasons, the loss of militarily relevant technology cannot be reduced to zero. It is not possible to eliminate espionage (more than 11,000 US companies alone are cleared to handle classified work) and it is impossible to police every unscrupulous businessman who is prepared to sell proscribed technology to the Soviet Union. It is inevitable that some weapons-related technology will slip away as a result of legitimate academic and commercial contacts. It is not always possible to identify future military applications of civilian technology and some militarily relevant technology is available from non-COCOM sources.

But it *is* possible, despite the political, economic and technical obstacles, to limit the loss. Some progress has been made. There is now greater appreciation of the magnitude of the problem in government agencies responsible for control and enforcement. A concrete effort is being made to reach a consensus with our Allies about the risks involved and how to combat them without trampling needlessly on academic freedom or commercial opportunity. There have been successes: plots have been foiled, rings broken up, arrests made and convictions obtained. Licences have been refused and the COCOM process has been used to prevent exports that if allowed would have strengthened the Soviet Union militarily. But the successes are still too few.

To match the Soviet Union's full-scale acquisition effort, the West needs a full-scale prevention effort and it must be a comprehensive Western effort. Since no one country – not even the United States – has a sufficient lock on Western technology to keep the Soviet Union from getting what she wants, it is crucial that the United States, Japan and their European Allies co-operate fully to protect the West's still adequate, but fast diminishing technological advantage. This co-operation must take into account historically different perspectives towards the

Soviet Union, international trade and detente.

For one thing, Western Europe lives in the shadow of the Soviet Union; Soviet power is simultaneously more familiar and more frightening. To many Europeans it seems more prudent to feed the bear rather than to cage it. Furthermore, the Soviet Union is seen in Western Europe as an important customer for countries that are more dependent on trade than the United States and as a source of energy for countries that are more dependent on imported oil than the United States.

Given all that, responsible West Europeans are as eager as the US to contain Soviet military power. The main challenge in pursuing that goal in the area of technology transfer is to articulate a clear policy that takes account of the inevitable conflicts between Western European and American views and economic political interests, while seeing to it that security is not compromised. Once the US and her Allies concur in such a policy, the means of enforcing it can be put in place and the will to carry it out will be strong.

At the heart of the policy there must be a clear consensus about precisely what constitutes military relevant technology. For some years the United States has been refining her definition. Possibly the single most important document in this area is 'An Analysis of Export Control of US Technology – a DOD Perspective'. This 39-page Paper, generally known as the Bucy Report because it was prepared by a task force headed by J. Fred Bucy Jr., then the Executive Vice-President of Texas Instruments, made an important breakthrough in the US approach to the problem. It placed the focus on the exporting of techniques and certain keystone technologies, not products. Bucy's approach reshaped US thinking about the definition of technology and it has led to important revisions in the categories of technology considered most important to protect.

A series of technology and equipment lists have been developed to provide basic guidelines. The key domestic lists are a Munitions Control List, administered by the State Department, and a Commodity Control List, administered by the Commerce Department. They are constantly being revised to take into account new developments in research and production-line methods, and new ideas about what constitutes dual-use technology. The Munitions List is straightforward. It proscribes the export of weapons and ordnance without a licence. The Commodity Control List is more problematic because it is not always evident that every item on it has clear military application, and many of the items have undeniable civilian uses. Because of this ambiguity, there is sometimes disagreement between companies whose business it is to make a profit and the government, which has a substantial interest in seeing US business prosper, but whose broader responsibility includes national security. Similar disagreements arise between academics, who have a fundamental interest in the free flow of scientific and technical information, and the government, which shares that interest, but whose first duty is to guarantee the safety of the state. The Defense Department places a high priority on resolving those differences.

There are also three international lists administered by COCOM. There is a Munitions List (similar to the domestic Munitions List administered by the State Department) and an Atomic Energy List. These lead to few disagreements. However, the third list, which is comparable to the US Commodity Control List, contains most of the dual-use technologies, some of which can be bought from neutrals or other third parties as well as from COCOM members. Most of the conflicts between the United States and her allies concern what should be included in this Industrial List and what exceptions to it should be granted. Here, too, sharper definitions are required, as is a better system of resolving disputes.

Over the last few years the US Commodity Control List and the COCOM Industrial List, which are virtually identical, have been substantially reshaped according to the standards proposed in the Bucy Report but the complexities of the COCOM list suggest the problems inherent in enforcement even after COCOM members have agreed on what the list should include. This list is made up of highly technical generic definitions of equipment.

The definition for computers, for example, exceeds thirty pages.

At President Reagan's request, the COCOM nations in January, 1982, for the first time in 25 years, convened a high-level meeting to discuss the technology-transfer problem. Various new initiatives have resulted. The US has suggested a number of ways to strengthen COCOM, including modernization of administrative methods and equipment, modernizing communication facilities and adding a computerized data base so that members can improve policy co-ordination and enforcement.

The US has also pressed for the establishment of a committee of military and technological experts to advise COCOM. She hopes that member nations will add defence experts to their COCOM delegations to work on strategic analysis in preparing control lists and the reviewing of difficult transfer cases. Until Defense Secretary Weinberger suggested that NATO interest itself in the implications of technology transfer, there was not a single body within the Alliance with responsibility for monitoring this crucial issue.

Domestically, the Export Administration Act directs the Secretary of Defense to prepare a list of 'military critical technologies'. That list, which provides advisory export guidelines, also follows the recommendations of the Bucy Panel by emphasizing design and manufacturing technique; keystone manufacturing, inspection, and test equipment; and goods accompanied by sophisticated operation, application, or maintenance techniques. More than 80 industrial firms reviewed and co-operated in establishing the first Militarily Critical Technologies List.

The Defense Department has also identified a group of industries in the USSR that can put Western technology to military use by monitoring the industries to which 'dual-use' technology is channelled. As a result, we can sometimes stop seemingly innocent, but potentially dangerous, technology transfers.

The US attempt to monitor and control the Soviet Union's acquisitions more carefully has required extensive co-operation among federal agencies. A National Command Centre co-ordinates their intelligence, inspection, and investigative activities. The Defense Department will soon begin to operate a training programme to help Customs officials to recognize high-technology items subject to national security controls. The FBI has provided major support, especially through its widespread experience with Soviet espionage, and the rest of the intelligence community has stepped up its efforts to prevent further losses in this area. Finally, the government has expanded security-assistance programmes to advise defence and defence-related concerns targeted by Soviet intelligence.

To improve the ability of the United States to curtail the flow of militarily relevant technology to the Soviet Union and her allies, President Reagan has proposed revisions in the Export Administration Act. The President's proposals would sharpen the distinction between critical and non-critical items, simultaneously making it easier to export technologies without significant military applications and more difficult for them to sell processes and products that have important military uses. The new rules would include: tougher sanctions on companies that violate export regulations; provisions for negotiating agreements with allies and neutrals to help to enforce US controls on a global basis, and controls on companies based abroad and on the activities of foreign nationals in the United States.

As we move further into the age of thinking computers, lasers and particle beams, it should be obvious to everyone that mastery of these technologies, and others still undreamed of, is vital to US national security and to the future of the US as a free nation.

The United States remains the pre-eminent innovator of high technology for defence and civilian purposes but, unless we are able to prevent the Soviet Union from rapidly duplicating our latest achievements, there is precious little advantage in being better and being first. We must protect our lead times but, if we err, it is surely better that we do so on the side of security.

Conclusion
The security of the United States, her allies and her friends, depends to a significant degree on the West's ability to preserve its advantage over the Soviet Union and the other Warsaw Pact nations in militarily relevant technology. If the West is going to maintain a margin of safety it is going to have to be a technological margin. Our past programme to prevent military, dual-use and other relevant technology from falling into Soviet hands has been inadequate. The Soviet Union has organized a major and generally effective effort to acquire Western techniques and equipment, both legally and illegally. If the West wants to stop this flow it must counter the effort successfully. That will require a broader international consensus than now exists, reached through NATO and COCOM, on precisely what items and classes of technology must be protected and a series of national political decisions to implement that consensus. These will require an even greater level of co-operation between governments and industries than now exists. Failing such action, the prospect is for a continuing erosion of our qualitative lead, which could ultimately turn the West's margin of security into a Soviet margin of terror.

Some Aspects of Technology Transfer

DR C. M. HERZFELD

Technology as a Factor in National Security

Technology impacts on national security in several ways: first, technology is a major determinant of the general economic strength and productivity of a nation, both of which are closely tied to the effective use of technology and, nowadays, particularly to such fundamentals as modern manufacturing technology, computerized design, manufacture and testing, the large infrastructure provided by modern communications, and by increasingly pervasive computer technology.

The second way in which technology impacts on national security is the narrower one of the application of modern technology to military capabilities, to weapons, and to military operations. The best known example is, of course, that of nuclear weapons. These have a major impact on national security, and have virtually no peace-time uses. Another example is the microelectronic processing of visual images. This is now important primarily in missile guidance using optical methods although it will later become important also in civil technology, particularly in providing robots with significant visual capability. Other well-known examples are high-performance aircraft, modern efficient jet engines, modern armour and munitions.

The third way concerns 'dual-use' technology. An example of such is provided by the so-called 'super-computers' which can be used both for military applications and for the solution of civilian technological problems. There are two kinds of super-computers evolving and they should be kept quite distinct. One is the so-called 'number cruncher' type of computer exemplified by machines built by Cray, Burroughs and others. These are used for the solution of very large and very complex scientific problems. Often these problems relate to military applications but such machines are also used to solve such problems as weather prediction, and the design of civil aircraft. The second kind of super-computer is quite different and will have quite different uses. An example is what the Japanese call the 'fifth generation' computer. These are complex electronic systems, whose subsystems are highly parallel collections of relatively small but very powerful computers which are tied together in a loose way that enables the system as a whole to perform a great variety of very complex functions. In the future, these super-computers will also have important civil and military applications.

Clearly, military technology increases the ability of a country to fight wars directly by providing better weapons and better ways of using them. Civilian technology can also help the military effort in a general way. The distinction between military and civil technology is not always easy to apply, although real differences exist with respect to the detailed specifications of the hardware. Thus, military computers have to be able to withstand much greater shock and vibration and to operate at lower and higher temperatures than civil computers. On a more general level, the distinction between military and civil technology is more clearly drawn in the West and blurred in the Soviet Bloc.

The Objectives of Control of Technology Leakage and the Risks in Leakage

The reasonable objectives that one might have in controlling leakage of technology from the West to the East range from the very broad to the very narrow. The choices made will obviously depend very much on the view one has of relations between the East and the West. If it is assumed that this relationship must be one of complete opposition carried on at a high level of tension, then a broad economic and technology policy is reasonable that gives no aid whatsoever, however indirectly, to the military capability of a potential enemy. Such a policy would allow no food export, no agricultural aid, no economic aid, no credits for any purpose, no tourism (because it contributes hard currency) and no or virtually no trade. This is a formula for economic warfare and as such lies at one end of the spectrum. The other end of the spectrum is, of course, a completely open relationship between East and West with respect to technology export and trade. Presumably such a policy would have to be based on an assumption of total agreement on all important issues between East and West.

Neither of these approaches is practical in the world of today. The first would bring an air of unprecedent tension and crisis and would only have a chance of succeeding if all or most of the Allies would agree to it and participated in it. On the other hand, the totally open approach cannot possibly be in the interest of the West because it would result in a very rapid closing of the technology gap which clearly exists between East and West resulting in a further erosion of our security. It is clear that we are all striving for a carefully calculated relationship with a concept of measured or tailored controls.

A spectrum of policies applicable to several levels of interactions between East and West seems appropriate. A few of the most important levels of interaction for our purpose are perhaps these, with some examples for each:

- *Level 1:* General trade of no stategic significance;
- *Level 2:* Civil technology of minor strategic or military significance (e.g. refrigerators);
- *Level 3:* Civil technology of major economic strategic significance (oil drilling equipment, food);
- *Level 4:* Dual-use technology (high performance computers, aircraft technology, advanced communications);
- *Level 5:* High-technology infra-structure material (microelectronic manufacture and test equipment);
- *Level 6:* High technology of direct military use.

These definitions allow one to construct a single diagram to show how a policy might be structured. (See Figure 1). The line drawn in the diagram sketches a particular policy approach.

Figure 1: A Policy for Restricting Access to Technology

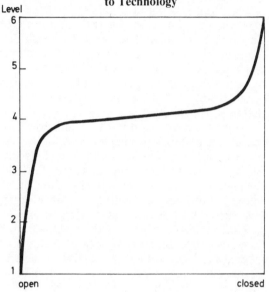

It is clear to all that advanced technology for direct military purposes should be strictly controlled. At the next level, that of the technology infra-structure, my own view is that the West should be very careful about the export of this technology and should in general lean towards rather tough controls. In the case of dual-use technology, such as general-purpose computers, advanced communications technology, and others. I also believe that the West should be fairly restrictive, but that considerations of international trade and politics should govern the details of the posture that is taken. A variety of approaches would seem appropriate and feasible at this level. At the next lower level, that of civil technology with major strategic impact, global political and economic considerations will dominate. Probably essentially free-market considerations should govern policy unless there is a strong need for economic sanctions for the purposes of political demonstration. It is clear that different policy profiles can make sense under different circumstances. It is also clear that the different levels of technology need to be rather clearly defined to make this approach useful.

Conditions for Controlling the Leakage of Technology

The conditions for controlling leakage are determined by a set of extrinsic and a set of intrinsic conditions. The extrinsic conditions concern the domestic policies of the Allies, Alliance politics, and the ability of all of us to influence governments and the private sector. Some of these are discussed briefly below.

The intrinsic conditions concern the nature of technology and its many uses, the nature of the Research and Development (R&D) process, and the nature of high-technology societies as distinguished from more mundane, emerging, or developing societies. These are discussed later.

Among the extrinsic conditions that must be satisfied to be able to control leakage of significant technology effectively, several stand out most strongly. Clearly, the most important is that the Western Allies (including Japan) must agree on the general desirability for control and on at least the broad concept of such tailored control. Furthermore, they must agree on some of the key details, particularly near the top of Figure 1. Not only must the Allies agree 'officially', but they must also participate in taking appropriate action. All this requires significant revitalization of COCOM which should become again a vital instrument of allied policy, and it must become strong enough to play this role.

Secondly, I believe that a more aggressive policy to enforce agreements against resale to third parties is needed. Such agreements may be difficult to enforce but ordinary publicity of proven or suspected resale of critical technology might be enough to deter large amounts of this.

A third condition for realistic control of technology leakage requires that we distinguish potential friends from potential foes, various shades of neutrality, and most importantly the difference between the Eastern Bloc regimes and their peoples. High technology, in the upper levels of Figure 1, can probably *not* be transferred to Eastern Bloc countries, because their regimes completely control the use of such technology. However, tailored approaches to lower levels of Figure 1, say levels 2 or 3, may make sense. Naturally, in this arena there will be much argument and perhaps disagreement among the Allies. What is important is that we face up to the issue, and are able to accept differences of viewpoint.

How to Assess the Importance of Technology and of the Leakage of Technology

The most important and most difficult problem intrinsic to technology management in general, and to technology flow control in particular, is to understand clearly the impact of different types of technology and different levels of sophistication of technology. It turns out that it is not at all easy to assess the importance of a given technology in most circumstances. For example, what does it matter if one uses several (say 16) 4K memory chips or a single 64K memory chip in a given application? It *may* matter a great deal or it may not matter very much, and the ways to decide the answers have to be thought through with great care and in a very professional way. I am convinced that we are relatively poorly prepared to assess the significance of this kind of detailed impact of technology, particularly in many areas of national security. A particular computer application needs, say, 64,000 bits of memory. Assume there are two options available. One is to use a board with 16 4K memory chips totalling 64K, the other is to use a single 64K memory chip. It is much simpler to make such choices in the commercial areas where a decision between two such memories can be made purely on a performance and cost basis. If 64K memory is needed for a particular application, it is now much cheaper to use one 64K memory chip than to use 16 4K memory chips. The reasons for this are obvious: it will take a larger box to house the 16 chips; it will take more power to run them; and they will probably be slower at whatever they are doing then a system using a single 64K memory chip. As a consequence, it is almost certain that in commercial applications the choice of a single 64K memory chip would be the proper one. In any case, a reasonable fully-worked-out design together with a reasonably realistic cost estimate, including cost to purchase the parts, cost to manufacture the systems, and cost of ownership of the system will give a very straightforward answer to the question of which level of technology to use in almost all commercial circumstances.

This decision is unfortunately not so simple in military applications. If a capability is needed that requires a total of 64K memory it may not matter that it is much more expensive to use 16 4K memory chips because the total cost of this memory subsystem is a very small fraction of the cost of the whole system, say a missile or a tank. The 4K memory chips can be bought off the shelf in thousands of places around the world. Their sale is probably no longer controllable. Indeed one could buy 4K memory chips by buying pocket calculators and taking them apart. On the other hand, from the point of view of military performance, it may not matter at all which way the memory is structured. Nor may the cost penalty matter greatly, if this penalty is a small fraction of the system cost, and if relatively few units of the systems are deployed. Thus a penalty of $1,000 per unit for ten thousand units is only $10 million, which is not much for an improved defence capability. On the civil side a cost penalty of $1,000 per unit (and for millions of units, say cars or TV sets) is the difference between feasibility and impossibility. The real problem in deciding what technologies to control for military purposes is that it is very difficult to tell what technologies make a major impact on a potential enemy who has a large number of ways of improving and substituting using less technologically advanced blocks or who may simply spend more money in order to obtain a given level of performance.

There is a disciplined way to make a rational examination of this problem. It is a rather specialized subject, which I believe, needs to be reconsidered and revitalized. It flourished in US defence circles in the 1970s

and was usually called 'net technical assessment' and, at a high level of aggregation, 'net assessment'. Net technical assessment is a systematic study of the impact of technology on the effectiveness of military systems and it is a fusion of intelligence analysis and operational analysis. I believe that it was a discovery of Andy Marshall and I am sure that his name will be attached to this subject for a very long time. After flourishing in the US in the 1970s, net technical assessment receded in influence and quality, and I consider it a tragedy that it did not continue to be used by decision-makers. In various ways most military analysts do net technical assessment and the good ones do it very well but the subject is genuinely complicated and requires complete analysis of very detailed information to come to really reliable conclusions. In particular, it depends upon an uncommon blend of real technical creativity and insight, real understanding of operational conditions, and real understanding of technical intelligence. During World War II, much of this was done quite regularly, often with spectacular results. Below are a few examples of the kind of things that are done in net technical assessment.

One can examine the effectiveness in combat of one Soviet aircraft, say a MiG-25 interceptor, against one US aircraft, say an F-15 fighter. One can work out in detail what each of these machines could do to each other at different altitudes, in different weather conditions, with different armament, employing different doctrines for the employment of electronic counter-measures (ECM) and so on. In this kind of a detailed analysis, such things as thrust, thrust-to-weight ratios, details of flight controls, the effects of different engines, the effects of different radars and so on can all be shown in rather explicit and dramatic form. Hence one can make estimates of the effect that the introduction of a better radar (either one that is more powerful or one that does a better job of processing clutter) would have on the eventual performance of each aircraft. This study can be done 'without any human effects present'. It is simply an engineering peformance analysis – very worthwhile but incomplete. It is more instructive to include in the analysis what is known about

85

the way that Soviet pilots are trained to fly their aircraft and the way US pilots fly theirs. In this way a more realistic assessment can be obtained about the combat performance of the two systems. To get a full understanding of the relative capabilities and also of the impact of different technologies on these capabilities one must, of course, extend the analysis. Firstly, several aircraft of one type meet in combat with several aircraft of the other; the numbers can be the same or different, say three against three or three against five. That is already rather difficult to do but some significant conclusions can usually be obtained.

The next level of complexity that must be taken into account is the ground environment, i.e. the presence or absence of surface-to-air missiles (SAM), anti-aircraft artillery (AA), air-borne warning and control aircraft (AWAC), and so on. At this stage, the analysis generally gets very complex and one has to do a large amount of computer modelling to get results. The importance of doing these studies is that one first analyses the contest with the equipments as one finds them; the analysis is repeated with various excursions based on different levels of technology. What is important for this analysis is that these excursions, assuming different levels of technology, give an indication of what technologies or levels of given technologies make a real difference to the military effectiveness of a given aircraft.

Naturally, this kind of analysis can cover one tank against another tank, several tanks against another number of tanks, tanks against anti-tank weapons, ships against each other, or ships against aircraft.

The analysis of this type is complicated and it takes many highly qualified people many months to complete. Often it has to be repeated after it is realized that some important feature has been taken only partially into account. For example, in the ground battle environment, the nature of terrain is not easy to model, nor is the effect of weather. Both are very important and the methods that are applied must be continuously improved. Finally the output of such studies must be compared to the results of field exercises.

On the whole, net technical assessment is a major intellectual activity and, at the height of its effectiveness in the United States, it involved large numbers of highly trained people and it was an important part of defence planning and thinking. This effort at net technical analysis needs to be recreated for at least two reasons. One is the reason relevant here, namely to get a better understanding of the impact of the flow of different kinds of technology, in particular of different *levels* of technology, on the combat effectiveness of different weapon systems. Secondly, our understanding of the military problems of the Alliance would be greatly improved if we conducted this kind of analysis at the national level and also at the Alliance level.

The R&D Process and the Control of the Flow of Technology

The second major intrinsic factor in the control of technology flow is closely involved in the process of conducting R&D and using its results.

To clarify some of the problems of control and to find solutions to them, a number of points about the R&D process need to be clarified. R&D turns fundamental laws of nature and the basic properties of materials into instruments of war or objects of commerce. Most of the points to be made are well known to practitioners and managers of the R&D process but some points are clearly controversial or not widely appreciated outside the R&D community. If progress is to be made in controlling the flow of critical technology, some of these questions must be examined and better understood.

It is a characteristic feature of the R&D process that it can be carried out in several distinct styles, ranging from a very orderly, step-by-step procedure, which is slow, systematic, and more or less predictable (and is here called Model A), all the way to a highly opportunistic or intuitive jump-like procedure which is very difficult to predict and to describe (here called Model B). Various mixed strategies also are feasible. In fact connoisseurs of the field can describe the R&D of organizations and even of individuals for purposes of R&D strategy description. It is this great variety of possible ways to conduct R&D which makes the security problems so difficult to attack.

The R&D Process: Model A

First the systematic, orderly, 'predictable' style of R&D. This is the description that is spontaneously used when R&D is described to the US Congress, to Boards of Directors, etc. It is a real description of a real process, but rather highly stylized for the sake of clarity and brevity.

The R&D process begins with Basic Research in physics, chemistry, mathematics, and any other fields relevant to the final product. (In US DOD parlance, money spent on this is called '6.1 money', from former Secretary of Defense McNamara's 'Package Six, R&D, category 1, research'. The DOD categories for these phases of the R&D process are useful and they are indeed generally used in equivalent form by most descriptions of the process). '6.1' is usually conducted in universities but a little is conducted in government laboratories and in a few industrial laboratories. It concerns the basic laws of nature, the properties of materials and the mathematical consequences of abstract logical conjectures. This part of science was totally open internationally before World War II, and remains very open in the Western democracies and in Japan. However, because so much basic science can be readily applied (for power and profit), the flow of ideas is more inhibited than it was.

The second R&D phase (Exploratory Development or '6.2') consists of applying the basic science to concepts that would have potentially significant uses. For example, a few lasers emitting very stable waves of light, some optical fibres, plus some special detection and signal processing equipment could make an exceptionally sensitive and accurate accelerometer, for missile guidance or for aircraft navigation. This idea is about 20 years old, but it is only now being put into practice. It has taken so long because it turned out in fact to be quite difficult to put into practice. This exploratory development phase of R&D is where the invention of what is really new happens and where the feasibility of the new concepts are proven.

The concepts are relatively freely communicated and published, usually after patent applications have been made. The concepts are often quite obvious, but success comes from ingenious ways to realize them. Usually the 'tricks of the trade' that make the concept easy to implement are closely guarded secrets that are not normally described in any publication.

The third phase (Advanced Development or '6.3') consists of working out the best and cheapest ways of implementing the concept 'invented' in 6.2. This is usually carried out in industry, some of the work is done in government laboratories, very little in universities (and if so then usually in the US in the so-called Federal Contract Research Centres like the Lincoln Laboratory). Industrial proprietary control of commercial applications and military security of military applications is the rule here.

The fourth phase, and the last that we need to describe here, is full scale development or '6.4', during which the final design of a product or weapon system is carried to completion. This phase is almost always done in industry and under all kinds of restrictions. It is followed by manufacture.

Table I summarizes the R&D steps and their related DOD planning phases. Table II (which should be thought of as being mounted parallel to Table I) identifies some salient features of each phase.

The R&D Process: Model B

Model B is a way of carrying out the R&D process which runs counter to, or differs greatly from, the orderly Model A described above. The importance of the existence and practice of Model B is that some features of it make control of the R&D process much more difficult.

Two characteristics dominate Model B. One is the fact that many ideas, concepts and inventions of phase 6.2 are either obvious or, if not obvious, are at least strongly suggested by concepts derived from the general 'state of the' art of applied science. A good example here is the atomic bomb. Once fission had been discovered in 1938, it was clear to all scientists that an energy-releasing technology was potentially possible. How best to realise

Table 1: R&D Planning and Process

DOD Planning Phases		R&D Process Phases
A.		Basic Research (6.1) laws of nature, properties of materials ↓
B. System Concepts Formulation ↓	← →	Exploratory Development (6.2) concepts for applications, proof of feasibility of concept ↓
C. Models, Prototypes ↓	←	Advanced Development (6.3) best implementation of concept, proof of feasibility of design
D. Full-Scale Development (6.4) ↓		
E. Production		

Table 2: The Nature and Scope of R&D

Phase	Who performs it	$ [a]	Numbers of organization	People involved	Character
A.	University (Government, Industry)	1 bn	500	5,000	Open
B.	Government and Industry (University)	3 bn	5,000	20,000	Open about concepts; closed about 'how'
C.	Industry	10 bn	100	100,000	Closed
D.	Industry	100 bn	100	10^6	Closed

[a] DOD & Industry $ are approximate and for illustrative purposes only

this potential, and whether an atomic bomb rather than an industrial power source or both was feasible, was *not* obvious. Once the feasibility of an atomic bomb had been demonstrated (which told *every* scientist that enough neutrons were released in each fission step to keep the chain reaction going), several approaches to bomb design were clearly seen to be possible.

There is an important message here. Once a concept applying to a weapon system is known to be feasible, *many* ways to implement it can be thought of quickly and can be found. Of course, some of these ways may be better, cheaper or easier than others, but even the more complex or clumsy implementations may be practical for the relatively few thousands of items typically needed for military hardware, though not perhaps for the typical millions of consumer items.

Another way to look at this matter is the truly remarkable substitutability of one technology for another if low cost and very large scale applications are not the dominating factor. Thus, military technology, rarely needing more than thousands of items of anything, with cost often being less important than availability, usually has available a large (even bewilderingly large) number of alternate ways of solving any given problem. For example, microelectronics is on a path of evolution to become more powerful and effective by several ord of magnitudes in the next 10 years or so. This is known to all competent technologists. Also known is the general way in which this will happen. Almost anyone can *follow* the leaders (US and Japan) in this process with a few years lag if they desire to do so; again it is relatively easy to make improved devices that are less than 'the best' but still very effective in a military system.

It is usual to think of technical substitution as favouring the Soviet Union. That is certainly not the whole story. The case can be made (and I believe it is correct to make it) that the true technological advantage of the US in particular and the West (including Japan) in general is our great ability flexibly and quickly to substitute better or cheaper technical options for lesser ones. This is done almost automatically in our non-military industries that are not constrained to follow the Model A R&D process rigidly. The agile, opportunistic approach of the Model B process is usually applied in Defence Industry only in war and it is forgotten or buried quickly at war's end. An obvious exception is in some intelligence collection related technologies (such as the Lockheed 'skunk works' producing the U-2).

How to Control Technology Leakage
How then do we control the leakage of vital technology? First of all, it must be clear that we need to be very explicit about our objectives; we must know what we want to control and what effect we wish to have. For example, in the general debate about 'control versus free flow' of technology, several factors

should be kept in mind. Clearly industry wishes to sell the advanced technology that is in demand and will lean in this direction. There are many reasons for this and the most important is the conviction of US technologists that the ability to exchange the 6.2 type of information freely amongst ourselves is one cause for the West's lead in technology. Routine and bureaucratic export control or secrecy classification of this type of information will kill the goose that lays the golden eggs.

Second, we have to be very clear about what technologies really matter and this knowledge should come out of a net technical assessment analysis and not just from information estimates or anecdotal judgments. The real problems are much too complicated and much too important to be solved by low level analysis.

Third, we have to be clear about what will work and what will not. It is my conviction that it is very difficult to stop completely the flow of a particular technology. The flow may be slowed by some years, but probably not by decades. We can probably stop the flow of some specific critical items, particularly those that relate to the building of the infrastructure of modern technology such as VLSI (Very Large Scale Integration) test equipment and VLSI manufacturing equipment. We can certainly also stop the export of certain very high-performance computers but it is already very difficult to stop the leakage of high-performance personal computers that sell for under $10,000 and have very significant computational capabilities.

Fourth, we must have a very vigorous strategy to keep ahead in the critical technologies. This should be an *allied* strategy and not just a set of competing national strategies.

Fifth, we must have more realistic classification policies and classify as secret or top secret only the technology that really matters and enforce this classification. As pointed out earlier there are some rather clear stages in the process where it makes a great deal of sense to classify and where it is relatively straightforward to do so. Conversely, we *should not* classify general technology, even if applicable to military systems, if it is not critically important or if it is in the early stages of development. We must be more selective and tougher about the secrets that really matter. This requires discipline and absolute commitment to the control of these technologies. I hope that the Alliance will make this commitment.

Finally, we must all agree to limit access to the key technologies by agents of unfriendly powers, and to the centres where these technologies are being developed.

Is an Anti-Soviet Embargo Desirable or Possible?

PROFESSOR PETER WILES

Totalitarian Regimes and Detente in History
The political basis of the Paper can be
quickly and briefly stated. The Soviet Union
is an 'armed territorial state on an ideological
base'. Past history is not encouraging about
detente with such states. They are governed
by dynamic internal ideological forces that
lead them constantly onward into new, ambitious, peculiar and tyrannical internal developments, and into new clashes with their
environment.[1] They all come to violent ends.

It is true that none of these regimes has
lasted as long as the Soviet Union, so that the
lessons of history are not unambiguous. It is
also true that not all of that first paragraph is
valid for other Communist countries. In
Poland, Hungary and Czechoslovakia, for
example, belief is dead. They are no longer
theocracies but 'logocracies', in which one
has only to repeat the correct words and even
most of the Party elite does nothing different.
These three countries, despite their great
differences, are (and always have been) ruled
with direct force, and the domestic part of
this force is dependent upon the foreign part.

These facts may raise reasonable hopes.
The negative argument for detente runs as
follows: military defeat is no longer possible
since nuclear weapons forbid it, and a *coup
d'état* from outside the Soviet ruling group is
extremely unlikely because the KGB functions
many times better even than the Gestapo. So
we are condemned to search for some other
policy and here positions divide into
Ostpolitik and 'old' and 'new' detente.

Ostpolitik in its original significance was
detente with satellites only: a purely West
German drive to make things difficult for the
GDR by obtaining Romanian and even other
diplomatic recognition. It rested, of course, on
the making of distinctions between the USSR
(which had already recognized the Federal
Republic) and her satellites. *Ostpolitik* was
very hard-nosed and quite successful.

'Old' detente included the USSR as well,
and other Western states. The 'old' position
characterizes the original Helsinki CSCE negotiations. The Western Foreign Offices still
took a tough line about what they were
doing. They thought of their new *Ostpolitik*
as a form of 'cold war by other means', as
Clausewitz would undoubtedly have called it.
They had nothing in general against the
prevailing US attitude; they only wanted to
do the same thing better, and with more concern for the interests of the countries they
represented. They were in particular reasonably contented with the general military technology embargo, the COCOM. They also had
practical political and social goals, such as
freedom for journalists to operate, and freedom for Jews to emigrate. These goals were
soon all reached, against the virtually costless
concession of recognizing East German frontiers. This was even a net gain, since it
entailed Communist recognition of West
Berlin's frontiers.

If the West had a longer-term policy at all,
it was that it need only wait. The
Polish/Czech/Hungarian infection will even
spread into the Soviet Union. It is an inner
change which the West did not begin from
outside and whose progress the West can
hardly influence. Actually, as is well known,
the publication of the Helsinki Agreement in
Pravda did encourage a good deal of dissi-
dence, and Jewish emigration led logically,
although unexpectedly, to *Volksdeutsch*
emigration.

But there followed the phase of 'new'
detente, which wishes to treat the concept of
detente as if it meant the end of the Cold
War. Quite especially in West Germany the
proponents of 'new' detente have much larger
goals than the proponents of 'old' detente:
the softening, even the pacification, of the
enemy. The means to these ends are mainly
economic: we must trade as much as

possible, and transfer technology too, because nations whose economies are closely involved with each other do not make war on each other, and in any case a fat Communist is more peaceful than a thin one. When we look away from the search for profit of particular capitalist enterprises and trade unions, in other words from the details and particularities of the daily external economic policy of any capitalist country, we still find that the main method, or should one say 'the great dream', is an economic one.

The proponents of an embargo, then, are not the only people who think in economic terms. The essence of 'new' detente is that you can buy peace. But it takes two to end the Cold War, which began in October 1917. And the English at least remember King Ethelred the Unready, whose Danegeld did not work – a story which forms, of course, no part of the German folk memory.

Would that the proponents of all forms of detente could recognize that only the negative argument, sketched above, has scientific validity. No historical event supports the positive policy of 'new' detente in comparison with, for example, the positive policy of a long-term embargo plus a return to 'old' detente. The defenders of both proposals are in the same position as all of us: they are only guessing. 'New' detente as *the* suitable alternative policy to direct military aggression has absolutely no basis in human experience: *'new' detente has no scientific foundation*. Indeed it is agreed by everyone to have altogether failed up to this point.

Embargoes: Political Aspects
On the other side, advocating embargoes, stands the US President, in whose company the author feels extremely uncomfortable. Let it be permitted to him to develop his own argument for this policy. What we want to know, after all, is what is right, not who says it.

So my counter-argument in favour of a policy of embargoes runs as follows, shorn of the irrational elements with which others have infected it.[2] The Soviet Union will not disappear of her own accord because of her inner ideological dynamics. Poland may cause some difficulties but there are no signs of the spread of political infection into the USSR: nor for that matter is political infection likely to spread into the GDR, Bulgaria, Cuba, Vietnam or (on balance) Romania. The Soviet system is meanwhile spreading successfully all over the Third World. War and *coups d'état* are, of course, not permitted but that does not mean that we have to be nice to the Soviet Union. The USSR – and Communists in a general way – all have the same weak points: agriculture and technology. From this we draw the conclusion of the *primacy of foreign trade*. The correct non-military *Ostpolitik* is that of the embargo.

An embargo is naturally cold war. Everything that is not what we have called here 'new' detente is plainly cold war. When we take into account the incontestable fact that the Communists have made cold war against us almost every year since 1917, it is hard to understand why this concept applied to our own policy here has an unpleasant ring about it. Anyone who has a permanent enemy, and is not seeking to soften him, is making cold war.

The Positive and Negative Economic Weapons
It seems that we have five main questions to answer.

- Is war always hindered by a close mutual involvement of the two economies of the potential enemies through international trade with each other?
- Is a fat Communist more peaceful than a thin Communist?

If we answer 'yes' to both these questions, then we take up the positive economic weapon. We enrich our enemy a little, through trade, or very greatly, through technology transfer. If the answer to these two questions is 'no', then the negative economic weapon lies to hand, namely an embargo.

But we must first face another three questions:

- Looking at it purely economically, how much in absolute *and in relative* terms does one lose and win through such an embargo?

92

- Can a short-term embargo even work?
- Is capitalism able to conduct a long-term embargo?

Peace Through Economic Involvement
It is clear that this goal can to some extent be subsumed into that of the general enrichment of the enemy. In this case simply the increased international division of labour leads to a higher real income of the enemy and therefore directly to peace: But what people mostly mean by this policy – for example Cobden and Bright in Britain in the nineteenth century – is something different. The prospect of enrichment may entice the enemy into a broader international division of labour, but the main effect of this is involvement with us, a current and long-lasting dependence on our materials and machines and on our markets for his products. For this reason, and not because he has become richer, he no longer wants to make war on us. That means that he is, in the last resort, not softened but simply threatened. He fears precisely our embargo in the worst case, to which the peaceful economic involvement will only be a run-up. It is this 'dialectical' form of the positive economic weapon that we are discussing in this section. This 'dialectic' is never stressed by the proponents of detente. In the literature 'involvement' and 'enrichment' are simply confused.

What kind of war is supposed to be hindered? A small peripheral war, as in Afghanistan? A small proxy war like, shall we say, the Cuban war in Angola? A short war like the latter? Or a long war like the former? Obviously no short war can be hindered by the negative economic weapon because its effect simply takes too long – unless one has already threatened very seriously the use of this weapon and established one's credibility in such use, so that the enemy knows that, even if he wins his small peripheral war, the weapon will still be used against him. But when one makes this threat seriously, the enemy avoids economic involvement. As to proxy wars, it is very difficult – both psychologically and diplomatically – to bring to a halt the enemy who is actually fighting by causing damage to his patron. President Castro and even General Jaruzelski have their own weaknesses and a substantial degree of independence. It is quite inefficient to work upon them only in this indirect manner.

A great European war on the other hand is shorter than 'short'. It can only last two weeks. At the beginning of the war one of course introduces the embargo, but the enemy has already a substantial war stock and the embargo makes no difference to him. Within two weeks both economies, nay the whole of the northern hemisphere, lie in ruins, and most of us are dead. Or we do not use nuclear weapons and then the Soviet Army simply wins the victory. In both cases further analysis is uninteresting.

From our categories there remains only to be discussed that of long small wars of the Afghan type. It seems that in this case mutual economic involvement with the ultimate goal of an embargo is – or ought to be – an effective weapon. Yet it is obviously not Western policy actually to use the present level of mutual involvement in this case; on the contrary the West seeks a higher level of mutual involvement (through wheat sales and natural gas imports). It is also hardly to be thought that we are building the natural gas pipeline in order later to cut it off for the sake of fifteen million Afghans. However, other Western governments of the future could indeed do just that.

A 'new' detente supporter might infer from this the importance of prior involvement: we must first of all give something before we can take it away. But this is not so. On the basis of zero trade you do not necessarily get zero embargo, since an embargo is an *ex ante* concept. If something, say the hard currency to be earned from natural gas exports, is merely possible, you are willing to make political sacrifices to achieve it. The prior existence of such exports is not required.

Softening Through Enrichment
Simple economic involvement, without the intention suddenly to strike with an embargo, is however only a part of the policy of enrichment. More important, because more effective, is technology transfer. The effect of enrichment is a very big subject that seems never to have been scientifically studied. Let

us begin with the non-Communist opponents of the most developed countries in the nineteenth century.

Japan is the *pons asinorum*. In 1868 this very militaristic people, after 200 years of isolation, reacted to a demonstration of the superiority of the American fleet with the overthrow of the Shogunate, the abolition of feudalism and industrialization. The imperialistic spirit was already there, and the new rulers began at once in the Cabinet to discuss the annexation of Taiwan and Korea. This discussion led to a half-hearted attack on Taiwan in 1874, for they had began to understand how weak, in an industrialized world, Japan really was. Thereafter, until 1894, they waited and learned. After the victory over China, Taiwan was at length taken and Korea half taken. In 1905 Russia was beaten and in 1910 Korea formally annexed. The rest is presumably well known to the reader. So the fat Japanese were just as bellicose as the thin Japanese; the difference was that they could buy or make better weapons.

The course of economic events is not so well known. Japan was *not* poor in 1868; the long Tokugawa peace had already enriched it far beyond China and Korea, up to approximately the Russian level. Her military expenditure and her lack of raw materials kept down the growth rate of GDP per head up to 1914, to 2–2.5% per annum – a good rate measured by contemporary standards but not in comparison with our times. This growth was, however, in comparison with the norms of the Tokugawa period, astonishing. Progress was very clearly perceived by the population.

Technology, and above all military technology, was imported on the grand scale. All Western countries were extremely helpful in this matter and so they created an enemy for more than China and Korea. The Japanese will to aggression remained firm whatever happened; economic progress had no effect on it. The single result of the 'positive economic weapon' was to arm this will. Only one thing could have avoided Pearl Harbour: the cessation of technology transfer. But in the years 1868 to 1941 this would have been ideologically impossible for the Western nations.

A similar but not so clear case was Germany. The time intervals were longer and Germany was already a world leader in many branches of technology (e.g. chemistry) before she made war. Also there were still, during the long period of the foundation of the German state, official restraints on technology transfer in Great Britain and France, which with Belgium were the only industrially-advanced countries.[3] These restraints were a part of the dying Mercantilist system. They were all repealed in the name of free trade before 1870.

In 1870 nobody asked where Germany had got her military technology from, but already in 1900, with the beginning of the construction of the Battle Fleet, a few Britons did begin to cast doubt on the results of free trade in ship construction technology. The majority of their compatriots laughed at them because Germany had by this time become Great Britain's best trading partner, for both imports and exports. Yet that was no kind of answer for wartime, and the volume of trade was not so important as technology, which conventional wisdom did not take into account. At Jutland and on the Somme the Allied Powers met the late results of their former free trade, just as the US did at Pearl Harbour.

We do not need to ask who was right in all these wars. We know that in 1914 masculine aggression, ever-expanding imperialism, and bellicose competition between races (which one identified at that time with nations) were the common ideology of all advanced countries.[4] '*La guerre fraîche et glorieuse*' is neither a German nor an English sentence. We need only observe that the latecomer had imported technology without hindrance and that German economic growth had in no way led Germany towards peace since, let us say, 1848. All it did was to enable Germany to buy or to make better weapons.

The history of other peoples from 1800 to 1914 tells us the same thing. In short the recent past of the capitalist world gives us *absolutely no scientific basis* for the doctrine that economic growth, whether developing from within or basing itself on other people's technology, leads human beings towards peace.

So what is it that has so obviously softened the developed capitalist nations latterly? Why is it today that only the nations of the Third World have nourished the above-mentioned 'common ideology'?[5] I suggest that a nation is 'softened' because:

- Of its incurable military weakness against its potential enemy. In this context we should note that economic growth can cure many things and that membership in an alliance permits a small country to adopt a bellicose posture (e.g. Cuba).
- Of recent experience of the horrors of war and the acquisition of nuclear weapons. It is certain that this generation of the peoples who have lived through the last war, including their general staffs and governments, are far more peaceful than other peoples, general staffs and governments.[6]
- Here however we must, unfortunately, make certain exceptions for USSR and GDR (see below).

It is certain that war is no longer amusing in Western Europe, and this remarkable change of spirit is contemporaneous with a remarkable period of economic growth. Most probably this is the reason for the suggestion to use the 'positive economic weapon' against the USSR. Western logic bases itself on Western experience, but which experience – the economic or the psychological?

Fat and Thin Communists
The doctrine of softening through enrichment is today mostly applied to Communist states and specifically to the USSR. A better example would have been China, which has indeed become more peaceful in theory since about 1965, and quite especially so since, under Deng Xiaoping, economic growth has started again. But the attack on Vietnam was not a peace-loving action, and it seems as usual better to dissociate aggression from real income. One must ask oneself why such an important principle is not tested also on the nations of the Third World, with their varying levels of wealth and their varying propensities to make war. An opponent of the doctrine can only conclude that dogmas are never tested.

Let us try to do so all the same. There are only three aggressive, adventurous, expanding Communist states: the USSR, Cuba and Vietnam. These show us that there is in Marxism itself no inner drive towards imperialism. One of these states is rich, when measured by Communist standards, one belongs to the 'middle class', one is poor. But it is neither their richness nor their poverty but their history that determines their attitudes to the outside world. Vietnam has simply a mediaeval empire to re-establish. Cuba's policy is probably Castro's personal policy: it seems to be that, if today Cuban blood is shed for Soviet interests in Africa, then one day Soviet blood will be shed for Cuba, in Cuba (or in Florida?). In other words, Cuba's adventures are in reality defensive.

The *application of the doctrine to the USSR* must mainly depend upon directly Sovietological considerations. What Japan was or Cuba is must weigh less with us than Soviet history. So can one, without regard to other nations, at least soften the Soviet Union by raising her real income per head with imported technology, or expect such a softening simply by waiting for a slower internally-generated increase? If the answer is 'yes', then the present policy of 'new' detente, despite its wholly unscientific character, is saved.

It is commonplace that this or that aspect of the USSR is a direct continuation of Tsarist Russia. This is nowhere clearer, naturally, than in foreign policy. The imperialism of the Tsars, which lies at the base of Soviet imperialism, was in no way softened by the slow growth of Russian real income over the centuries.

I had wanted to say that this imperialism had certain ideologically natural boundaries: Slavonic speech or Orthodox belief. But that is not so. The advance into Central Asia and the Far East had nothing to do with these ideological criteria. It is not true that Belgrade, Prague, Sofia and – however improbable it may seem – Addis Ababa would probably have satisfied the Third Rome. Now the USSR has taken the latter three, but she is still expanding in all directions. The old ideology certainly played its part here,[7] but also the new ideology was more important, which sets the natural boundaries of Soviet power with those of the whole world.

So the Empire is expanding despite an undeniable increase in consumption – often, until recently, faster than in the surrounding capitalist world. Admittedly a certain softening is to be found. Thus, under the Tsars official torture of accused people and legal mutilation of condemned people were gradually given up and, from time to time, also the death penalty. The Communists did not bring back mutilation, but they did bring back torture and the death penalty. The latter still remains, and theoretically in sharper form than before (and also for economic crimes). But torture has, for the second time in Russian history, almost disappeared. The official theology has in its turn traced the same zig-zag course: from primitive semi-illiteracy to sophisticated higher learning; then revolution and primitive semi-illiteracy again; and then higher learning again.

These tendencies are international. Under the Tsars the country was obviously behind the West, but the direction of movement was the same. Then the Revolution broadened the gap severalfold but the direction still remained the same. This moral gap is a great military advantage, for civilized is civilian. The man who prefers reason to force makes a bad soldier. The general will of the Russian (Soviet?) people to make war if need be is in consequence less disputable than in the American case. So the Empire spreads wider.

The Chronology of Soviet Foreign Policy
Let us now look a little closer at the chronology. Foreign policy was at its most aggressive in 1917–23, that is when people were much poorer than they had been in 1913. In this period quite obviously not poverty but the primitiveness of the ideology and the objectively unstable situation of European politics were the cause: all that encouraged false hope. There followed a period of growing isolation until 1939. The treaty with Hitler, the quintessence of a defensive measure, rested clearly on a military appreciation that the country could not resist Germany, and upon a certain sympathy for Hitler on the part of Stalin personally. In these years, too, people had

fallen back into poverty (the Great Purge), but with plainly opposed effect to the previous case. The explanation is that in neither case had real income anything to do with foreign policy. Then Eastern Europe was annexed, admittedly under circumstances of the greatest poverty at home. But the point is that the Red Army was already there, so the measure was objectively possible. Would a prosperous USSR not have done the same thing?

In Khrushchev's time there was peace. That was his personal inclination. He kept hold of what already belonged to him (Hungary) with great brutality, but he expressed himself against the 'export of revolution', thus incurring Suslov's displeasure. He remained in practice true to this promise. Was all that 'on account of' the higher real income of his people? Thereafter came Brezhnev Africanus who 'in spite of' the further increase of real income in the USSR exported revolution to three African countries plus Afghanistan, brought Cuba and Vietnam into the CMEA, suppressed the peaceful Czechoslovak Revolution (peaceful compared with Hungary) – and began detente and sought technology transfer.

The rationalization and softening of the ideology on the other hand was, under these two leaders, a continuous process. Nevertheless the process has never been so sharp and so quick as in 1921, when Lenin introduced the New Economic Policy precisely *because of* the poverty of the people. The greatest ideological 'progress' therefore happened because economic failure had cleared people's brains. Economic success, on the other hand, makes one complacent.

I conclude from all this that the USSR is like every other 'armed territorial state on an ideological base', indeed probably like every other state: she attacks when ideology 'justifies' the war, and the military situation is favourable. It is favourable when the enemy is relatively weak, and so war springs more naturally from one's prosperity than from one's poverty. With the course of history it is true that one becomes more soft and more rational, but that is with the course of history as a whole not with the course of real income in particular. So the doctrine of softening through enriching has no more scientific foundation when we apply it to the Soviet Union than to any other state. I conclude from this that a fat Communist is not peaceful and a thin one is not bellicose, but that the opposite is also not true. A Communist as such (and above all a Russian Communist) is bellicose and as he becomes fatter he buys and makes more and better weapons. One cannot buy peace with him but, on the contrary, he becomes fat from profitable trade.

The Missing Science of 'Embargology'[8]

An embargo is a complicated and surprising weapon. The most elementary mistakes are still made very frequently. In the end the instructed errors of professionals who have mastered a science are not quite so great.

For instance Mr Caspar Weinberger suggested in 1982 that we must drive Poland immediately into bankruptcy. But our goal with regard to the Polish debt is not to punish the country but to influence it. What Poland needs from us, she can in any case hardly finance. For either the coal goes straight into Western debt service (if Poland does not go bankrupt) or, in the case of bankruptcy the coal can no longer be sold because it would be confiscated. But then Poland would no longer have a Western debt and she sends all her coal automatically to the CMEA so as to service her debt with those countries, or indeed to buy Western articles indirectly. We on the other hand have lost all influence. In war no general would have made so gross an error. One should enter upon an economic war with no less care than a shooting war.

A second example is that it very seldom happens that an embargo alone can work decisively in a short time; patience is needed. However, oil is an exception. In 1936 Italy needed only one thing for her Abyssinian aggression – oil – and only this material was not embargoed by the League of Nations – but that was perhaps nearer to cowardice than to error. In 1941 there was less cowardice, with still worse dramatic results. In July 1941 Japan faced a complete US oil embargo. Some at any rate of her staff officers calculated that her stock would last two years, and her capacity to make war would

seriously decline. Pearl Harbour followed within five months.

The third example is not economic, but uses the same principles. It was no bad idea of President Carter to boycott the Olympic Games in Moscow after the invasion of Afghanistan, but did he calculate? He certainly did not ask what the opinion of the British Olympic Office was, or whether the British government had any influence upon it, or whether the absence of Arab teams would take away many athletes of world renown.

The first rule then is to let the head govern the heart; but there are no professional 'embargologists', no generally accepted doctrine, which can advise the inexperienced, haphazardly chosen, temporary 'generals' in these conflicts. In the age of Mercantilism on the contrary there was a well developed if not always correct scientific basis for policy.[9] However, the fact that a weapon has fallen into incompetent hands proves nothing against the weapon.

It is certainly not the case that the weapon has never been effective. The Italo-Abyssinian case is almost a positive proof of its effectiveness: people were *afraid* of the success of the weapon. The case of Japan in 1941 shows how right they were. The widely-spread opinion that the British embargo against Rhodesia (1966–77) had no success rests upon a technical error. It is certainly correct to say that British Petroleum (a nationalized firm, and so the property of the government that introduced the embargo) and other oil firms evaded the oil embargo, but we must look away from this well-known scandal to the neglected results of the Portuguese Revolution of 1974. In March 1976 Mozambique, after long hesitation in view of the losses she would herself suffer, at last closed the Rhodesian border, and so closed also the only railway line to the sea that did not go through Johannesburg. Mr Vorster, annoyed by the resulting transport bottleneck in Johannesburg, used his new monopoly position to force Mr Smith to the conference table in Geneva. When, on 24 September 1976, the latter announced to his people his intention after all to negotiate with the black revolutionaries in Geneva, everyone in Rhodesia felt that the end was near. This day marked the beginning of the surrender even if the immediate military situation was not at that time bad.

All these facts were there to be read at the time in the better international newspapers. Prejudice against embargoes must indeed be running high if, only seven years later, this victory is interpreted as a defeat. One must not say that a weapon has failed, when simply the inexperienced 'general' (Mr Wilson in this case) promised too much with it. Until 1974–76 Rhodesia had too many open borders with friendly powers. The embargo was successful, and its 'general' was not Harold Wilson but Samora Machel.

A more important example of success is Senator Jackson's threat in 1970 not to repeal the prohibition on capital transfers to the USSR unless Jewish emigration was allowed. In entirely informal ways – but without public negotiation with Senator Jackson – the emigration thereupon began. However, during the next election the Senator spoke too much in public about this matter and the Russians gave up their attempt to gain access to the American capital market. Nevertheless, once it had begun, Jewish emigration went on, to be followed by the CSCE Accords at Helsinki and the *Volksdeutsch* emigration. It is astounding how the proponents of 'new' detente feel themselves bound to oppose embargoes and to maintain that the weapon is useless or counter-productive.[10] Detente, whether 'old' or 'new', was the direct child of the great American embargo, as the Kremlin sought to enlarge its opportunities to import technology and capital by making political concessions.

Is This Embargo Practical?

We have ascertained the general practicability of an embargo in skilled hands. To go into technical details would be to write the missing 'Introduction to Embargology'. More interesting for us is this question: is the USSR a suitable victim for an embargo?

The answer has little historical basis but is very positive.

– The USSR needs our technology, because the KGB, the enemy of all international communications, hinders pure research and because the centrally-planned economy can neither organize applied research not the development of new products.

– The USSR needs wheat because climatically and geographicaly she is a Canada with a US-sized population (she has not the Middle West), because her agriculture was collectivized and because Communist ideology does not permit the relaxation of this system, at least as regards the internal functioning of the *Kolkhoz*.

– The Soviet economy swallows up very large investment outlays (particularly in agriculture) per rouble of output, and needs especially foreign capital which comes in the form of hard currency.

The influence of Senator Jackson shows us indisputably the extent to which the country is dependent on technology, wheat and capital.

But the aim of the embargo can scarcely be some short-term attempt to stop this or that Soviet foreign policy measure: for instance the Afghan War or the Polish 'auto-invasion'. The USSR is a proud imperialist power whose present real income can finance such policies. Moreover, for such important goals, *once undertaken*, the government will sacrifice everything.

Rather the goal of an embargo should be to constrain, not modify, the decision-making process in the long term. All these Soviet adventures cost a great deal. Above all, Afghanistan and Angola were not necessary, and Angola indeed cost hard currency. The economic situation in the Soviet Union is serious: she needs growth and she does not get it.[11] People are working less and stealing more. The Soviet Union hesitates before making the expenditures necessary for the SS-20 missiles or for Nicaragua. Without Western technology, wheat and capital, she would hesitate a lot longer. What has not already been undertaken perhaps one will never undertake. Gradually, the Soviet state is becoming relatively, maybe even absolutely, weaker – first in civilian investment, then in consumption and therefore, later, also in defence. *The right embargo is, then, a long-term one, aimed simply at Soviet econ-*

omic growth, and so not conditional upon minor changes in behaviour.

Figure 1: Relationship of Defence Growth and Consumption Growth

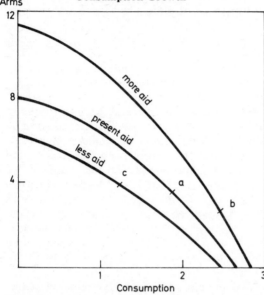

The arms consumption trade-off (percent per annum increases, very approximate). 'Aid' includes credits and technology transfer.

Source: M. M. Hopkins and M. Kennedy, *The Trade-off between Consumption and Military Expenditures for the Soviet Union during the 1980s* (Santa Monica, Ca: Rand, 1982).

Charles Wolf has put the point as follows. There is a trade-off between growth in defence and growth in consumption (mainly a trade-off between returns from the two kinds of investment) as in Figure 1, which is approximately valid for 1980–90. This trade-off is largely economic, and is largely an objective constraint. By more foreign aid we raise, and by less we lower, the trade-off line. Incidentally we affect the growth of arms more than that of consumption because the latter is three or four times larger in absolute size than the former, and because of the weight in the latter of the low technology sectors. We necessarily leave the Russians free to choose their point in whichever line they are on. We 'constrain behaviour' by lowering the line; we 'modify behaviour' by persuading them to choose a more pro-

consumption point on a constant or on a higher line. Our ability to constrain is clear enough, our ability to modify is inscrutable. 'New' detente expected the USSR to move from point *(a)* to point *(b)* and has been proved wrong. The long-term unconditional embargo policy is more modest, and claims only to be able to lower the line. But note that it would be hard, because of the way the lines are drawn, to *maintain* the growth of arms at a%, i.e. 4% (while consumption of course grows at 2%). Thus, the point *(c)* promises virtually zero growth in *per capita* consumption.

But what of the 'doves' in the Kremlin? There is much paranoia among anti-Soviet writers, and this is nowhere more evident than in the denial that there are 'hawks' or 'doves' at all. Yet in the 1920s and 1930s the distinction is perfectly clear. Moreover Beria *did* want to give up the GDR in 1952 – and was overruled. Malenkov *was* more cautious about nuclear weapons than Khrushchev. The latter *was* opposed to the 'export of revolution' but, at the height of his power, he could not stop Suslov from contradicting him publicly. The Army *did* disapprove of Brezhnev's visit to Bonn. And so one could go on. Yet my conviction remains that these disagreements are generally small and always tactical, and make no difference to the grand end of world conquest.

All the politicians mentioned did use violence; all of them remained within the pale of orthodoxy. Given the opportunity, the 'dove' of the previous paragraph will catch the rabbit – it is his duty, and he is really only a 'dawk'. There is also nothing to stop 'hawks' succeeding 'doves' in power, or 'dovish' moods succeeding 'hawkish' moods in one Communist breast (as in Khrushchev, above). The differences are perfectly genuine, but simply too small to affect the long-term foreign policy of the West. True 'doves', with whom one might collaborate in a safe world, were Bukharin, Nagy and Dubcek. It is self-evident that if such 'doves' definitely take power in the Kremlin we must abandon our embargo. Indeed we must make the same point clear in advance, since precisely this event is the long-term hope of humanity. But so far, in 64 years of Soviet power, just one

99

	Year 1	Year 2	Year 12	Year 13
GNP	100	99.95	99.95	do
Exports to USSR	1	0.75	0.75	”
Rest of GNP	99	99.20	99.20	”
Defence Burden	5	5	4.5	”
Other Expenditures	95	94.95	95.45	”
Loss(−) or Gain(+)		−0.05	+0.45	+0.45

person securely identifiable as a true 'dove' has ever reached the Politburo. There is a great arrogance in asserting that the West can install doves in the Politburo. This is a typical over-optimistic claim of the 'behaviour modification' school. A long-term embargo is, to repeat, more intellectually modest.

It has another advantage: it is something we can *do*. In an abstract way the advice 'Don't just do something: stand there' is as valid as its opposite. But in this concrete case inaction is a sure recipe for defeat. Our adversary is always inching forward: territory and military technology are stolen or simply accrue to him. Whatever his problems he still can and will inflict upon us the death of a thousand cuts. Inaction also raises problems of morale, and is in the long run *worse* for an alliance than a positive but controversial policy.

Yet again an embargo on the USSR is compatible with the favourable economic treatment of Romania and Hungary, and with that elusive ideal, an 'appropriate' yet imaginative and practical economic treatment of Poland. The first two of these countries are not in need of such high technology as the USSR, and receive no aid from her: so help to them cannot be passed on.

Are not embargoes highly provocative? Yes – and they should never go so far as Roosevelt's embargo on Japan. But they are hardly so provocative as, and certainly more moral than, the only defensible alternative – a spiralling arms race.

For there is a trade-off. It would be extremely rash to quantify the results of a long-term unconditional embargo. But all military and indeed economic policies are extremely rash, and honest quantification

tends to make them at least more transparent. So let us consider a few purely illustrative numbers. Most COCOM members export 1% of their national product to the USSR, and have a defence burden of 5%. Suppose we decide that one quarter of those exports is dangerous. Then 0.25% of our resources must be diverted to less profitable uses, where they earn 20% less, or 0.20%. So we lose 0.05% of GNP. The sequence is presented above for simplicity, without growth of GNP.

The effects on Soviet economic performance are serious, and eventually, in face of generally slowed productivity growth, military expenditures fall. So in the tenth year after the increased embargo we all decide to lower our own defence burden by 10% because we have achieved a sufficient superiority. Then the sacrifices due to the embargo have all been recouped by the end of year 13, for by then the present value of losses and gains is positive at virtually any reasonable rate of futurity discount. This is at any rate the kind of sum that must be done.

Take too the much more subtle and complicated case of the Polish debt. The West has been, quite unconsciously, engaged in a 'khedival' operation: we lent to Gierek, as we lent in 1863–76 to the Khedive Ismail of Egypt, irresponsibly to an irresponsible borrower (cf. Landers, 1958). In nineteenth century circumstances, Ismail's bankruptcy led to Britain acquiring the Suez Canal and occupying the country. In the twentieth century, bankrupt sovereigns fare better but Poland – still not quite bankrupt – has suffered a shattering blow. *Solidarność* grew up under Gierek's economic failure – and that failure prevented him from borrowing his way out of the problem *Solidarność* presented. The military result has been the destruction of Poland as a fighting member of the Warsaw Pact.

What has this cost the West? Some $26 billion at current prices, in that Poland's service on this debt is now reduced to a negligible trickle. Suppose that $13 billion of this is owned by the US: that is 8% of US *annual* defence expenditure.

Was Lenin Right About Capitalism?

A single long-term aim recommends itself also when we consider the weaknesses of the embargo-makers. A general aim, which quarrelsome and economically competitive COCOM powers can agree on at rare intervals, in solemn conclave, is perhaps possible. But more ambitious, fine-tuned, off-again-on-again, *short-term conditional* embargoes are certainly not. They will not command the unanimity of all Western Foreign Offices and, for that reason alone, they will fail. The USSR will simply face them out.

The right embargo, then, is a *long-term unconditional* embargo, a much expanded COCOM. Let us not forget that COCOM is itself just such an embargo, and it has at least not worked badly. It should be expanded to include much more technology. There should similarly be *special export taxes* on exports of wheat and capital to the USSR, plus a boycott of natural gas.

I name only these very few commodities out of political realism and a desire to avoid giving way to paranoia. Strictly speaking lipstick too is a strategic good, for foreign lipstick is popular in the USSR and high-priced. It therefore carries a high turnover tax – and taxes are useful for defence. Moreover, there is not only a financial but also a technological argument of the same kind:

Of course, anything one pleases can be regarded as strategic material, even a button, because it can be sewn onto a soldier's trousers. A soldier will not wear trousers without buttons, since otherwise he would have to hold them up with his hands. And then what can he do with his weapon? If one reasons thus, then buttons also are a particularly strategic material.

But if buttons really had such great importance and we could find no substitute for them, then I am sure that our soldiers would even learn to keep their up with their teeth, so that their hands would be free to hold weapons. [Nikita S. Khrushchev, *Pravda*, 28 February 1963.]

However, these more comprehensive doctrines, though absolutely correct, would be too unpopular to apply.

In any case the whole aim of a long-term unconditional embargo would be not to influence current policy but to prevent growth.[12] The philosophy behind the embargo should be like that of NATO itself: to deter the Soviet Union from military adventure. This is just possibly something on which the capitalist countries might agree, particularly if the idea is presented as a cold cost-benefit analysis: we will be able to cut our defence budget by so much if we sacrifice so much profit on foreign trade.

However, the argument for a truly scientific short-term and conditional embargo is not dead. Let us suppose, having considered things 'scientifically' and at leisure, that we set as goal some specific change in Soviet behaviour and overtly attach to it a specific embargo. What if the required change in behaviour is not vouchsafed to us in the long term? Do we give up the specific embargo and thus lose credibility? Or do we continue it, so making it long-term and virtually unconditional? I have quoted above Senator Jackson as an overwhelming and supremely relevant example of a successful embargo leader but with hindsight it can be seen to have been the risky short-term and conditional type. A little more Soviet will-power and he would have failed.

Lenin is reputed to have said somewhere that the capitalists are so blind that they will even sell us the rope with which we shall hang them.[13] Are the (state) capitalist nations of the OECD, which are always competing one against another, capable of sustaining a long-run embargo? Certainly they would lose very little by it. The Communists have recently shown, after long years of perfect reliability, that they are not the best debtors in the world.[14] Western capital can therefore be

101

exported to other unreliable countries instead. Technology is never a very profitable sale in any case. The man who profits from it is the one who first uses it. There remain only wheat and its *Doppelgänger*, natural gas. Is it better, as Mr Caspar Weinberger said in August 1982, to sell wheat because it removes hard currency from the enemy, or to buy natural gas and so to replenish his stock of it? If we forget that in this way the natural gas finances the wheat, the old-fashioned mercantilism of Mr Weinberger is probably right this time. Hard currency is the sinew of war: if one has it one can suddenly buy things more military than wheat. So here lies the 'guilt' of Western Europe, and other arguments like the energy dependency that results from it, seem hardly valid (5% is a small proportion).

The USSR can drill but it cannot harvest or make pipes. The NATO powers can harvest and make pipes, but they have nothing worthwhile to drill. In relative terms both the opponents are as unequal after the exchange as before, and here a good professional 'embargologist' could make a contribution. Here is the outline of a policy, derived from the following four premises:

– Strictly speaking the absolute profit must be the same on both sides before we pronounce the exchange 'embargo-neutral'.
– If one opponent cannot tolerate at all the loss of the profit then the other should not make the exchange and should give up his own profit. It is certain that the 'marginal utility to the state of real income for the people' is greater in the Soviet Union. For example, stagnation of consumption is ideologically unacceptable. Sixty-five years after the Revolution, the regime has still a serious legitimacy problem. One of the pillars of its precarious legitimacy, and at the same time a much-trumpeted promise, is precisely rising real income. What Mrs Thatcher, freely elected, can do deliberately, the Soviet leadership must not for one moment allow.
– The fungibility of hard currency is extremely important, as noted above. With bad Soviet harvests this is an almost decisive consideration. On the other hand,

the foreign trade roubles which come into our hands are almost totally without fungibility.
– Above all the embargo measures have to enjoy political respect at home. If the American farmer or the French housewife does not tolerate these measures, then their validity will last about a year.[15] The long-term goal will be forgotten and the whole future of all embargoes will be called in question. The directly interested parties – entrepreneurs and their labour who export, consumers or industrial users who import – will always have a strong 'democratic' case.

The policy concerns wheat and gas together. We must acknowledge that it is psychologically impossible to solve these two issues separately. For instance to demand a gas boycott without imposing a wheat embargo is sheer hypocrisy. It might then be best to tie them tightly together. The EEC would undertake to buy so much North American wheat at a discounted price with the discount set to compensate the EEC for the loss of its Soviet gas – on condition that neither party trade in these two commodities with the USSR. There should also be, if it is at all administratively possible, an export tax on wheat for the USSR.

We cannot avoid saying a few words about cultural embargos and boycotts. These, to our disgrace, arouse less opposition than the economic ones that are so much more effective. The reasons are surely economic: the cancellation of a cultural tour destroys no-one's livelihood, be he the importing impresario or the exported artist; and the former must reckon too with a spontaneous consumer boycott in any case. Moreover, such culture is subsidized, so the less of it the better for the taxpayer. But it is also not to be denied that artists are more altruistic than the owners of and workers in ordinary enterprises; they regularly submit to, even personally initiate, that which the Ohian farmer schemes to render impossible for all time. This fact can be used. Our natural indignation against specific Soviet crimes needs after all an outlet at the time, even if we know that it will not 'modify behaviour'. Perhaps then

102

there *should* be the short and emotional cultural embargoes that in fact there are, and for once our weaknesses have not betrayed us. Certainly they should be neither long nor dispassionate: our interest is in having as much contact with the Soviet people as possible, and one of the few serious arguments against a long-term economic embargo is the *Soviet cultural reaction*.

All this implies that the good professional 'embargologist' is not necessarily a narrow specialist but is capable of putting forward practical policies. He thinks that Lenin was probably right. Although he hates war, he does not wish to lose the conflict with Communism; yet he remains pessimistic. War, at any rate a small war, seems to come more easily to a capitalist country than a long-term embargo; and this for at least two good reasons. Firstly, war may no longer be fun but at least it remains heroic. Second, small wars distribute their burdens fairly. Those who fight are usually volunteers: they seek and get glory, at the known price of a little death. Those who don't fight *all* pay extra taxes, according to some mild scheme of fiscal progression. By contrast embargoes generate no glory, last a long time and distribute their burdens most unevenly. This is why we have raised above the question of fiscal compensation. As a result, the Bellona of the Falkland Islands still delivered parts of pumps for the gas pipeline. Our sharpest but most peaceful weapon is too heavy for us to handle.

NOTES

[1] On non-Communist states of this type, see Wiles 1984. (This contribution is a revized version of that article, further revized after listening to the debate.)

[2] Notably, I do not accept for one minute the argument, pushed by the White House but not the CIA, that the Soviet economy is collapsing, and a strong embargo will push it over the brink.

[3] The repeal in principle of the British 'Artisans and Machinery Acts' was in 1825 – before the *Zollverein*. The final repeal of all provisions came in 1843. I cannot find a date for France or Belgium, probably, however,the French repeal came in 1860 with the Cobden–Chevalier Treaty (the famous trade treaty between France and Great Britain). In the standard texts on Mercantilism these restraints on technology transfer are mentioned only in passing (and never indexed). They were valid for civilian industry as much as for military. Compare for instance Heckscher 1934, vol. II, p. 145; Cole 1939, vol. I, pp. 55–6, 110–11, 237–40, vol. II, pp. 139–41, 304–8.

[4] Clarke 1966, Tuchman 1966.

[5] Including South Africa and Israel.

[6] A few examples are worth airing. During the Falklands War of 1982 there was not one single demonstration against the enemy or for the war in Great Britain, but a great many in Argentina. For this latter people, and for the peoples of Spanish culture in general, '*la guerre*' was still '*fraîche et glorieuse*' There were only two exceptions: Chile (frontier quarrel with Argentina) and Spain, which has gone through a long civil war. If on the other hand we look at the Vietnam War, the US in 1964 had not suffered gravely from war since 1865. For this reason the people went willingly into the war and it is Vietnam itself that was their psychological turning point.

[7] In particular, the Russians preferred Addis Ababa to Mogadishu. On the traditional interest in Addis Ababa, compare Jesman 1958.

[8] We owe the concept and word to Georges Sokoloff (1980).

[9] And not so very incorrect. See Wiles 1968, ch. 16.

[10] An example of this total neglect of elementary fact can be found in Wolff von Amerongen (1980) p. 65: 'Embargoes have indeed caused economic losses – for both parties – 'but the political aim was never achieved'.

[11] Probably real consumption per head in 1979–81 has been stable, while investment has fallen and only defence expenditures have risen (also per head). Hidden inflation is running at about 3–4% per annum. See Wiles in *Soviet Studies*, nos. 1 & 3, 1982.

[12] We can also imagine short-term unconditional and long-term conditional embargoes, but these seem to be empty logical categories.

[13] I cannot find this sentence in the *Sochineniya* or in Annenkov's document (1961) but it sounds genuine.

[14] North Korea 1978, Poland 1981, Romania 1982 – and now even Cuba is threatening to stop debt service.

[15] *Fallait-il ajouter au drame des Polonais le drame des Francais qui seraient privés d'approvisionnement en gaz?* M. Pierre Mauroy, at Cambrai, 25 January 1982.

BIBLIOGRAPHY

(I include some sources not referred to in the text. Thus this list is also a selective reading list).

Gunnar Adler-Karlsson, *Western Economic Warfare 1947–1967* (Stockholm: Almqvist and Wiksell, 1968).

Yuri Annenkov, in *Nowy Zhurnal*, New York, September 1961.

Roger Carrick, *East–West Technology Transfer in Perspective* (University of California Policy Papers in International Affairs, no. 9, 1978).

I. F. Clarke, *Voices Prophesying War, 1763–1984*, (Oxford: O.U.P. 1966).

Charles W. Cole, *Colbert and a Century of French Mercantilism* (New York: Columbia U.P., 1939).

Eli Heckscher, *Mercantilism* (London: George Allen & Unwin, 1934).

M. M. Hopkins and M. Kennedy, *The Trade-off between Consumption and Military Expenditures for the Soviet Union during the 1980s* (Santa Monica, Ca: Rand, 1982).

Gary C. Hufbauer and Jeffrey J. Schott, *Economic Sanctions Reconsidered: History and Current Policy*, (California: The Institute of International Economics, 1984).

David S. Landers, *Bankers and Pashas* (London: Heinemann, 1958).

Marie Lavigne, in *Le Monde Diplomatique*, September 1968.

Les Relations Economiques Est–Ouest (Paris: Presses Universitaires de France, 1979)

Friedemann Mueller, *Sicherheitspolitische Aspekte der Ost–West Wirtschaftsbeziehungen* (Ebenhausen: Stiftung Wissenschaft und Politik, 1977)

Juergen Noetzold, *Die Bedeutung des Technologietransfers in der wirtschaftlichen Ost–West Kooperation* (Stiftung Wissenschaft und Politik: Ebenhausen 1974)

Alec Nove, in *La Repubblica*, 25 January 1980.

Georges Sokoloff, 'Exercises d'Embargologie' in *Politique Internationale*, no. 8, 1980.

Angela Stent, '*West German, British and French Export Controls and Technology Transfer Policies Towards the Communist Nations*' (report for the US Congress' Office of Technology Assessment, East–West Technology Transfer Project, 26 June 1979).

From Embargo to Ostpolitik, The Political Economy of West German–Soviet relations, 1955–1980 (Cambridge: C.U.P. 1981).

Barbara Tuchman, *The Proud Tower* (London: Hamish Hamilton, 1966).

Heinrich Vogel, 'Die Embargo-Politik der USA . . .' in *Europa Archiv*, 201981.

Joseph Wilczynski in *Soviet–Studies*, July 1967.

Technology in COMECON (London: Macmillan, 1974).

Peter Wiles, *Communist International Economics* (Oxford: Blackwell, 1968), chs. 16 and 17.

in *Probleme des Industrialismus in Ost und West* (Munich: Festschrift für Hans Raupach, Gunter Olzog Verlag GmbH, 1973, (in English)).

'On the Prevention of Technology Transfer', in NATO, Directorate of Economic Affairs, *East–West Technological Co-operation*, (NATO: Brussels 1977).

'Ost–West-Handel und Technologischer Vorsprung . . . ' in *Verein für Sozialpolitik, neue Folge*, Band 102, Staat und Wirtschaft, 1979.

'Embargologie', in *Ost-Europa*, 1984.

Ist eine Wirtschaftskooperation . . . Vorteilhaft?' in ed. Gottfried Zieger und Axel Lebahn, *Rechtliche und Wirtschaftliche Beziehungen . . .* (Baden-Baden: Nomos, 1980).

'Quelques Reflexions sur l'Embargologie' in *Politique Internationale*, no. 11 1980.

Otto Wolff von Amerongen, 'Economic Sanctions as a Foreign Policy Tool' in *International Security* (Cambridge, Mass.: Harvard University Press, 1980).

Economic Relations Between East and West

DR DALE R. TAHTINEN

The purpose of this Paper is to discuss some of the principal issues involved in East–West economic relations, including the topic of sanctions. A key element of our relationship with countries around the world is the economic tie that brings us together as trading partners. Since the USSR represents the main threat to Western security, Western economic trade policy towards the Soviet Union and her Warsaw Pact allies in Eastern Europe cannot be separated from Western security needs and objectives. Consequently, our trade policy vis-à-vis the East contains some basic and significant aspects that are different from our trade policies towards other trading partners. In discussing that trade policy, I wish to focus 'mainly on the effort which the US and her Japanese, Canadian, and European partners are making to fashion a collective approach to their economic relations with the Warsaw Pact members. This has been a particularly difficult undertaking but the undertaking is succeeding, with important results, from our common efforts.

Review of East–West Relations

Obviously many factors contribute to East–West tension. The Soviet Union's physical location places her in close proximity to Western interests on two continents. Her desire to increase her international influence prompts the USSR to challenge those interests. Her Marxist–Leninist ideology gives Soviet leaders a historical perspective and a vision of the future that differs fundamentally from our own.

We do not have to agree with the Soviet Union on all the fundamentals of morals or politics. Moscow's behaviour, must, however, be subject to that degree of restraint necessary to our living together on this planet in the nuclear age but we cannot hope to influence all the external and internal factors which determine Soviet behaviour. Obviously we would like to encourage the gradual evolution of the Soviet system towards political and economic pluralism but, if we cannot do that, we must at least counter Soviet expansionism by sustained and effective political, economic and military competition.

To meet these goals, the US intends to draw in part upon past strategies ranging from containment to detente. There is, after all, substantial continuity in US policy, a continuity that reflects the consistency of US values and US interests. The US has put aside, however, assumptions about US–Soviet relations that have been refuted by experience or overtaken by events.

Consider the changes that the world has witnessed since the Truman Administration developed the doctrine of containment. Soviet ambitions and capabilities have long since exceeded the geographic limits which the architects of this doctrine took for granted. Today, the Soviet Union conducts a global foreign and military policy. Any strategy that aims to counter it must be equally far-reaching. Where it was once, in the immediate post-war period, the US goal to contain Soviet influence within the limits of its reach, the US goal is now to foreclose Soviet challenges where possible and actively to contest them where necessary wherever US interests are threatened.

The policy of detente, of course, represented an effort to induce Soviet restraint. In 1972, a Strategic Arms Limitation Agreement (SALT I) was signed. President Nixon and Premier Brezhnev exchanged visits and signed numerous agreements. Both the US and the allies of the US joined the USSR and her allies to create a widespread spirit of East–West detente.

Economic relations were a key part of the overall thaw in East–West relations. Lenient Western credit terms permitted the East to increase the purchases of Western grain that

105

they needed and of technology and equipment that they could make only with difficulty or not at all. Truck assembly lines, entire chemical plants, and innumerable types of capital equipment were bought by the East.

Underlying detente was the theory that a web of economic, scientific, cultural, and political relationships would bring Soviet and Western views on security and other core issues closer together. It was believed that the tangible benefits flowing from economic and other interchanges would encourage Soviet restraint in foreign policy.

In forging economic links with the Soviet Union, we must admit that the US was as eager as her allies to increase her exports. From 1972 to 1975, US trade with the Eastern Bloc nearly tripled. While much of this increase resulted from greater grain sales, the Soviet Union also stepped up her purchases of US equipment and technology. The Pullman Corporation helped the Soviet Union to set up production lines at the Kama River Truck Plant, and the Bryant Manufacturing Company sold the Soviet Union equipment that allowed it to make miniature ball bearings with extreme precision.

We all know how the optimistic views of East–West relations of the early part of the decade were quickly dashed. Detente, despite its economic benefits for Soviet society, was no barrier at all when Soviet decision-makers saw opportunities to advance their strategic position through overseas adventurism or outright military aggression. Anyone with illusions that fundamental Soviet behaviour had changed by detente should have been disabused of them by more recent events.

It is a familiar litany to describe how the Soviet Union, in the late 1970s and after, failed to live up to the hopes associated with detente. Her sponsorship of Cuban adventures in Africa and of Vietnamese imperialism in Indochina, her invasion of Afghanistan, her violation of the Helsinki Accords, her crackdown in Poland, and her present involvement in Central America are visible indications that her fundamental values and policies had not been changed at all by a more lenient, friendly, and co-operative attitude on the part of the West. Lying behind all of these aggressive acts was the massive and unrelenting Soviet military build-up that went far beyond any reasonable notion of what would be needed to defend the USSR. Even in the area of strategic arms, supposedly restrained by the SALT Agreement, the USSR continued the most massive arms build-up in history. The SALT I and SALT II processes did little to curb the strategic arms build-up but they did encourage many in the West to imagine that security concerns had somehow become less pressing.

As the Soviet Union demonstrated that her fundamental values and policies had not changed, Western Governments began to re-evaluate their economic, political, and security relationships with the East. The changes we have witnessed in recent years mean that we could not be content merely to tinker with past strategies. Unlike containment, US policy begins now with the clear recognition that the Soviet Union is and will remain a super-power with global reach. This global super-power's conduct in recent years has taught the US that her policy must assume that the USSR is more likely to be deterred by actions that make clear the costs of aggression than by the delicate web of interdependence central to some visions of detente.

Western Re-evaluation of Detente
The Western governments, with the US acting most quickly, began to re-examine their basic economic, political and security relationships with the East in 1980, following the Soviet invasion of Afghanistan. It was realized rather suddenly as world events go that the Soviet Union had demonstrated conclusively that none of her fundamental values or policies had changed. In January 1980, ministerial level discussions were held in NATO on the most appropriate economic responses to Soviet aggression. The following summer, in Ottawa, President Reagan urged the Allies to re-examine East–West relations and the Allies concluded that co-ordination was necessary 'to ensure that, in the field of East–West relations, our economic policies continue to be *compatible with our political and security objectives*'. The Allied reorientation was given further impetus by the Soviet-inspired imposition of martial law in Poland in December 1981. The US and

106

her allies imposed economic sanctions on Poland, while the US went further and, acting unilaterally, imposed restrictions on shipments of oil and gas extraction and transmission equipment by US firms to the USSR.

It is hardly surprising that US attitudes in the economic sphere evolved more rapidly than those of her European and Japanese allies. The trade of the key allies of the US with the East has, since the days of Imperial Russia, always surpassed US trade with the East. This has been natural, given the proximity of the trading partners and the mutual comparative advantage which results from an exchange of the East's raw materials for the West's manufactured goods and services. In short, East–West trade is more important to the allies of the US than it is to the United States.

In the spring of 1982, the US indicated her concern over Western subsidies of credit for the Eastern Bloc. The US began intensive discussions with her Western industrial partners and, subsequently, the Soviet Union and other countries were put into the same OECD consensus category with developed countries. At the Versailles Summit in June 1982, East–West economic relations were mentioned in the communiqué but, following that meeting, it became clear that there were significant differences in interpretation among the allied leaders.

When President Reagan observed that there was no movement on important issues by either the Poles or the Soviet Union, he extended the sanctions on oil and gas equipment to subsidiaries of US firms and to licensees of US technology. Although the President would have preferred not to act unilaterally in this matter, his overriding priority was to demonstrate US resolve to oppose continued brutality and supression of human rights in Poland. The extension of the oil and gas sanctions provoked severe protests from the allies of the US.

As soon as Secretary Shultz took office in the summer of 1982, he was asked by the President to listen carefully to what America's allies were saying. He came to two conclusions after meeting with the NATO Foreign Ministers at La Sapinere in Quebec in the autumn of 1982. First, that there was enough convergence in the views he heard for there to be a good chance of reaching agreement on a collective approach to East–West economic relations; and, second, that a collective approach would be much more effective than a unilateral approach.

On Secretary Shultz's recommendation, the President lifted the pipeline sanctions in November 1982 because a broad consensus was emerging on the nature of the economic relationship with the East and because the US and her European, Japanese, and Canadian partners agreed to the basic principles on economic relations with the USSR and undertook to carry out a series of analyses of East–West economic relations designed to provide a framework for a collective approach to these relations. The analyses were undertaken in a variety of locations.

East–West Studies
In December, 1982, the governments concerned agreed on a programme of analyses and discussions of East–West economic relations in the following institutions:

- In NATO, the overall security implications of East–West economic relations were to be examined.
- In the OECD, East–West financial relations and credit terms, as well as problems stemming from the Eastern nations' centralized control or trade, were to be studied.
- In COCOM (the Co-ordinating Committee for Multilateral Export Controls), measures for improved surveillance and control over Western exports with strategic or military implications were to be reviewed.
- And finally, the International Energy Agency (IEA) was to analyse the energy security of its members in a broader context in order to highlight the dangers created by undue energy dependence on any single insecure source while identifying alternative sources of energy.

The major segments of those analyses have been completed, but some work continues. The results have provided us with a framework that has been agreed by the US and her partners for the conduct of East–West economic relations. US hopes in undertaking these studies were amply borne out by the co-operative spirit with which the studies were conducted and by the results achieved. The conclusions from those studies were endorsed at the ministerial level prior to the Williamsburg Summit and this made it unnecessary for the seven Heads of Government to spend much time at Williamsburg on this subject.

The Williamsburg declaration concluded:

East–West economic relations should be compatible with our security interests. We take note with approval of the work of the multilateral organizations which have in recent months analysed and drawn conclusions regarding the key aspects of East–West economic relations. We encourage continuing work by these organizations, as appropriate.

Let us review conclusions upon which the Heads of State based that statement.

NATO's Economic Committee had undertaken an extensive review of the security implications of East–West economic relations. At the June 1983 meeting, the Foreign Ministers concluded that trade must be consistent with 'commercially sound terms and mutual advantage, that avoids preferential treatment of the Soviet Union and remains consistent with broad Allied security concerns'. The Ministers specifically called for avoiding dependence on the Soviet Union and encouraged the development of Western energy resources.

In the OECD, the members had completed the first phase of a thorough economic analysis of trade and financial relations with the East. This analysis concluded that East–West trade had not developed as rapidly as once expected and still remains of marginal importance to the West. Western gains from this trade have been disappointing, especially when it is considered that half the increased level of exports to the East in the late 1970s was financed by borrowing. Debt obligations have not been met despite a sharp cut in imports by the Eastern nations. Most interesting is the basic reason ascribed for these trends: the nature of the planned economic system of socialist states which makes it difficult for the East effectively to use imported capital equipment and technology and to produce goods which are competitive in Western markets.

In the export credit area, the OECD agreed that subsidized credits should not be made and that the Soviet Union should not be given the same concessionary interest rates as are given to developing countries. Since July 1982 the minimum interest rate applicable to direct government provided credit to the Soviet Union and other developed countries is 12.4%. The Allies are working to extend and strengthen this export credit arrangement. Over the long term, the Allies are also working to improve statistics on trade flows and foreign indebtedness in order to be certain that data is current and based on common definitions.

At COCOM, the members have recently taken a number of significant actions to further strengthen what has been a reasonably effective effort to prevent the transfer of strategic technology to the East. In January 1982 and in April 1983, High Level Meetings were held, the first in many years. While the details of both the High Level Meetings and of routine COCOM activities are confidential, the Allies have agreed to take steps to strengthen the effectiveness of the organization and the national control systems, to improve co-ordination between member governments to strengthen national licencing and endorsement methods, and to adapt COCOM controls to keep pace with technological developments. The Member Governments have also agreed to study whether security interests require controls on certain categories of high technology not now controlled. It looks as if the allies are prepared to work together to ensure that high-technology trade with the East does not undermine Western security.

Finally, in the global context at the IEA, the US and her partners agreed that they should avoid undue dependence on any one source for energy supplies. Such dependence on one source could potentially enable the source to exercise monopoly power and exert political pressures. While Ministers agreed that gas has an important part to play in reducing dependence on imported oil, they also agreed on the importance of avoiding a situation where imports of gas could weaken rather than strengthen the energy security and thus the overall economic stability of member countries.

Before arriving at this conclusion, a detailed study of global energy requirements and security was undertaken to assess the energy vulnerability of individual nations by each type of fuel and to identify policies which could enhance energy security. This study shows that an interruption in the supply of oil remains the major risk, but that rapidly rising imports of natural gas from non-OECD sources pose a significant challenge to the energy security of Europe. On the subject of natural gas, the US and her partners undertook the following: to recognize the need to rely where possible on secure and diversified sources; to take actions necessary to strengthen their ability to deal with supply interruptions that may nevertheless occur; to advance development of such important indigenous gas resources as the Troll Field in Norway or the gas resources of North America; and finally to give special attention to their progress in implementing these measures on an annual basis. There would appear to be, for the first time, a coherent framework for the continuous examination of energy security issues.

It is important to remember that neither the conduct nor the implementation of these studies took place under any formally legally-binding scheme. None of the organizations which sponsored the studies is a supranational body whose recommendations are binding on the members. Indeed, such a rigid arrangement would be antithetical to the spirit of alliances or friendships with other democratic countries. We continue to depend upon consensus.

Earlier I mentioned the pipeline sanctions. It should be made clear that the US does not want – did not want in June 1982 and does not want now – the friction, tension, and bickering associated with those export restrictions. But the US did want to ensure (and there seems now to be a consensus within the Alliance over this) that economic relations were 'compatible with our political and security interests'. The

President lifted the sanctions because he believed that a basic consensus had been reached, and the efforts in NATO, OECD, COCOM, and the IEA confirm the details of that consensus and the direction in which the Allies intend to head.

With respect to sanctions, we should not forget that the Soviet Union has not hesitated to use economic measures to extract political gain. In an interesting article in the *Los Angeles Times*, Dr Elliott Hurwitz, Special Assistant to the US Under Secretary of State for Economic Affairs, Allen Wallis, reviewed major attempts by the Soviet Union to use economic measures since World War II to compel changes in the policies or actions of other nations. These include: severing trade with Yugoslavia in 1948; reducing it again across the board in 1958 because of Yugoslavian independence over international issues such as the 1956 Hungarian uprising; breaking relations and terminating purchases of wool from Australia in 1958 because a Soviet diplomat's wife sought asylum along with her husband; cancelling trade contracts, withdrawing their Ambassador, and stalling discussion of aid in Finland in 1958 when one of her political parties took a less pro-Soviet line; reducing trade by more than 75% with China in 1960 over ideological differences; severing of all trade with Albania after she accepted an industrial-development loan from China in 1961; and reducing oil supplies to Cuba in 1967 until she brought her foreign policy closer in line with the USSR. More recently, in 1981, Poland was threatened with a cut-off in supplies of oil and other raw materials unless the Solidarity labour unions were halted. Late last year, an Italian business delegation was warned that Italian commercial interests would suffer if Italy did not take significant steps towards 'economic normalization'. Despite Soviet cultivation of an image among Western trading partners as a 'reliable supplier', the USSR is (as are other nations) quite capable of using economic measures in areas in which she has leverage and in which she sees the promise of political gain outweighing the short-term economic costs. Soviet ideology emphasizes the political consequences of economic relations, and the USSR would view it as naïve to try to divorce the two.

Work in Progress
Before concluding, I should like to view briefly how the Allies are planning to build on the results that have been achieved thus far and we plan to maintain the awareness of the security dimension of East–West economic relations. What we have done is to begin a continuing process which will include:

- Work in NATO on the general security implications of East–West economic relations;
- A more detailed analysis in the OECD of the balance of economic advantages in East–West trade;
- An effort in COCOM to strengthen that organization and to examine whether members' security interests require controls on additional high-technology items;
- A study in the IEA on national energy policies and Western security.

In reviewing East–West economic relations, we must keep in mind that the United States spent $183 billion on defence in fiscal year 1982 or 6.6% gross domestic product. The US plans to spend $1.4 trillion over the next five years. The European and Japanese allies are spending smaller but still very significant sums. The central question is to what extent are our economic relations with the Soviet Union helping her to build up her military forces and thus forcing us to spend even more on defence. The studies that have been reviewed here are devoted to a careful evaluation of whether and when our economic ties with the USSR are indirectly facilitating these huge Soviet expenditures on defence.

Conclusion
The process of turning away from the economics of detente has not been a smooth one. Differences in perception within the Alliance of the strategic importance of East–West trade have evolved at different rates and have sometimes caused the path to be rocky. We should be pleased that that period is behind us and that we have now strengthened our common security through the forging of a collective approach to Western economic policy towards the East – one which we believe will be valid for the rest of the decade and perhaps beyond.

The Reagan Administration supports trade between the West and the Communist nations – as between any nations – where that trade is conducted at prevailing market prices and terms, where there is a mutual balance of advantage, and where the specific transaction (or category of transactions) does not contribute directly to the strategic advantage of the Soviet Union. Western consumers and producers, both agricultural and industrial, can benefit from such trade.

Let me emphasize we should be prepared to accept that Soviet priorities and Soviet behaviour are very likely to be governed by factors inherent in the Soviet system, rather than by changes in Western economic policy, and these factors are not very different for Andropov than they were for Brezhnev. But, at the least, a policy of restricting high technology exports and removing the preferential advantages which the Soviet Union has often exploited in the past would place greater pressure on Soviet decision-makers to face the consequences of their resource allocation policy on the Soviet economy in the middle and longer run. This is simply a policy of economic realism designed to protect Western security interests; it is not a policy for bringing the USSR 'to its knees', or to bring about the 'collapse of the Soviet system'.

The effects on Soviet behaviour of such a policy of resource restriction will be gradual and will be felt only over the long run. This argues for the implementation of Western policy on East–West economic relations in this direction now rather than later.

Our policy is not based on trusting the Soviet Union, or on expectations that they will undergo a change of heart. It is based on our firm belief that, faced with demonstrated Western determination to strengthen its defences, to increase its political and economic cohesion, and to oppose adventurism, the Soviet Union will accept that restraint is her most attractive, indeed her only viable, option. Perhaps, over time, this restraint will become an ingrained habit in the USSR; perhaps not. Either way, our responsibility to remain vigilant is the same.

Considering the East–West Military Balance

DR BO HULDT

In September 1979, in a perhaps somewhat less than Metternichean mood and moment, Henry Kissinger made his much commented upon observation about the changing strategic situation with parity between the super-powers making the United States nuclear umbrella over Europe increasingly symbolic. With the arrival of the Reagan Administration such 'revelations' became the order of the day. Secretary of Defense Caspar Weinberger, in his rather low-key style, made one of the most chilling comments of all when he observed that the United States no longer had any margin for error.

On 31 March 1982 President Reagan himself declared that 'on balance the Soviet Union does have a definite margin of superiority' over the US strategic arsenal. Weinberger supported him: '. . . there is a degree of superiority and strategic edge on the Soviet side, that is necessarily a matter of great concern'. Since these statements were made, a certain amount of modification and backtracking has taken place. Pentagon spokesmen, commenting upon the IISS *Military Balance 1982–1983* in the autumn of 1982, maintained that 'the United States no longer enjoys strategic superiority', and that 'the overall effectiveness of our retaliatory capacity has become increasingly uncertain'. Former Defense Secretaries Schlesinger and Brown joined in the debate: the United States had in their view lost superiority – but rather than the Soviet Union being on top, there was thought to be a stand-off.

By then, however, we were all becoming rather accustomed to stunning news – having also reflected on, for example, Colin Gray's encouraging words: 'We will be fortunate if we survive the 1980s'.[1]

Against this background, it is with some trepidation that one ventures into the realm of sweeping statements about the military balance between East and West.

All these statements, however, bear witness to the breakneck pace at which the world has changed since 1945, when the United States was supreme, as the only nuclear power and with over 60% of the world's total industrial output, to the relative decline of American power by the 1970s and 1980s and the rise of the Soviet Union as a global military power.

The Soviet 'prisoner', contained within a network of Western alliances, base systems and economic blockade established in the 1940s and early 50s, had by the 1970s broken out of his confinement. If not exactly a reformed personality, the Soviet Union by then appeared to most of the world as greatly changed in some key respects: little was left of the ideological appeal which still exercised a pull in the 1950s; Soviet leadership in a united world Communist movement was long gone and was conceivably beyond recapturing; and much of the revolutionary gesturing had been replaced by something beginning to resemble the priorities of a traditional European great power. Nothing seemed more appropriate than that this new Soviet Union should be granted the status of strategic peer in the SALT negotiations by Nixon and Kissinger, those contemporary heirs of Kaunitz and Talleyrand.

Having been rejected by the West in the 1950s (Hungary and the Middle East) and again in the 1960s (in the Congo and Cuba), it was now above all as a world *military* power that the Soviet Union was granted parity in strategic terms and with this presumably she also expected that recognition which Presidents Kennedy, Eisenhower and Truman had refused. When Leonid Brezhnev stated in 1970 that now there was no question of any significance in the world that could be decided without consideration being paid to the views of the Soviet Union, he was in effect silently mouthing the wisdom of the Great Elector of

Brandenburg: 'Alliances, to be sure, are good, but forces of one's own, upon which one can rely, are better . . . and it is these, thank God!, that have made me *considerable* since the time when I began to have them'.[2]

Still, the 'breakout' remains limited in that it has not changed the immediately surrounding political geography – as was feared in the late 1940s. The 'rim-land' around the Soviet 'heartland' still looks much the same as it did in the 1950s. The Soviet Union has not obtained control over the North and Norwegian Seas, she has not opened the gates to the Baltic, nor pushed NATO back to the Rhine, nor destroyed the independence of Finland, Sweden, Austria or Yugoslavia. She has not even succeeded in establishing a non-conflictual relationship with the Eastern Europeans corresponding to the integration process in Western Europe – rather the contrary. The Soviet Union has not unlocked the Dardanelles, nor established mastery over the Mediterranean. And though she has made some headway, she has not overrun Turkey and Iran, captured the warm water ports on the Indian Ocean or secured the Japanese seas and straits.

Instead, the Soviet Union has bypassed the rim, establishing bridgeheads in Africa, Asia and Latin America. Even these advances, however, *could* be described as rather modest successes: a kaleidoscope of disappointments and partial gains, mixed results from efforts to arrange 'collective security', arms and 'ideology' transfers, hurt feelings and great expectations. These advances hardly represent a steady 'geopolitical momentum' from 1945 to 1980.[3] The picture is very much one of over-extension (the USSR – rather than the West – is presently the power directly or indirectly involved in guerrilla warfare in the Third World), a picture of the Soviet Union busily building strategic sandcastles in the Third World that if anything show rather less durability than those made by the West.

In two respects, however, the world *has* changed fundamentally. First, as a result of long-term historical trends but also aided by Soviet policies, a new international climate has emerged, characterized by more fluid international relationships that tend to recall traditional balance-of-power politics, with a wide number of operators, all actively pursuing their own interests.

Secondly, since the definite quashing of Nikita Khrushchev's half-hearted efforts before 1962 to limit military expenditure, the Soviet Union has built a military machine of unprecedented dimensions. Few analysts in the West seem to question the reality of this build-up. The quarrel is rather over percentages and, above all, its political significance.

The Soviet Military Build-up

After the Cuban debacle, Ambassador Kuznetsov told his counterparts: 'You Americans will never be able to do this to us again'. Whether that is so remains to be seen; the military build-up, however, is a fact. The message remains the same: there has been a steady rise in Soviet military capabilities at a pace considerably greater than the West's and the momentum of his process will also carry on through the 1980s.[4]

With this the Soviet arms build-up appears to have developed an *autonomous* character – largely unconnected with Western actions – and it becomes legitimate to ask whether a continuing armaments process can be politically controlled at all, what the motives are and what the long-term impact upon international security will be.

The history of the SS-20s here becomes a case very much in point. We now know that offers were made by the Carter Administration to the Russians in 1979 – after the abortive deep-cuts proposal made by the United States in the SALT negotiations in 1977 – to agree on a general freeze that might conceivably have prevented the whole Euro-missile controversy from ever developing. These offers were rejected by Brezhnev and, in spite of repeated signals from the West, the Soviet Union continued the deployment of these missiles at an unrelenting pace.

It is not easy to discover any Soviet counterpart to a 'dual track' here and one may choose to question *either* the intentions of the Soviet leadership *or* the extent to which these same leaders really exercise effective control over their weapons acquisition process.[5]

During the history of the Cold War we have become accustomed to a picture of ups and downs and wide swings in the defence efforts of the West. Soviet arms expenditures, on the other hand, are supposed to have followed a more stable, upward trend – at least since the early 1960s. The real arms race began with the Korean War, showing signs of a slowdown in the mid-1950s with the 'Geneva spirit', again picking up speed after *Sputnik*, with the Eisenhower and Kennedy Administrations laying the ground-work for the United States' strategic deterrent today as it has largely remained structured since the mid-1960s. The Vietnam War implied new peaks, followed by the 'contrac-tion' of the early 1970s. Already by 1976, however, the United States had begun to rearm and since then we have witnessed a continuing effort to counter the effects of the march that the Soviet Union – the tortoise racing the hare – has stolen on the West.

The Soviet build-up during the years of detente, when the balance was, in Richard Burt's choice of word, 'disturbed',[6] has raised very basic questions about Soviet society. *One* answer has been provided by Cornelius Castoriadis with the concept of the 'strato-cracy', the totally militarized society where all resources and priorities remain subor-dinate to the military sector and to the wishes and whims of the lords military.[7]

In a way, this represents somewhat of a Sovietologist's parallel to the *Limits to Growth* report from the Club of Rome in 1972: 'Demand will continue to grow exponentially with no conceivable point of saturation or levelling out short of some unspecified disaster'. Military expenditures are really, in Khrushchev's words, 'a bottom-less pit'.

In the West, being 'hooked' on welfare just as much as the Soviets to us appear obsessed by (military) security, rising worries concern the dangers emanating both from growing Soviet capabilities *and* from the remedies, rearmament or 'Nachrüestung', which could both threaten welfare and increase the original dangers further. (If this latter view, the 'fear-of-causing-provocation' theme, catches on, it will obviously by itself imply a success for the Soviet leadership.) Much more than a mere tactical victory, such a development could signify a fundamental

breakthrough in Soviet capacity to exercise direct influence over Western Europe – and attain that hegemony which Stalin thought 'natural' in 1945 when he regretted not having been able to emulate Czar Alexander's entry into Paris after the fall of Napoleon. The present situation, however, may seem 'a plague on both houses' with the Soviet leaders possibly fearing that a new armaments race would undo all that has been gained through the efforts of two decades and again distract their leadership from those social and economic reforms that even the military, the 'stratocracy', must realize are necessary.[8] Thus the Russians may worry that the West will somehow repeat the strategic 'quantum jump' performed during the Eisenhower and Kennedy Administra-tions. The Soviet response to such a develop-ment has been made abundantly clear: 'No matter what type of weapons may appear in the USA and in what quantities . . . the Soviet Armed Forces will have an appro-priate counterbalance for such weapons'.[9]

One might here refer to a vicious circle created by the combined effects of the dyna-mism of American technology and an uncompromising Soviet concept of 'security' that has in the past led to the Russians 'doing the same thing' as the Americans, with a few years' delay but then doing it *en masse*'.[10]

At present, the Soviet leadership may face a dilemma. Assuming that the military build-up has been undertaken for 'political' purposes, depreciation of Soviet capabilities as compared with American military resources – which is the theme of the official propaganda pamphlet *Whence the Threat to Peace* – would seem to be dysfunctional. The middle road would be a combination of 'threat' and 'reassurance' aimed at dissuading the West from 'Nachrüestung'. Such a mixed policy would be consistent with Soviet postures towards Western Europe since Stalin's efforts in 1949 to undo the damage of the Berlin blockade.

From the point of view of the Soviet leadership, the worse case would conceivably be Western all-out rearmament which, given superior Western resources, would inevitably leave the Soviet Union behind if pursued with resolve and for the duration. It goes without saying that although this would be a *worst* case from the Kremlin's perspective, it is not necessarily the *best* from the Western viewpoint.

The Concept of 'Balance'

The very use of the 'balance' concept merits scepticism. Ernst B. Haas' analysis of the term 'balance of power' uncovered at least eight different meanings of the term.[11] His colleague Nicholas Spykman noted that 'The truth of the matter is that states are interested only in a balance which is in their favor. Not an equilibrium, but a generous margin is their objective. There is no real security in being just as strong as a potential enemy; there is security only in being a little stronger . . . The balance desired is the one which neutralizes other states, leaving the home state free to be the deciding force . . .'[12] Or put even more directly: 'The equality meaning commands it [balance of power] as propaganda; the advantage is a mental reservation for private use'.[13]

During the deployment of the SS-20 missiles we have been treated to a sequence of official Soviet statements about an existing 'balance' or 'approximate parity' in Europe – regardless of the gradual rise in the number of SS-20s deployed. Likewise, Western comments made about the present military balance frequently mix 'parity' with 'Soviet superiority' with almost total abandon – even in one and the same context. The Reagan Administration has variously expressed as its goal superiority (as President Carter did when stating that no price would be too high to ensure that the United States remain the strongest power in the world) and a 'balance' restored.

With all this in mind one may have a certain sympathy with the observation made in a Hungarian source: 'The balance . . . is a highly complex and constantly changing concept, which cannot be easily defined . . . In fact, 'balance' can never be defined on a global or regional level, either concurrently or in an exact way, because of various structural demands by armaments modernization processes, their dynamics and phase shifts and also because of military geographic disparities'.[14]

This is very wise but not very helpful. Obviously, the use of the concept 'balance' has strong connotations of a safe margin, and a true equilibrium of just 50/50 may not be seen as such at all. Our Hungarian authority, looking for ways out of the dilemma, suggests 'a balance of reciprocal perception' and quotes Western sources on 'a balance of vulnerability' and 'a situation in which neither side is able to exert its political will on the other'.[15]

There are also instructive historical examples. British governments paid limited attention to the Prussian and Imperial German armies – to which there was no counterpart in the British Empire – but once Germany began her naval build-up a totally new situation developed. In a similar way, 'parity' at sea today would conceivably imply greater risks for the West, dependent on transoceanic communications, than for the East.

That 'balance' does not necessarily imply symmetry has been repeatedly underlined by NATO spokesmen – there is no point in matching 'tank for tank' – and the IISS summaries have previously referred to an 'overall balance' or to (an acceptable) 'zone of insecurity' as to the military relationship in Europe.[16]

On the Soviet side numerical imbalances have seldom been looked upon with similar 'generosity'. On the contrary (as to the Euro-nuclear balance) '. . . the Russians do think that formal equality matters'.[17] Furthermore there is a Soviet concept of 'equal security', supposedly intended to answer the question whether Soviet security is 'safeguarded in equal measure with what it [the Soviet Union] conceives to be the security of Western nations'.[18] This may sound most reasonable and even compatible with the 'common security' suggested by the report of the Palme Commission. But it might also appear a formula for *compensation* for those special disadvantages and handicaps that trouble the Soviet leadership. With such an interpretation it would be difficult to talk about similarly 'equal' security for *other* states. One would assume that it is in the recognition of this *mutuality* of claims on 'equal security' that the true message lies from the Palme Commission to the Kremlin.

'Equal Security' for the Heartland Encircled

Far from flouting military superiority as the result of the armaments efforts of two decades, the Soviet leadership has strongly protested against what Marshal Ustinov has labelled 'a fabricated, malicious lie', i.e. Western claims about such Soviet superiority.[19] Instead, the Soviet view has repeatedly emphasized the constraints under which they are operating and the advantages open to their opponents: '. . . due to its geographical situation, the Soviet Union is potentially still at disadvantage as compared to the United States . . . Actually, the Soviet Union has to face immediate military threats from three directions. In addition, the Soviet Union is surrounded by several countries, alliances or groups that are directly or indirectly backed by the United States . . . '[20]

It may appear incredible to us that the Soviet Union could ever have seriously considered the possibility of an all-out offensive from Western Europe, also given existing military capabilities.[21] However, *if* the Soviet Union really did expect (and still expects) a concerted attack from all directions at one and the same time, 'equal security' would seem to dictate a 'balance' of power between the Soviet Union on the one hand and, for all practical purposes, a very substantial part of the rest of the world. A worst case as seen by the Soviet High Command might be a co-ordinated NATO attack in Europe, a Chinese invasion from the East and a full-scale rebellion in Eastern Europe.[22] (One might add that to make this worst case even worse, the Red Army could also be engaged in the Southern Theatre – as it is today and by Soviet initiative.) To us such a scenario appears fantastic but the West has its own obsessions and 'windows of vulnerability'.

To the West, the Red Army with a nominal strength of some 180–190 divisions seems an outrageously outsized force – far beyond the requirements of Soviet security demands.[23] From the Soviet perspective things obviously appear in a different light. These forces are deployed (in varying states of readiness) in the following way: 30 divisions in Eastern Europe (which together with 55 non-Soviet Warsaw Pact divisions face a theoretical potential of 84 NATO divisions); 29 in the Southern Theatre (with some 5–10 tied up in Afghanistan); 47 in the Far East (facing some 120 Chinese divisions – and possible Japanese forces); and in the central parts of the Soviet Union some 80 divisions. If we subtract the 30-odd divisions in the peripheral Baltic, Leningrad and Odessa Military Districts (MD), this leaves the Soviet High Command with a central reserve of some 50 divisions, a sum which incidentally just about equals the non-Soviet Warsaw Pact component in Eastern Europe. Also incidentally, this would roughly match what reserves NATO would be able to field should the West decide to scratch up its remaining resources.

Planning for such a worst case may, from the Moscow horizon, appear prudent, aiming for defence with 'equal security' in relationship to that 'unfriendly' world which surrounds the USSR. It should also be noted that, on the perimeter around the USSR, it is possible to identify several of the *potential* nuclear powers – none of which could be expected to threaten United States' territory, at least not with their first generation nuclear arsenals, *if* such arsenals materialize.

Geography is also a state of mind, and Soviet protestations about being 'alone in the world' and encircled by 'enemies' could be described just as much in such 'mental' terms as a geopolitical fact.[24]

'Balance of power' is a traditional European concept. The Soviet Union uses her own terminology: 'the correlation of world forces' which, in contrast to balance of power, has an explicitly dualistic connotation – it is 'them' against 'us' – and which consists of a compound of *social*, *political* and *military* dimensions.[25] The concept has been given considerable complexity and elaboration but the basically dualistic character has remained. In the view of the Soviet leadership, this correlation has changed to the advantage of the socialist camp during the most recent decades. The terminology as such is extremely vague and the analytical concept 'the correlation of forces' should be seen just as much as a most flexible instrument for political struggle.

The concept could provide theoretical underpinnings for truly imperial pretensions with deep roots in Russian history. As an expression of practical politics it would imply Soviet claims to parity with the United States in strategic systems, but it could also justify a 'right' to a 'balance' on the theatre nuclear level with all other 'enemies' put together. The mobile SS-20 missile here appears a solution to most challenges covering a 'glacis' including Greenland, Djibouti and South Korea. The inclusion of British and French nuclear forces in the INF talks has now been declared 'an objective necessity from the point of view of Soviet security interests'[26] and the Kremlin may also be looking for future agreements with those countries against which the some 100 SS-20s east of the Urals are directed.

Possible Soviet aspirations to a 'balance' or 'equal security' in their relations with the outside world *could* imply hegemonial claims (compare British naval policy prior to World War I) with the most far-reaching implications for a world order still to a large extent carrying the imprint of a European imperial past and an American international 'system' established after World War II.[27] But Soviet aspirations along the lines suggested above do not necessarily have to be seen in exclusively 'aggressive' terms. The imperial analogy – the Soviet Union as a Roman Empire with a strong perimeter defence and a deep concern with internal control – could accommodate both Colin Gray's 'offensive' scenario and Christopher Jones' 'defensive' aims in Eastern Europe.[28] Above all, this analogy would help us to some healthy scepticism about the unqualified and unreflecting use of the terms 'defensive' and 'offensive' about Soviet performance and intentions – as distinct from those of other states or groups of states.

Balances

Thus, while the West tends to see security in terms of one single balance, i.e. that with the Soviet Union, the situation from the Soviet point of view may be considerably more complex. To ward off reality with conceptual means (the 'correlation of forces' formula) will not eliminate the problems posed by Chinese forces or by (future) increased Japanese military resources. In this section, however, we will leave aside the complexities of the balancing situation as seen from Moscow's perspective. *The* 'balance' remains that between NATO (US) and the Warsaw Pact (Soviet Union) and will be commented upon in terms of three 'separate' balances: the *strategic* balance, the *European* balance, and '*global reach*'.

The Strategic Balance

This is the sphere of recognized parity. The Reagan Administration, however, has made this the chief focus of the arguments about Soviet 'superiority': Soviet superior resources in land-based ICBM supposedly offer the Kremlin a window of opportunity (and thus create a 'window of vulnerability' for the West) should the Soviets decide to go for a first strike. This is no doubt a most fascinating scenario, crediting the Soviet leaders with iron nerves and an unlimited belief in the rationality of the US leaders who will be expected to surrender after receiving a first counterforce strike rather than risk losing their cities. There seems very little reason why the Kremlin should have such faith in common sense on the part of an opponent whose inconsistencies the Soviet leadership has frequently lamented.[29]

Greater concern should be caused by the tendencies towards instability resulting from the pursuance of several and perhaps contradictory concepts at the same time. Since the McNamara years, the United States has tried to educate Moscow on mutual vulnerability and mutual assured destruction – teachings which the Soviet leaders have obviously not taken to with either ease or speed. Reagan's 'star wars' concept, with an 'absolute' defence, opens up totally new perspectives (assuming that this is either technically or politically possible). Earlier wisdoms are now apparently to be un-learned by us all. Likewise, the United States led the MIRVing process, now, supposedly, to be reversed with a return to small, mobile, single-headed missiles. Previously the US has also aimed at 'driving the Russians to sea' by emphasizing 'invulnerable' submarine-launched systems. Here the USSR still appears to stick to her concept: land-based ICBM systems, which constitute the bulk of Soviet strategic forces,

116

still remain in her view the most *stabilizing* components also because they can be directly led and controlled.

While new 'strategies' may be highly appropriate *per se*, cross-currents of concepts and purposes may themselves create instability and uncertainty, both as to capabilities and intentions.

The European Balance

The European situation has been 'unstable' for the whole of the post-war period. Present observers tend to forget, most conveniently, previous moments of panic – for example in connection with the Berlin crises from 1958 to 1961 – when there were indications of just as much (if not more) political disarray under Soviet pressure as we have witnessed during the last few years. (Most instructive, perhaps, are the events immediately preceding the meeting between Eisenhower and Khruschev at Camp David in 1959). This observation is not intended to belittle NATO worries about an imbalance in conventional and theatre nuclear forces but even the most urgent of worries ought to be placed in some perspective.

Strong arguments are now building up for a strengthening of NATO conventional capabilities in Europe with an arsenal of technical, organizational, tactical and financial solutions proposed. Whether these arguments will penetrate to national finance ministries remains to be seen. There are also obvious political constraints. The possibility of a force restructuring within NATO with a stronger role for the Federal Republic of Germany would be 'a situation that the Western countries would hardly welcome' – at least not according to an East European view![30] Whether that is in itself true or not, a substantial conventional NATO build-up may not be regarded as much more attractive to the Soviet Union than the *Pershing* II are today, however much NATO invokes the numerical imbalances now existing in most weapons-system categories.

The Europeans initiated the fears of Soviet theatre nuclear superiority. Since then, American worries over European wavering under the threat of the SS-20s have almost seemed to overshadow the original concerns.

This is undoubtedly to the point insofar as the balance in Europe rests upon *political* complexities and that European 'capitulationism' could be the result of a *self-inflicted* political process rather than of a Soviet open show of arms. On the other hand, the tendency to ascribe the vagaries of European politics to growing Soviet military superiority in Europe seems a dangerous oversimplification. Europe – and transatlantic relations – would not necessarily be 'straightened out' even if the balance was put right.

That there *is* a numerical imbalance (although frequently overdramatized) is not in doubt, but the calculus about Soviet superiority also rests on assumptions about a Soviet freedom of choice and timing and about *Warsaw Pact cohesion* that the present crisis in Poland hardly substantiates. So far, there seems no way in which the Soviet leadership can escape the problems generated by the 'security' zone in Eastern Europe. To push the logic of the situation to the limits, disorder and unrest in Eastern Europe would make a Soviet westward thrust extremely difficult (despite the fact that this remains one of the favourite scenarios for the outbreak of a third World War), while an 'organic' relationship and greater independence for the satellites might make it infeasible (as well as unnecessary) for quite other reasons.

The second great imponderable of the European balance concerns aspects of *quality*. The official NATO view is that the Alliance has lost 'much of the technological advantage which permitted NATO to rely on the view that quality could compensate for quantity'. Continued reliance by NATO on new technologies is the course projected. Recent experiences in the Middle East – the Israeli successes against the Soviet-armed Syrians – suggest that NATO could be in a considerably better position than present Alliance spokesmen profess (although the victories in the Bekaa in Lebanon could also be seen as favouring the *offensive* party).

However, a pronounced reliance on repeated injections of high technology will also bring instabilities through continuous organizational and tactical changes. Uncertainties about performance in war may thus increase rather than decrease, and mutual East–West understandings of the state of the balance become more complicated. Such a development might seem a strong motivation for advancing the MBRF negotiations beyond the level of manpower figures.

An increased conventional effort – or a 'modernization' – on the NATO side may now appear inescapable because of the high stakes – the danger of 'intimidation' – that NATO itself has publicly identified as a result of Soviet theatre nuclear *and* conventional superiority. The assumption so far has been to counter the danger through a combination of conventional build-up, additional theatre-nuclear forces and arms-control agreements. A more deliberate *conventional* build-up would aim at raising the nuclear threshold, conceivably also the abolition of (parts of) the tactical nuclear arsenal and a confirmation of the shift in the direction of *no early* first nuclear use that has already been indicated. A denuclearization of Europe today would not be feasible (perhaps not even desirable) because of the general image of imbalance and instability that this would project.[31]

'Global Reach'
No-one denies the growing Soviet capabilities to project power on a global scale. No doubt too the situation today is greatly different from that of the early 1960s. At the same time the attention given to these changes tends to obscure the actual *balance* between Western and Soviet capabilities in this respect.

In terms of airlift and sealift – and in terms of sea control generally – the West remains clearly superior. (The assumed Western lead in anti-submarine warfare should support such a view). The dramatic transformation of the Soviet Navy from a coastal defence force to a high seas fleet has narrowed the margins but not changed the basic force relationship with the West. This is also an area where the contributions of the United States' allies are substantial while, despite *land* forces supplied by proxies, the Soviet Union has no comparable naval support.

However, one might hold that the Soviet Union has done rather well with her limited naval support resources – also beyond the seas. While outclassed by the West on the high seas she has still been able to 'land' in the Third World and, once ashore and 'entrenched', her land force potential (or rather that of her clients and arms users) has become more important.

If, on the other hand, the forces of the West were to be tied down in substantial and protracted operations calling for large reserves – as might be a consequence of the more active policies suggested by the Reagan Administration – severe manpower problems will arise. In 1953 French Premier Pierre Mendès-France chose withdrawal from Indo-china rather than the calling up of conscript forces. The revitalization of the American draft system still appears a difficult decision in peacetime.

Rapid deployment forces – or equivalent formations – are now being organized by the United States (7-plus divisions) and by France (some 5 divisions). A smaller force has been deployed 'in anger' by the British – with both rapidity and success. A substantial Soviet force is presently engaged in operations in Afghanistan – but with little rapid success.

With their 'bridge' in 1977–8 to Ethiopia, however, the Russians demonstrated a capacity for speedy operations on a very large scale – just as their arms transfers generally to the Third World have involved larger quantities of hardware than comparable Western transfers. To the extent that arms transfers to the Third World shape long-term security relationships, such transfers will also have an impact upon 'allies' and 'access' for East and West. President Carter's efforts in 1977 to limit the arms trade have been replaced by a totally different policy by the Reagan Administration. On the other hand, tendencies towards 'differentiation' in arms acquisition processes in third-world countries – and the historical record generally – suggest that gratitude and loyalties (as well as dependence) may be of a most fleeting character.

The unstable situation in the Third World, where regions and individual countries now seem to enter a second post-colonial phase with considerable political reorganization and tendencies towards the remaking of colonial maps, offers opportunities for that power which wishes to challenge the old world order. The Soviet advances into Angola, Mozambique, Ethiopia and also Afghanistan have been seen in this light. But to opportunities should be added risks. These risks pertain both to local and regional conditions but also to a growing danger of collisions with the West – presenting the world with possible reruns of Fashoda. What party will play Major Marchand's role tomorrow may not be self-evident.

Given possible super-power ambitions to engage in a new 'Great Game' in the Third World, it is hard to believe in such iron discipline and clear-cut delimitation of the respective interests that confrontations could be wholly avoided. Furthermore, large-scale super-power engagements in the Third World would also promote resentment and resistance and perhaps, ultimately, provoke nuclear proliferation.

As seen from the perspective of *status quo* and stability, *third-world nationalism* and what inter-state loyalty remains within the non-aligned movement (although there seems precious little of it) should – in general – appear a better bulwark against outside penetration or subversion than any rapid deployment forces. In the 1500s, England's King Henry VIII, finding himself in the midst of the struggle between Hapsburg and Valois, is supposed to have observed that 'he who has my support will win'. Today, the Third World carries no political weight of a similar order and the King's words might need a little rephrasing: he who takes on the Third World will *not* win.

An Effort at Evaluation
We have in the most recent years been treated to a continuous flow of force level assessments presenting East–West comparisons in tables and graphs. At the same time, men of wisdom have issued warnings against such excess of apparent exactitude, pointing instead to 'the forgotten dimensions of strategy'.

The appearance of Ayatollah Khomeini did seem to overthrow many of our paradigms for political, rational analysis – and so much for all the Shah's men and horses – but having now contemplated him and his

Revolution for some time (and witnessing the war of attrition between Iran and Iraq), analysts may be even more strongly tempted than before to return to old habits of book-keeping. The Treaty of Chaumont in 1814 – where all the bean-counting may be said to have originated – still throws a long shadow over our conceptions of how international relations are conducted.[32] This is all inescapable, of course, but our counting of tanks, missiles and aircraft also tends to turn our very *analyses* into arithmetic of a not very sophisticated kind. Discussing nuclear arsenals lends itself exceptionally well to this – their character is slightly out of this world anyway – but there has so far been no nuclear war, and any strategist's view of what one would be like may be as good as any other's.

Where greater efforts should be placed would be in the qualitative analyses of balance interaction or 'spillover': how do factors of balance or imbalance interrelate at various 'levels' (and how are these 'levels' to be defined)? While the outcome of the Cuban missile crisis in 1962 was certainly a factor of US *strategic* (nuclear) superiority, it was perhaps even more a result of American *local* (conventional) preponderance making it impossible for Khrushchev and his Marshals to defend their missiles. At the moment, there are those who maintain that strategic parity will open up possibilities for 'enterprising action' on local levels: with the US nuclear superiority lost, 'peace-keeping' power and all traces of *Pax Americana* will also be gone. This might be so, but still we do not know much about the exercise of power – and the usability of military force (including *nuclear*) – in a system where the rank-ordering of the strongest powers seems increasingly in doubt.

It might be timely to resurrect A. F. K. Organski's theory from 1961 about the 'dominating world power'.[33] Organski's view is that, to a far greater extent than has been appreciated by historians and international relations experts, international politics have been characterized by hegemonial relations, the paramountcy of *one* power, rather than by traditional balance of power patterns. In the post-war period, the United States has been the *hegemon* dominating an essentially unipolar system,[34] but with the 1970s – and applying Organski – we seem to have entered a new phase with a true challenger, the Soviet Union, which in Organski's terminology would also be described as an 'unsatisfied' state, demanding 'a place in the sun'. From Organski it would not necessarily follow that we are witnessing a true power transition from one *hegemon* to another but that, whatever the outcome, we are heading for dangerous years.

The Cuban case just referred to suggests the importance of *local preponderence*. In a situation as described by Organski, the superpower's clients, as well as the smaller states in general, would have to carry a heavier load for their own security – 'to hold their own' – either through national efforts or through regional co-operation.

Doubts may attach to the readiness of the Western democracies to defend their interests (short of being the object of a direct assault upon the national territory) by the use of force if necessary. The Falklands campaign may have had a symbolic and, for some a heartening, effect but in other respects the record of Western resolution may be less impressive. The very considerable amount of 'back-seat driving' provided by the press of Britain's continental allies also indicated the division between a 'leftist' (force is illegitimate) and a 'rightist' (force is legitimate if necessary) conception of international relations that was also apparent in Britain.

There have been tendencies in Europe to see Afghanistan as 'a country far away' (suggesting uncomfortable historical parallels), but the real test in terms of dangers beyond the national territories has not yet materialized. Awaiting its appearance, and remembering the loss of HMS Sheffield, no-one can safely assume that the peaceful welfare democracies of Western Europe – constituting among themselves the world's only 'security community', and certainly not the seasoned leadership in the Kremlin – would not accept the costs and fight, if so compelled.

Conclusion

Analyses of the over-all military balance between East and West made in the West tend to agree on the basic facts: that there has been a strong Soviet military build-up in the last two decades; that this pertains to both quantitative and qualitative factors; and that the Western technological edge has been blunted. From the Soviet perspective this represents 'a military equilibrium shaped during the past decade between the United States and the Soviet Union'.[35] To the West it implies instead a balance 'disturbed' and a long-term threat of even greater proportions.

An effort at evaluation, however, would be that the probabilities of any political cashing-in on these changes on the part of the ascending power, the Soviet Union, still remain limited. Apparently few, if any, believe that the Soviet Union plans for a violent take-over; many, on the other hand, believe in a Soviet willingness to play chess – or to take greater risks – from positions of strength offered by putative military superiority.

On the *strategic* level, a fundamental deadlock remains which seems threatened less by imaginative first-strike scenarios than through a proliferation of nuclear concepts and lack of inter-party communication. There seems no reason not to expect an agreement on the basis of common interests in the regulation of the SALT heritage.

In the *European* arena, NATO official confidence (and the reasons for such confidence) seems greater today than a year or two ago, in spite of impending nuclear deployment. The balance in Europe remains a *political* game loaded with uncertainties, but these uncertainties still seem rather to favour the West than the East as long as the Alliance remains politically intact. Despite Soviet tank inventories and various pronouncements on the demise of extended deterrence, NATO should certainly be in the position to refuse intimidation.

The *Third World* is sometimes pictured as a kind of no-man's-land, open for the manipulations of alien forces and the first claimant. Such notions are both dubious and risky; instead, the difficulties and hazards involved should be underlined as well as the prohibitive costs of 'Sicilian' expeditions intended to yield major strategic gains. The Soviet Union considered herself on the verge of a breakthrough in the Third World in the early 1960s. Twenty years later, after some gains and some losses, the Soviet Union holds a number of strongpoints but she has certainly not captured the Third World which rather continues to lead its own life, with increasing economic and social problems which neither super-power seems now to have much interest in or ability to solve.

The United States' response during the post-war period to indications of the Soviet Union catching up militarily have invariably been to go into higher gear and to deploy new technologies – and again to leave the Russians behind. These have also been the signals issued so far by the present US Administration. But, judging from the current American debate, much of the present build-up seems more a question of money being thrown at the problems, strong on statements about new levels of ambition but weaker on hardware – all in all, more sound than fury.

We are now witnessing economic constraints working on both sides. It is true that neither side represents fully mobilized forces. The East operates a semi-war economy, but within an extremely inefficient total economy that, through lack of dynamism, may also limit the total volume attainable for armaments. The West operates no war economy at all, but here societal forces and welfare ideals impose limitations. So far, however, these limitations seem to have been considerably more compelling in Western Europe than in the US. This phenomenon constitutes an irony of history: a key factor behind the American Revolution of 1776 was the British effort to tax the colonials to pay for their own defence!

Both super-powers may now be facing outer limits. In the United States original popular support for greater military efforts has flagged – even though threat perceptions may not have changed. Deficit problems and the rising need for domestic priorities now pose hard choices. In the East, Secretary-General Yuri Andropov indicated before his death a new course of economic reforms and priorities which even the 'stratocracy' may understand to be a necessity from the point of view of its long-term interests.

With these weak signals, to which one might also add genuine and growing fears on both sides, we could be facing a new situation, presenting us with a breathing space – and, one might hope – opportunities for renewed arms-control efforts on a more realistic basis – both balanced and equal – than during the heyday of detente expectations in the early 1970s.

A very different kind of projection could take as its starting point present tendencies on the part of the super-powers to dig in along their own predefined positions, demonstrating a *preference for unilateralism* (or even isolationism) rather than dialogue. Such invocations of *Dieu et mon droit* – less lion-hearted than *laager*-minded – would suggest more sinister prospects in perspective.

It may be easy to find fault with the current notion of 'common security'. That the idea as such is no novelty is obvious (see Brodie, McNamara and many others). It is also clear that the term could become a popular but meaningless catchword but the very basic recognition of our shared interest in global security, across the great political divides, seems a fact that not even the most hard-bitten 'cold warrior' should be able to escape.

NOTES

[1] Colin Gray, 'The Most Dangerous Decade: Historic Mission, Legitimacy, and Dynamics of the Soviet Empire in the 1980s', *Orbis*, Spring 1981, p. 13. I am not making these introductory observations to criticize the rhetoric employed by responsible politicians and analysts. That criticism seems by now to speak for itself. One would rather like to make the point that in spite of this rhetoric there has been a remarkable steadfastness among US allies and the influence of the peace movements has actually been limited (when considering Mr Gray's exclamation one might even be tempted to charge the latter with moderation). Small states – insofar as we have any systematic knowledge about small state behaviour – supposedly respond to changes in the balance of power by rushing to the side of the ascending power, putting distance between themselves and the 'loser'. (See Annette Baker Fox, *The Power of Small States*, (Chicago: University of Chicago Press, 1957).) Given the enormity

of the messages dropped, one can only marvel at the *lack* of panic in the West. Using Michael Howard's terminology, one might say that, while the wording used by President Truman in 1947 gave the Europeans 'reassurance', the same kind of rhetoric employed in the 1980s has not had the same effect.

2 I am obliged to Professor Gordon Craig for this quotation from his book, *The Germans* (New York: Putmans, 1982), p. 238. The original text is in G. Küntzel and M. Haar, *Die Politischen Testamente der Hohenzollern*, (Leipzig, 1919), vol. I, p. 56.

3 Compare 'Soviet Geopolitical Momentum: Myth or Menace?' *The Defense Monitor*, January 1980.

4 Thus according to Phillip Karber (in Uwe Nerlich (ed.), *Sowjetische Macht und Westliche Verhandlungspolitik im Wandel militaerischer Kraefteverhaeltnisse* (Baden-Baden: Nomos, 1983)) between 1968 and 1978 there has been a rise in Soviet military expenditures by 75%, while US expenditures declined in real terms by some 40%. Warsaw Pact troops in Europe increased by 150,000 men, while NATO instead cut its forces by some 50,000. The way the time period is cut, US increased military spending in the late 1970s has thus not yet taken effect. The official US position is presented in *Soviet Military Power* (Washington DC: USGPO, 2nd edition, 1983). This should be read parallel with its Soviet counterpart, *Whence the Threat to Peace* (Moscow: Military Publishing House, 2nd edition, 1983), which provides detailed counter-arguments together with indignant protestations against Western 'propaganda pamphlets'.

5 A study on the Euro-missile issue-touching *inter alia* upon the problems referred to here – is presently being prepared at the Swedish Institute of International Affairs by Milton Leitenberg. See also Raymond Garthoff, 'The Soviet SS-20 Decision' (*Survival*, vol. XXV, no. 3, May/June 1983).

6 Interview with *Der Spiegel*, no. 18, 1983.

7 Cornelius Castoriadis, *Devant la Guerre* (Paris: Fayard, 1981).

8 Compare Coit Blacker, 'Military Power and Prospects' *Washington Quarterly*, Spring 1983: 'The fear that the United States will again widen the technological imbalance enlivens a pervasive historical concern for security, even survival' (p. 59).

9 Marshal Ustinov, *Pravda*, 12 July 1942. Among more recent statements see G. Arbatov, *Tass*, 10 August, 1983: '. . . we shall do everything within our power to create it [a counter to any new US weapons system] . . . that may occur in 3, 4 or 5 years time, but it will be done'.

10 See Tomas Bertelman, *De sovjetiska-rustningarnas drivkrafter* [*The Motivating Forces Behind Soviet Armaments*] (SSLP/Swedish Department of Defence: 1983).

11 Ernst B. Haas, 'The Balance of Power: Prescription, Concept, or Propaganda?', *World Politics*, July 1953.

12 Nicholas Spykman, *America's Strategy in World Politics* (New York, 1942), pp. 21–5.

13 A. F. Pollard, 'The Balance of Power' *Journal of the British Institute of International Affairs*, 1923, p. 59.

14 Lazlo Kiss, 'Some Methodological Problems in Comparing Military Powers', *Kuhlpolitika*, The Hungarian Institute of International Relations, 1983/1,

pp. 6–10. A somewhat heroic effort to come to grips with the problems of measuring the military balance is the proposal submitted in 1981 to the UN by the Austrian delegation on the creation of a data base for 'objective' knowledge on military matters (UN Doc. A/C. 1/36/14)

15 Kiss, *ibid.*, p. 10.

16 See, *inter alia*, the summary in *The Military Balance 1979–1980* (London: IISS, 1979) p. 117; compare the introduction to *NATO and the Warsaw Pact. Force Comparisons* (Brussels: NATO Information Service, 1982) and *The Guardian* interview with Robert McNamara, 9 August 1982.

17 Lawrence Freedman in letter to *The Times*, 7 April 1983.

18 Gerhard Wettig, 'The Garthoff–Pipes Debate on Soviet Strategic Doctrine: A European Perspective', *Strategic Review*, Spring 1983, p. 73. Christopher Jones has elaborated on the Soviet concept in 'Equality and Equal Security in Europe', *Orbis*, Fall 1982, where he argues that 'the mission of Soviet nuclear and conventional forces in Europe is to secure an unchallenged Soviet capability for military intervention in Eastern Europe . . . the objective of Soviet proposals for a balance of intermediate nuclear forces is to deny NATO a capability of deterring the Soviet Union from such interventions'. (p. 637). Whether the Soviet Union would really need *any* theatre nuclear forces for such a purpose is certainly open to question.

19 See *International Herald Tribune*, 1 August 1983: 'Ustinov warns again for NATO missiles'.

20 Kiss, *op.cit* in note 14, p. 11.

21 One should not, however, forget the climate at the peak of the Cold War when the Kremlin no doubt found reasons to contemplate extreme alternatives, regardless of the scarcity of Western resources. See *Life* magazine, 6 June 1951, which depicts in detail a scenario for a full-scale attack on the Soviet positions in Eastern Europe aiming at the liberation of the People's Democracies and the crushing of the Soviet state ('Airhead Warsaw'). Wishful thinking, no doubt, but also perhaps giving the Soviet leadership at the time food for thought.

22 See also Jerry Hough, 'The World as Viewed from Moscow', *International Journal*, Spring 1982.

23 *The Military Balance 1982–1983* (London: IISS, 1982), gives a grand total of 185 divisions; *Soviet Military Power*, *op. cit.* in note 4) gives the total as 191 divisions. Whichever figure one chooses, a very substantial portion (more than 100 divisions) represents skeleton forces (category 3 units with 25% strength).

24 See also Uri Ra'anan, 'The USSR and the "Encirclement" Fear: Soviet Logic or Western Legend?' (*Strategic Review* Winter 1980). Ra'anan totally rejects the whole notion of 'encirclement'. Thus would a doctor to a paranoid patient, but the Soviet Union is certainly no ordinary patient – and there are 'objective' reasons for such a state of mind. One of the objective reasons would be the self-fulfilling potential of Soviet attitudes to the surrounding world.

25 See Julian Lider, *Military Force* (Aldershot, Hants.: Gower Publishing Co., 1981), ch. 10.

26 Statement by Marshal Ustinov on 5 August 1983.

One might here sense some of the difficulties (to put it mildly) that the Soviet Union will have to face when the arsenals of the smaller nuclear powers, all more or less inimical to the USSR, start to grow through modernization in the late 1980s and 1990s, (several thousand nuclear warheads planned for France, Britain and China). The USSR could hardly expect the US to agree to a definition of 'parity' that would put the USSR's strategic arsenal on an equal footing with *all* non-Soviet arsenals combined. How would 'equal security' (*à la* Ustinov) fare in a world of increasing nuclear multipolarity?

[27] The Cold War seems now supplanted by a historically more familiar pattern – a traditional great power rivalry with a marked effort on the part of a growing number of international actors to dissociate themselves from the rivalry as such. Ironically enough, the efforts of the Reagan Administration to re-establish the ideological confrontation of the 1940s and 1950s seems to have contributed to this.

[28] Some may no doubt find it a bit difficult to view the Soviet leadership, ideology and party politics as the successors of Marcus Ulpius Trajanus (98–117), 'Optimus Princeps', or Lucius Domitius Aurelianus (270–275), 'Restitutor Orbis'. Historical analogies, however, are intended to widen perspective and broaden the mind – not to suggest common identities.

[29] The 'window-of-vulnerability' scenario seems also to have been if not played down, at least redesigned since the report of the Scowcroft Commission. See Blair Stewart, 'The Scowcroft Commission and the "Window

of Coercion" ' (*Strategic Review*, Summer 1983). While the incredulous reactions, perhaps above all on the part of Western Europeans, to various first-strike scenarios seem extremely well-founded, there is every reason to underline – also to fellow Europeans – the utter seriousness of the matter of strategic deterrence. General Haig remarked at Georgetown University on 6 April 1982: 'Let us recall that nuclear deterrence must work not just in times of peace, and moments of calm. Deterrence faces its true test at the time of maximum tension, even in the midst of actual conflict. In such extreme circumstances, when the stakes on the table may already be immense. . . .'

[30] Kiss, *op.cit.* in note 14, p. 12.

[31] See J. J. Holst, 'INF and Political Equilibrium in Europe', NUPI *notat*, no. 274B (Oslo: Norwegian Institute of International Affairs, 1983).

[32] The Chaumont Treaty, part of the groundwork for the Vienna Congress, established a hierarchical order for the European state system, based on the ability to field armies of varying sizes. The requirement for entering the select great power club was a force in excess of 60,000 men.

[33] A. F. K. Organski 'The Power Transition' in James Rosenau (ed.), *International Politics and Foreign Policy* (Englewood Cliffs: Free Press, 1961).

[34] Compare George Liska's *Imperial America*, Baltimore: Johns Hopkins UP, 1967 with his *Russia and the Road to Appeasement* (Baltimore: Johns Hopkins UP, 1982).

[35] Mikhail Borisov, 'The American Threat to Peace', *New Times* 1982, no. 3, p. 18.

Trends in the Balance of Military Power Between East and West

MAJ.-GEN. WILLIAM E. ODOM

In the 1950s and 1960s the US enjoyed clear primacy in the East–West military balance, permitting no confusion or misperception about who was number one and who was number two in the hierarchy of super-powers. Not only was the US nuclear arsenal superior in numbers and quality of weapons, but the American technological and industrial potential were also so far ahead of what the USSR could bring to the competition that few observers took seriously the Soviet bid to achieve a reversal of the balance. More important for peace between East and West in the Third World was the West's great advantage in capabilities for projecting power – naval forces, air forces, air and sea lift, communications, economic infrastructure in those regions, and transportable ground forces. Thus, the post-war international order rested on the basis of this highly unequal military balance between East and West, a condition, however, that was not to remain static.

The 1970s marked a dramatic qualitative change in the geostrategic nature of East–West relations. While the shift in the military balance was the single most important factor of change, it was not the only one. At least three others should be kept in mind as creating the larger strategic context which affects directly the balance in Europe. The first was the normalization of relations between the US and China. Marking the culmination of a major strategic reconfiguration between East and West, it provides an equilibrium in the Far East that lowers the threat of war and thereby reduces US military requirements for that region.

The second change concerns two other regions of the world which interact strategically with the defence of Europe. The Persian Gulf region, under the impact of rapid modernization of conservative Islamic societies, intra-regional wars, and greater Soviet power projection, could now easily become the basis for a super-power confrontation. Vital Western interests in Middle East oil make it imperative to prevent the increase of Soviet influence in the region. In fact, it is difficult to conceive of a sucessful defence of Western Europe that does not include a successful defence of access to Middle East oil.

A similar but less clearly recognized strategic interaction is growing between the Caribbean Basin and Western Europe. The Soviet–Cuban military connection would have a critical influence on the ability of the US to project forces to Europe in the event of a crisis there. Soviet intelligence facilities, use of Cuban naval ports, and growing Cuban fighter aviation capabilities give Cuba and other pro-Soviet states in the Caribbean a military significance for the defence of Western Europe that cannot be overlooked.

The third change is the diffusion of economic wealth within the Western Alliance. Defence requirements have increased while the relative US share of Western wealth has decreased. Sharing the military burden, therefore, is of much greater significance in the European military balance than in earlier decades. To borrow a Marxist image, the economic 'base' of the Alliance has changed; accordingly, the Alliance's institutional 'super-structure' is experiencing tensions caused by the changing economic realities.

These larger strategic relationships have indeed altered the nature of the East–West military balance, so much so that we should recognize that we are in a qualitatively new era in the East–West competition. It is imperative to keep this global strategic context in mind as a backdrop as we assess the Soviet military build-up, its rationale, its future trends, and its implications for the balance of forces in Europe. Many post-war concepts and formulae are no longer relevant for diagnoses of, and solutions to, our military problems in Europe for the remainder of the century.

The Record of the Soviet Build-up

Over the past two decades the USSR has accomplished the most comprehensive peacetime military build-up in history. A brief summary of Soviet programmes in the following categories of military capabilities will demonstrate the extent of this reality:

- Strategic forces;
- Theatre forces;
- Naval forces;
- Forces for power projection.

Moreover, there is no sign of abatement in this steady growth of the Soviet Union's military power.

Strategic Forces

The USSR has moved ahead in intercontinental ballistic missiles (ICBM), enjoys a quantitative edge in nuclear-powered ballistic missile submarines (SSBN) but has not matched US quality in this area, appears determined to compete in bombers although the gap remains large, and continues a massive strategic defence effort.

The number of Soviet land-based ICBM rose to about 1,600 launchers in the mid-1970s but dropped back to approximately 1,400 as older systems were phased out. The fourth generation of new systems includes ten models in the SS-17, SS-18, and SS-19 types. Fractionation of warheads and increased accuracy make this a formidable force and the basis of concern about US ICBM vulnerability.[1]

While the US holds the lead in numbers of submarine-launched ballistic missile (SLBM) re-entry vehicles (RV) (about 5,600 to 1,500), the Soviet SLBM inventory is larger (about 950 to 650). The very large *Typhoon* submarine, now entering service with the new SS-NX-20 SLBM, will increase the number of RV, their range, and their accuracy. Furthermore, a sea-launched cruise missile (SLCM), the SS-NX-21, is expected to

be operational in the near future, launchable from a submarine torpedo tube, and with an estimated range of 3,000 km. In many respects, the US SSBN fleet retains its significant edge, but the Soviet Union is narrowing the gap.[2]

The Soviet strategic bomber fleet consists of almost 900 strike and support aircraft, but their quality is not high except for the *Backfire*. The appearance of a new bomber, the *Blackjack*, similar to the US B-1 bomber, suggests that the USSR has not dropped out of the bomber competition and is determined to lengthen this leg of her strategic triad.[3]

Less well appreciated in the West is the Soviet effort to achieve a comprehensive strategic defence capability. Civil defence and high-altitude air defence have long been parts of their system. New pieces, however, are appearing to fill the gaps. The mobile SA-10 air defence missile has a significant low altitude capability, and the *Foxhound* interceptor has look-down/shoot-down capability. Both are now being deployed. While adhering to the Anti-Ballistic Missile (ABM) Treaty, the Soviet Union has, nevertheless, maintained a large ABM research and development (R&D) programme, and deployment at the site around Moscow proceeds apace, providing protection to the large number of military and key industrial facilities located there.[4]

Soviet efforts in space are primarily military, including an anti-satellite (ASAT) programme and improving quality in intelligence collection capabilities.[5]

Theatre Forces

Following Soviet doctrinal tenets for the 'theatre strategic operation', Soviet theatre force programmes include a panoply of weapons ranging from deep-fire support systems to large mobile and armour protected ground forces designed to operate under either conventional or nuclear and chemical battlefield conditions.

While the SS-20 deployments, numbering more than 350 missiles and some 1,050 warheads, are well-known, less attention has been given to the modernization of surface-to-surface missile (SSM) forces found at the front, army, and division levels. The new family of short-range ballistic missiles (SRBM) includes the SS-21, the SS-23 and, the SS-22 with ranges of 120, 500, and 900 km respectively, distances that in some cases reach deep into West Germany, the *Benelux* countries, France, Britain, and Italy.[6] Nuclear artillery is also appearing in greater numbers, including a new 152mm self-propelled gun.

Frontal aviation is changing, not so much in numbers, where it already exceeds NATO's tactical aviation strength, as in quality, where it has lagged behind Western air forces. The *Fencer, Flogger*, and *Fitter* aircraft have all been upgraded, and the *Frogfoot, Flanker*, and *Fulcrum* are new fighters.[7]

Soviet tactical air defence is now fully mobile, integral to every command level, and capable of providing an extremely lethal mobile air defence umbrella for offensive ground operations. The SA-4, SA-6, SA-8, SA-9, SA-11, and SA-13 are now in the force, and will continue to be modernized in the future.[8]

The ground forces are now receiving the T-80 tank and increasing numbers of self-propelled howitzers and guns. The already large number of infantry fighting vehicles (IFV), supported by mobile engineer, NBC, and signal capabilities, give the ground forces an impressive offensive structure which could fight under both nuclear and non-nuclear, chemical and non-chemical conditions. Attack helicopters are rapidly entering the division and army organizations at a rapid rate, providing yet another means of supplying high mobility and fire power. The *Hind* and the *Hip* are heavily armed helicopters, and the *Hook* and *Halo* provide a large troop lift capability.[6]

The number of divisions has grown considerably in the last decade, totalling 191 when all categories are included.[10] Although most of these are not fully manned, they can be brought to full strength quickly from the pool of 40 million reservists. The majority of the growth has occurred in the Far East where the number has risen from some 15 divisions in the 1960s to 52 divisions today. In the European theatre the change has been largely in improved weapons and reorganization to provide a better combined arms capability for high speed operations.

Naval Forces
The size and vigour of Soviet naval programmes indicate a clear determination to build a blue-water navy, as well as to provide for the defence of coastal waters. Seven classes of surface ships, five classes of submarines, and four types of aircraft make up this force-building effort. The *Kiev* class V/STOL (Vertical/short take-off and landing) aircraft carrier is the largest surface vessel. The third of the class joined the fleet in 1982 and a fourth should be launched in 1984. The *Kirov*-class cruiser is the first Soviet nuclear-powered surface ship. The second of these is nearing completion. The first *Krasina*-class guided-missile cruiser has entered the fleet, and the two classes of guided-missile destroyers, the *Sovremennyy* and the *Udaloy*, continue to be built.[11]

The attack submarine programme includes three nuclear and two diesel classes. The largest nuclear attack submarine, the *Oscar*, is followed by the *Alfa* class, at 40 knots the world's fastest, and the *Victor* III, fitted with the USSR's first towed array ASW sensor. The *Tango* and *Kilo* classes of diesel-powered submarines continue to augment the fleet.[12]

Power Projection
This category of military capability is less precise than others because it does not end with purely military forces. To appreciate its full dimensions, we must consider a number of non-military capabilities and activities.

Naval forces, of course, permit power projection, but they are supplemented by the large Soviet commercial fleet, particularly the roll-on/roll-off (RoRo) ships which can handle amphibious forces. The same is true for military airlift. Although the present fleet of the *Cock*, the *Candid*, and the *Cub* will be augmented by a new transport similar to the US C-5A, *Aeroflot*, the largest airline in the world which can be turned to military support, remains the backbone.

Arms-sales agreements between 1977 and 1982 alone totalled $47.5 billion. The regions of North Africa, the Middle East, and South-west Asia receive the majority of these arms transfers, but Cuba and South-east Asia are also significant recipients.[13] With arms transfers frequently go military advisers, larger diplomatic and espionage teams, and non-military commercial activity. The 125 to 150 advisers in Peru alone exceed the total number of US military advisers in all of Latin America.[14] Unlike most Western states, the USSR can, for political and subversive aims, co-ordinate all these resources – banks, trading organizations, commercial shipping, and air flights, as well as diplomatic and military assistance programmes. The trends in all these activities have been upward over the last two decades, growing with surprising rapidity since the mid-1970s.

Finally, the use of surrogate forces, particularly Cuban, has added dramatically to the Soviet power projection capability in recent years. The rapid movement of a two-division force to Ethiopia in 1978 was an operation of greater speed reaching a non-contiguous country than any other we have seen from the USSR.

Taken together, this array of Soviet programmes, ranging from strategic forces through theatre forces, naval forces, and means of power projection, exceeds the combined military efforts of the Western Alliance. The trends in the military balance are not only adverse, they are dramatically adverse. We must, therefore, try to understand what inspires Soviet military programmes, where they will go in the future, and the constraints they face. Then we can speculate on their implications for the West.

Why the Soviet Military Build-up?

No very compelling hypothesis has been articulated to explain why the Soviet Union perseveres in accumulating military power far beyond what is clearly adequate for defence of the territorial *status quo*. The popular answer, encouraged by Soviet spokesmen, is that historical experience with foreign invasions inspires large defensive programmes regardless of the unlikelihood of such invasions today. The historical record, of course, is quite at odds with this assertion: Russian and Soviet invasions of neighbours have been far more numerous than foreign invasions of Russian and Soviet territory.

Another answer with some currency is that it stems from a deeply-rooted bureaucratic dynamic. In this view, the military-industrial sector has transcended policy control to acquire a momentum of its own.[15] If this were true, several military developments would be difficult to explain. The reorganization in the late 1950s, leading to the establishment of the Strategic Rocket Forces (SRF), and the emergence of the General Staff's authority in the early 1970s is unlikely to have bubbled up as the result of bureaucratic momentum. They suggest 'top down' reforms, driven by a policy perception of military need.

Although historical and bureaucratic factors certainly play a role, they are inadequate as an explanation. They omit the critical causal role of the Party leadership's policy aims and the development of military doctrine to implement them. If we are to anticipate future trends in the military balance, we must better understand policy and doctrinal factors. While they, too, are not the whole story, they seem to be a central but somewhat neglected part of the story.

The basic policy guidance for the Soviet military has long been 'peaceful co-existence' as Lenin originally defined this 'alternative form' of the 'international class struggle'. Disappointed at the failure of revolution in Western Europe where the working class was strong, Lenin was, nonetheless, not willing to admit the failure of the socialist revolution in Russia. His 'peaceful co-existence' policy recognized the military and economic superiority of the West. On that front, correct state-to-state relations would be pursued, and capital credits and technology would be sought to build what Stalin soon defined as 'socialism in one country'. In the Third World, Moscow would support revolution against 'imperialism', international capitalism's 'weakest link'. This was a key feature of 'peaceful co-existence'. And as the Soviet industrial base grew adequate to challenge the industrial West militarily, the overall correlation of forces between the socialist and capitalist camps would shift in favour of socialism. Under those conditions, revolution in the West would become possible.[16]

This strategy is well enough known. It was interrupted only by World War II, reinstated by Khrushchev, and continued through different tactics by Brezhnev. It is critical to remember this, however, if we are to understand Soviet military policy and doctrinal development, because it is the political context in which Soviet military science and doctrine have grown, the nuclear age not being as exceptional as is sometimes believed. Two revolutions in Soviet military affairs have occurred in the history of the regime and, more recently, an evolutionary third stage of doctrinal development has begun. Each will be briefly reviewed.

The First Revolution in Soviet Military Affairs
After World War I, a great blossoming of military thought occurred, leading to debate and policy disputes over the extent to which Marxism demanded a unique military science and doctrine. The appearance of new military technologies, specifically aviation, poison gas and motorization, added to the debate and affected the parallel debate on how the new regime should approach economic development. Frunze brought the military debate under control and gave it synthesis in two essays, 'A Unified Military Doctrine' and 'Front and Rear in Future War'. The essence of Frunze's analysis was that new weapons not only changed the nature of war, making the old concept of the 'front' inadequate in light of air forces' ability to bomb the 'rear' and of motorized ground forces to engage in deep mobile operations, but they also had enormous implications for the organization and priority of Soviet industrialization.[17]

In retrospect, it is clear that military requisites did indeed drive many aspects of Soviet industrialization, and military doctrine was designed to exploit the new weapons. In the late 1920s and early 1930s, the concept of 'deep operations' was worked out in practice and articulated in the Field Regulations for the Red Army.[18] While the Red Army did not initially match the Wehrmacht in 'blitzkrieg' operations, it was not behind in its doctrinal thinking. In fact, the early Soviet descriptions of the 'character of future war' proved quite perspicacious.

The Second Revolution in Soviet Military Affairs
After World War II, Soviet military leaders found themselves in much the same situation that confronted them after World War I. Once again they lacked a modern industrial base. Much of what had been built in the First and Second Five Year Plans had been destroyed. Once again, new technologies had emerged on the battlefield. Nuclear weapons, rocketry and cybernetics promised to alter the nature of war even more dramatically than aviation, gas and motorization.

The tendency in Western analysis of this Soviet 'revolution in military affairs' has been to treat it out of the Soviet historical context and to assess it largely through the prism of Western experience with the new technologies. Typical is Lawrence Freedman's exhaustive study of the evolution of Western nuclear strategy.[19] Insofar as it deals with the Soviet side, it is a very poor reflection of the realities because it accepts the view that emerged among many Soviet specialists in the West that Stalin stifled all progress in coming to grips with the new military realities. Stalin did not stifle technical developments; his R&D programme produced a bomb earlier than the West expected. As for Stalin's 'permanently operating factors' being inadequate for nuclear strategy, Maj.-Gen. Talenskii made that assertion shortly after Stalin's death when he invited a discussion of nuclear doctrine in the classified page of his journal, *Military Thought*.[20] But is that conclusive evidence? Are 'the permanently operating factors' incompatible with Soviet nuclear doctrine as it has developed? Hardly. Evolving Soviet doctrine appears more as a filling out of those general maxims with specific operational guidance. Furthermore, as long as the USSR did not have a nuclear bomb and could not develop empirical evidence about its effects, how were her officers to theorize on its military applications with confidence? In retrospect, the debate and discussion that followed in *Military Thought*[21] occurred at about the time when testing data would have been available. It not so much broke with the tradition of pre-war doctrinal development as adapted and built on it.

The major synthesis of the Soviet military analysis of the impact on future war of nuclear weapons, rockets and cybernetics appeared in 1962 in Marshal Sokolovskii's celebrated *Military Strategy*. It not only

128

described the implications of nuclear weapons for future war but set forth the criteria that Soviet force building would have to meet. It was a road map for future force development the same way Frunze's essays had been in the 1920s.

The key difference between the Soviet approach to the new technologies and the approach in the West is her insistence on considering all levels of war – the strategic, the operational, and the tactical. The operational and tactical levels received attention in the West, particularly with the development of tactical nuclear weapons in the 1950s, but it was not sustained, and it faded in the 1960s and 1970s as the idea of 'assured destruction' took on a doctrinal role in Western force building. Even in the 1950s, concern with tactical nuclear weapons was driven by the search for an alternative to dealing with them at the strategic level. Later, the belief took hold that once they come into play at the strategic level, the operational and tactical levels become irrelevant.[22] While some observers assert that Khrushchev wanted to build only a 'minimum deterrence' capability, the evidence is far from conclusive and can be interpreted in quite the oppositive way.[23] The more recent Soviet literature is explicit on the necessity to deal with all three levels.[24]

In any event, when one looks at the Soviet military capabilities today and reads Sokolovskii, one finds a remarkable consistency in working from theory to practice, in anticipating what a global war would demand and methodically pursuing the programmes to acquire it. John Erickson has described this evolution of Soviet forces and doctrine as having created a Soviet 'combined arms' capability that permits the General Staff to operate at either the conventional level or the nuclear level without a modification in doctrine and tactics.[25] They have provided the dispersal of forces to make them less vulnerable under nuclear conditions, called for by Sokolosvkii, by the deep echeloning of highly mechanized and armour-protected formations, and they seek concentration of forces through a high speed of advance (60-100 km per day), allowing a rapid accumulation of combat power at places of contact with the enemy's defence. When this is understood properly, the Soviet emphasis on a mobile air defence umbrella and large amounts of long-range nuclear fire support – the SS-21, -23, and -22 – make very good sense, providing continuous air defence and long-range fire support for operations in great depth.

The Third Change: Evolution in Military Affairs

In the late 1970s, when Marshal Ogarkov became Chief of the General Staff, yet another basic review of Soviet doctrine and force development seems to have occurred. Once again the Soviet Union saw new technologies having a fundamental impact on the nature of future war, not causing a break as sharp as nuclear weapons but nevertheless demanding reformulations and changes. The new triad of technology areas includes microcircuitry, directed energy systems, and the use of space, especially for reconnaissance and communications. The key question for Soviet military science remains the same: how to exploit them in Soviet doctrine and organization?

In the late 1970s we began to see significant changes in Soviet divisional organization.[26] More artillery, especially self-propelled artillery, was added, and a number of other changes seemed designed to provide a better combined arms capability to the division. At higher echelons, we began to read about a new kind of formation, the 'operational manoeuvre group (OMG)', which promised 'deep operations' both earlier and deeper than before.[27] In 1982 Marshal Ogarkov published a small book reviewing many aspects of the aims of Soviet force development, providing an overall perspective to these changes. He chided his officer corps for not exploiting new technologies and described a new 'theatre strategic' concept of operations. Of particular interest is his emphasis on the speed of operations now required and the new levels of command and control that are imperative. In World War II, pauses between frontal operations lasted days; in a future war they must be continuous. Only at the beginning of this Century did 'front' level operations come into practice, making war a series of multiple-army frontal operations. By the end of World War II, that was proving inadequate. A new level, the 'theatre of military operations' (or TVD), was beginning to evolve as the level of command necessary to co-ordinate multiple-front operations. The major task now, according to Ogarkov, is to perfect and elaborate this level of command and control.[28]

Ogarkov expressed concern about the speed of staff work needed to manage this evolving new concept of the 'theatre strategic operation'. It will require particular emphasis in the years ahead. He also emphasized adoption of new battlefield applications of technology, not only automation for troop control but also for aviation, air defence, rocketry, and means of destroying tanks. All of these things have to take into account the possibility of the use of nuclear and other weapons of mass destruction. One gets the sense that Ogarkov feels that his army has been lethargic about modernizing in light of new technical possibilities. He certainly does not seem inclined to rest on the laurels of the enormous military modernization programme that has already been achieved by the Soviet Union.

If we take Ogarkov's strictures as playing a role analogous to Sokolovskii's dictates in *Military Strategy*, we see not an announcement of a present Soviet capability but rather a road map of where force development should go in the future. The 'theatre strategic operation' is a capability to be attained, a faster and better-controlled capability than the one now in place.

A number of the weapons being fielded make more sense in this context. The family of more accurate short-range and inter-mediate-range ballistic missiles can provide very deep fire support. If that is to be exploited at ranges out to 900 km, then ground forces must be capable of reaching those depths earlier, not weeks after such deep strikes have been made. And the emphasis on strategic defence also makes sense. If a nuclear theatre strategic operation is contemplated, then the USSR must expect to be hit by US strategic forces. While the Soviet Union certainly does not desire that

kind of exchange, it makes sense to limit its damage by all means possible, defensive as well as offensive.

As this military capability grows, the Politburo can begin to dream of the kind of shift in the correlation of forces between the socialist and capitalist camps that make political change in the West possible. It creates the imbalance in power that can support a bolder policy towards 'progressive' forces and 'realistic' circles in the West. Such a gradual shift in Soviet policy is by no means confined to Europe. It is part of a co-ordinated effort with power projection into the Third World of the kind that we have witnessed in Cuba, Vietnam, Angola and Ethiopia.

Likely Trends in Soviet Force Development
New Technologies
Given the new technologies, including integrated circuitry, directed energy weapons, and space potential, we should expect to see vigorous efforts to field applications of all three areas. Integrated circuitry holds the greatest potential for improved command and control at all levels. At the lowest level, 'smart' munitions with closed intelligence-operations loops (that is, systems that can acquire and guide munitions to a target without a man in the loop) are certain to receive great emphasis. At a higher level much effort is already apparent, such as radar netting to support air defence. And, in light of Ogarkov's strictures about better command and control of combat formations, we can expect applications in communications, intelligence and operations staff support at all levels at least down to division.

Directed energy applications are already appearing to assist fire control, as for example in the laser rangefinder on tanks. Applications in intelligence acquisition systems are certain to follow as well as in communications. Directed energy weapons systems depend on advances in power generation, advances that are not far off. And as those advances occur, the kinds of weapons applications will be numerous, including space-based as well as ground-based systems.

In space, two main directions of Soviet engineering and development can be anticipated. First, better capabilities for reconnaissance and target acquisition are essential for current short-range and intermediate-range ballistic missiles. The improved accuracies of those weapons cannot be exploited fully without timely reconnaissance from space. Second, the Soviet Union will seek to improve her ability to destroy adversary space reconnaissance systems.

Organization and Command and Control
New technologies inevitably cause changes in organization and command and control. The general directions have been set by Ogarkov. The new divisional organizations show greater emphasis in 'combined arms' balance, requiring little or no 'task organizing' for each new operation below division level. That step can shorten the time required for initiating operations for new and changing objectives. The army and the front levels are bound to undergo changes just as extensive as those at division. We are already seeing that process in the concern for the OMG and the re-organization of air defence and frontal aviation. The front commander now has direct command of the air defence and frontal aviation within his sector. Finally, the attention given to the TVD, a command including two or more fronts, suggests an effort to free the front commander from a number of tasks so that he can, as Ogarkov insists that he must, sustain a series of operations without pauses between them.

The Soviet emphasis on speed and depth in theatre operations makes no sense at all unless staffs at all levels can receive tasks and translate them into orders for subordinate units with much greater speed than heretofore seen in warfare. Not surprisingly, one finds even in the open literature an obsession with this problem. Game theory, net-working theory, and computer applications occupy a central place in their thinking about solutions for this general problem.[29]

The command and control problem also has implications for authority within the Warsaw Pact. Unless the East European armies follow suit in all aspects of this Soviet transformation, including the national command authority decision process as it relates to the leading role of the USSR,

Ogarkov's image of the 'theatre strategic operation' will not be realizable. Yet if they do follow suit, the economic cost will be high, and it will amount to a virtual surrender of any residual threads of political authority by East European governments over military matters.

Strategic Defence
Strategic defence too is likely to receive a great deal of attention in the decade ahead. Here the improvements are already appearing, as mentioned earlier in low-altitude air defence with the SA-10 deployments and the look-down/shoot-down interceptor capability.[30] The very large Soviet investment in civil defence and strategic air defence make little sense unless it is eventually capped with an ABM defence, if not country-wide, then at least over many key areas. Whether the ABM Treaty is adequate to prevent this development in spite of new technologies has yet to be seen but we certainly cannot be confident that it will or that the Soviet Union may not abrogate the Treaty. The Soviet Union has never forsworn strategic defence, notwithstanding the Treaty, and it is imperative as a backdrop for managing theatre warfare of the kind she is preparing for.

Ground Force Strength
It seems unlikely that ground force strength in numbers of divisions will grow as rapidly in the decade ahead as in the past fifteen years. In the European theatre they seem to have reached a peak. In the Caucasus and Central Asia, the trend is more likely to be modernization of existing divisions than in expansion. In the Far East, the future is less clear. The transportation constraints and the distances from European Russia are so great that Soviet forces in the Far East must be adequate to deal with any eventuality without significant reinforcement. The space there is large, and conceivably the General Staff could see the need for additional forces.

Constraints on Soviet Military Programmes
The 'Ogarkov Plan' for Soviet force development will not be easy to realize. There are four major constraints which will cause delays and difficulties.

First, the health of the overall economy is sufficiently weak to lead even the senior military leaders to worry.[31] Some military industries can be redirected to civil production to help overcome certain bottlenecks that are becoming quite severe, particularly in transportation. That shift should not seriously deflect the larger goals of the military plan, but it can slow their attainment.

Second, the cost and complexity of R&D for new weapons systems are exceeding the capability of the military industrial sector alone to carry out.[32] The civil scientific community is playing a greater role, and with it comes some of the lesser efficiencies of inter-ministerial and inter-sector co-ordination.

Third, access to Western technology and credits has played a key role in the past decade of Soviet military modernization. If it is restricted, even partially, Soviet military programmes, particularly R&D and the manufacture of new weapons components, can be considerably delayed.

Fourth, the Warsaw Pact forces must keep pace in modernization programmes. Yet the Eastern European economies are hardly able to support them to the degree that the USSR desires. Moreover Eastern European leaders can be expected to drag their feet, holding out wherever they can against Soviet demands for greater allocations to the defence sector. Finally, their credit and trade difficulties with the West provide them with strong arguments for resisting Soviet military programme plans.

Implications for the East–West Military Balance

What the Soviet Union has already achieved in her military forces gives her a significant advantage in Europe and in other contiguous areas. Furthermore, growing means of Soviet power projection to non-contiguous areas in both hemispheres, while not yet matching US power projection, have become a very serious challenge, particularly in the Middle East, Africa and the Caribbean. Both of these threats must, of course, be viewed against the Soviet strategic capabilities, offensive and defensive. The interaction of the three components of Soviet military power – strategic, theatre and power projection –

presents the West with a genuine qualitative change in its own security requirements.

The Western habit in past decades has often been to focus on a static assessment of the military balance. The concept of 'nuclear superiority' implied, for example, essentially a tally of numbers of nuclear weapons and delivery systems. Moreover, nuclear superiority was seen as compensating for a deficit in the static conventional force balance. In the new conditions created by Soviet military capabilities, numerical superiority not only looks unattainable politically in the West, but it would not necessarily be desirable. Certainly, an effective military defence for the West for the remainder of the century will require significant increases in numbers of some kinds of capabilities, but we cannot choose those categories without determining first what kind of military doctrine is required to counter the Soviet concept of the 'theatre strategic operation'.

Such a doctrine must take advantage of Soviet weaknesses and Western strengths. The recent and numerous arguments that a conventional defence of Europe is both possible and adequate may be valid if we assume away the reality of Soviet nuclear weapons capabilities and doctrine. Unfortunately, that does not seem wise, but to take them into account does not make our case hopeless. Samuel Huntington has challenged us lately to 'renew strategy' and rethink the problem of Western security in light of the qualitatively new realities.[33] He suggests that we consider shifting from a defensive orientation in our general purpose forces to a retaliatory offensive orientation, particularly in Europe, and that we shift the emphasis in strategic forces from offensive systems to defensive capabilities.

The logic of his proposal takes into account key Soviet weaknesses and Western operational requirements. Soviet political difficulties with Warsaw Pact allies could be more fully exploited if those countries expected a NATO retaliatory offensive into Eastern Europe. At the same time, the West will need not only nuclear deterrence in the future but an ability to deter other things, such as Soviet military aggression against a Warsaw Pact ally. In the nuclear case, it is more likely that the Soviet Union may threaten with her nuclear arsenal to prevent US power projection in support of an imperilled ally, much as the US threatened the Soviet Union in 1973 when the USSR wanted to support her ally, Egypt, with ground forces. In such cases, even a 'leaky' strategic defence capability might be more reassuring to an American President than additional offensive nuclear capabilities.

At a lesser level of doctrinal concern, the European theatre, the US Army's concept of AirLand Battle is designed precisely to exploit the offensive form of combat against the large Soviet ground force offensive. It links the attack of the deeply-echeloned Soviet forces before they arrive at the line of contact with the ground commander's scheme of manoeuvre. The deep attack is to be conducted not only by fire – by artillery, rockets, and tactical aircraft – but may also include ground forces penetrating the front and seeking objectives scores of kilometres deep in the Warsaw Pact rear.

While AirLand Battle doctrine may be applied at the tactical level in a limited fashion with today's capabilities, the West's lead in technology gives it a real advantage in the future fielding of systems that would allow retaliatory offensives quite deep into Eastern Europe. A 'deep attack' doctrine for the 'operational' as well as the 'tactical' level certainly deserves consideration in NATO. Intelligence and reconnaissance systems, highly accurate conventional munitions, attack helicopters, high-speed armoured formations, and superior air power might well neutralize the large Soviet land force capability without matching it piece for piece. To achieve and retain such a military edge, the West must not only deploy new systems but it must also control its own technology advantages by preventing easy Soviet access to them, thereby exploiting another Soviet weakness.

Strategic defence is of course necessary if we hope to keep a conflict below the nuclear threshold. There can be no assurance on that point, but even a limited defence capability would greatly improve the prospects of doing so, and it would add measurably to the credibility of the West's deterrent posture.

Two rather difficult problems – in addition to the costs of these new military capabilities – must be addressed effectively if a restoration of Western military pre-eminence is to be achieved. The first concerns command control. The more attention one pays to Soviet command and control changes, the more apparent it becomes that the Soviet General Staff seeks to exploit NATO's weaknesses in this regard. The 'theatre of military operations' and its nexus with 'fronts' provides the Soviet General Staff with a much better chance of getting 'inside' the NATO command and control cycle, that is assessing the operational situation and responding to it with new orders and offensive action.

The second problem concerns Soviet power projection to non-NATO regions of the world. Although NATO may remain limited geographically in its area of operational responsibility, its objective security is not attainable within that region alone. The strategic inter-relationship between Europe and South-west Asia is simply a reality. One theatre cannot be defended without successfully defending the other as long as Western Europe is dependent on Persian Gulf oil. An adverse shift in the balance of US–Soviet influence in the Persian Gulf and Middle East region is equally an adverse shift in the strategic balance on the Central Front. This was not a significant factor in the two decades before the Soviet Union acquired a large and diverse capability to project power into the Third World, but the events in Angola in 1975 and in Ethiopia in 1977–78 demonstrated a major change, giving that factor new importance.

A similar inter-relationship is developing with another theatre as a result of the Soviet–Cuban military position in the Caribbean. The growth of military and intelligence capabilities in Cuba, created by Soviet supplies and deployments, now make it problematic whether the United States could deploy to Europe in a crisis without diverting some forces for the contingency of hostilities with Cuba and with Soviet forces that might deploy there. As Cuban–Soviet influence spreads to Nicaragua, Grenada, and possibly to other states in the Caribbean Basin, such potential force diversions become even greater. Some military resource diversions are already necessary merely to deal with the present insurgencies in that region. In other words, it is not possible to deal with a major crisis in Europe without consideration of the Caribbean.

The trends in Soviet power projection capabilities suggest that the relationship between Third World regional disturbance and the defence of Europe will increase in military importance in the 1980s. Whatever one's view about where the limit of NATO's concerns should be, one cannot responsibly ignore these factors as they affect the military balance in Europe.

The Trends in Summary

East–West relations have crossed a qualitative threshold in the last decade. The diffusion of Western economic power, the emergence of the strategic importance of the Persian Gulf region and the Caribbean Basin, and US–Chinese normalization have created a new East–West strategic configuration. Even more important in this change is the increase of Soviet military power. It has transformed the character of the competition, not only militarily but also economically and diplomatically.

The West does not have to accept this military change as permanent although it is sometimes asserted that military superiority, the basis of Western security in the 1950s and 1960s, cannot be restored. In its old form, it is true, it cannot be. But it simply is not true that a new form of Western military pre-eminence is not attainable. It will require, however, modifications of our military doctrine, acknowledging that nuclear weapons affect not only the strategic level of war but also the operational and tactical levels in the sense that the Soviet General staff understands this. And it will require basic shifts in emphasis with respect to offensive and defensive doctrine, shifts that will raise the long-unresolved issues of command and control arrangements for coalition warfare as well as types of forces and weapons systems. It will also depend on exploiting Western advantages in technology as well as denying the transfer of those advantages to the USSR through economic interaction. Finally, the new third-world regional strategic inter-relationships with Western Europe on security must be recognized and taken into account when assessing the military balance in Europe.

NOTES

[1] *Soviet Military Power* (Washington DC: USGPO, 2nd Edition 1983) pp. 19-20.

[2] *Ibid*, pp. 21–3.

[3] *Ibid*, pp. 23–4.

[4] *Ibid*, pp. 24–31.

[5] *Ibid*, pp. 65–9.

[6] *Ibid*, pp. 37–8.

[7] *Ibid*, p. 42.

[8] *Ibid*, p. 38.

[9] *Ibid*, pp. 38–42.

[10] *Ibid*, p. 34.

[11] *Ibid*, pp. 55–8.

[12] *Ibid*, pp. 58–60.

[13] *Ibid*, p. 91.

[14] *Ibid*, p. 90.

[15] See Edward L. Warner, III, *The Military in Contemporary Soviet Politics* (New York: Praeger Special Studies, 1977), for a development of this explanation.

[16] For an example of Soviet military policy articulated in the context of the shifting correlation of forces, see V. G. Kulikov, 'Army of a Developed Socialist Society', *Red Star*, 23 February 1973. The Red Army, according to Kulikov, had both an 'internal and external' role. Today, the internal role has dropped off, and the external role has become greater for the bloc of Socialist states.

[17] M. V. Frunze, *Izbrannye proizvedeniia* (Moscow: Voenizdat, 1957), pp. 4–21, 133–42.

[18] David M. Glantz, 'Soviet Operational Formation for Battle', *Military Review*, February 1983, vol. LXIII, no. 2, pp. 2–12.

[19] Lawrence Freedman, *Evolution of Nuclear Strategy* (New York: St Martin's Press, 1981) particularly pp. 58–9.

[20] See Harriet Fast and William F. Scott (eds), *The Soviet Art of War* (Boulder, Colo.: Westview Press, 1982), p. 124.

[21] *Ibid*, pp. 123–56. Much of this classified journal is now available in unclassified form in the US today.

[22] See Albert Wohlstetter, 'Bishops, Statesmen, and Other Strategists on the Bombing of Innocents', *Commentary*, June 1983, vol. 76, no. 6, pp. 15–35.

[23] See W. E. Odom, 'The Soviet Approach to Nuclear Weapons', in the *Annals of the American Academy of Political and Social Science*, September 1983, pp. 117–35.

[24] See, for example, V. E. Savkin, *Osnovnyye printsipi operativnogo isskustva i taktiki* (Moscow: Voenizdat, 1972).

[25] *The College Station Papers, No.2, Soviet Combined Arms: Theory and Practice* (College Station: Center for

Strategic Technology, Texas A&M, 1980), p.58.

[26] *Soviet Military Power, op. cit.*, in note 1, p. 40.

[27] C. N. Donnelly, 'The Soviet Operational Manoeuvre Group: A New Challenge for NATO', *Military Review*, March 1983, vol. LXIII, no. 3, pp. 43–60.

[28] *Vsegda v gotovnosti k zashite otechestva* (Moscow: *Voenizdat*, 1982).

[29] K. V. Tarakanov, *Matematika i vooruzhenniia* (Moscow: *Voenizdat*, 1974).

[30] *Soviet Military Power op. cit.* in note 1, pp. 27–31.

[31] Ogarkov, '*As Nashu Sovetskuyu rodinu: zashishchaya mirovoi trud*', *Kommunist*, 1981, no. 10, pp. 80–91, admits that the economic costs of full military readiness in peacetime are not affordable.

[32] Arthur J. Alexander, *Soviet Science and Weapons Acquisition*, no. R-2942-NAS (Santa Monica, Ca.: August 1982, Rand) for a cogent analysis of this problem.

[33] Samuel Huntington, *The Strategic Imperative: New Policies for American Security* (Cambridge, Mass.: Ballinger Publishers, 1982), pp. 1–52.

Public Opinion as Both Means and Ends for Policy-Makers: I

MICHEL TATU

The role of public opinion has never been negligible in the conduct of governments, whatever their nature and whether democratic or authoritarian. Even the latter, with a few exceptions, wish to have the support of their publics (even if they manage not to rely on public opinion) and they tend to legitimize dictatorships by the promise of happiness if not now, at least in the future. However, in terms of international relations, the role of public opinion has been limited (until now) to periods of war and social upheaval. Indeed, even in the cases of wars, it was only in the Napoleonic Wars that we saw the population as a whole involved in the fighting, for the *'levée masse'* introduced a new dimension as against the 'professional' wars of the past. A more recent example is the case of Khomeini's Iran, but revolutions do not last for long: either the mobilizing consensus recedes quickly on its own, or it has to be artificialy maintained by repressive measures.

The modern era has introduced two contradictory factors into the relationship between governments and public opinion as far as international relations are concerned. On the one hand, nuclear weapons have turned back the 'post-Napoleonic' revolution in the conduct of war. They render obsolete the concept of *'levée en masse'* and have ensured a return to the 'professional' wars of the past: nuclear wars are now supposed to be conducted not by the masses but against the masses, by a few professional soldiers of the General Staff and in isolated units, such as strategic submarines or strategic missile bases. On the other hand, the development of rapid world-wide communications and of media diffusion, have placed the general public in direct contact with nearly every facet of foreign policy formulation and made

every citizen, who chooses to be, aware of any potential tension in foreign relations. Not surprisingly, the combination of these two factors has increased the salience of public opinion in the foreign-policy formulation of most governments: diplomacy can lead to precipitate escalation of crises, and so towards nuclear holocaust. The population would know that there was a crisis, but would have no possibility of controlling it.

Hence it is necessary, at least in the eyes of the most motivated segments of public opinion, to have some say in the conduct of foreign policy *before* any danger arises. While it was said in the past that war was too dangerous to be left to the generals (implying that politicians should be involved), one might now say that foreign policy is too dangerous a matter to be left to the politicians. Public opinion must be taken into account. And, since war is likely to be short and brutal, public opinion, if it is to intervene at all, must intervene in the early stage of preparation for war i.e. during the period of military build-up.

This is a desirable development, but its impact on the conduct of governments will heavily depend on their nature. In the democractic states, all opinions carry equal weight and the political impact of an idea will depend mainly on the amount of support it can rally. Normally the 'most successful opinion' will reflect the internal values of a particular society and the dominant ideological trends in that society at a given moment. It will be difficult to take into account external factors and ideas, or the realization that other nations do not necessarily share the same values and can behave differently. For example, the citizen of a society founded on the rule of law, brought up to believe in the Christian virtues of good faith and accommodation with his neighbours, may fail to understand how and why his government does not always succeed in negotiating with other governments: something must be wrong with his own government, since there is nothing which cannot be achieved by peaceful negotiation and persuasion. Moreover, he will naturally criticize his own government more than any foreign government, since his government is assumed to be under his influence and is supposed to share his values.

Any democratic government has thus to prove that it is is behaving properly and 'morally', in line with the wishes of the people: the very fact that it must sometimes act otherwise under the pressure of necessity puts a democratically-elected government on the defensive: it has to explain those necessities and its intentions; in fact it has often to apologize to its people for its conduct. For such a government, public opinion is both a means to rally the necessary support among its constituents and voters, and an end in itself, since the *raison d'être* of democratic rule is the broadest possible identification between collective and individual values.

The situation is quite different for an authoritarian government, and even more so for a totalitarian one. Indeed the chief difference between those two forms of dictatorship is that an authoritarian regime tends to limit the expression of public opinion in order to gain a greater margin of freedom for government policy, but without suppressing public opinion completely or denying that it exists; the totalitarian system, on the other hand, does not conceive of a public opinion outside the values and ideology it has defined for itself: public opinion has to be shaped. All media will be concentrated on this task and it will be judged preferable that, short of this ideally 'monolithic' public opinion, there be no public opinion at all.

At the same time, totalitarian rulers do not ignore public opinion in other countries. They will try to use it for their own ends, to propagate their own ideas among foreign populations and to open another means of applying pressure on the governments with which they have to deal. Thus they take a full part in the battle for public opinion, like the democratic governments, but only on the other's ground, while preventing their own population from expressing an opinion.

Consequently, public opinion for a totalitarian system is not an end in itself, but a means as far as foreign relations are concerned. Popular sympathy, whether domestic or foreign, is not necessary to the perpetuation of the system: it is only an instrument to promote foreign policy goals. The only problem will be to adapt this instrument of propaganda to different audiences and to foreign ideological values in order to make it effective. This can be achieved by playing upon the same broad notions – peace, justice, happiness – which are the universal individual values.

Before outlining some specific causes of the manipulation of public opinion in the present context of East–West relations, there are three main areas in which this manipulation takes place.

Information Release
The earliest stage, and the one most often forgotten, relates to the release of factual information and to the various degrees of *secrecy* applied by governments. To be effective, any public opinion campaign needs to be based on facts. Those facts can simply be invented by imaginative propaganda (as in the case of the campaign regarding the alleged use of bacteriological weapons by the American forces in Korea in the early 1950s), but a more effective way to manipulate public opinion is to select from among true facts those most suited to the desired purpose, and to keep the others secret.

In fact, any release of information is selective, whatever the real intentions of the regime which controls this information, and Western governments are not immune from accusations in this respect. Beginning with the 'missile gap' in the early 1960s, Pentagon officials have often overestimated the Soviet military potential in certain areas, in order to get approval for new weapons programmes. Sometimes the distortion comes simply from the fact there is only one main source of information (the US Administration as far as the 'arms race' is concerned), and that this source is inclined to focus public interest more or less exclusively on those matters which are of concern to it.

For example, up to 1979–80, the main preoccupation in Washington was the SALT II Treaty and the state of the Soviet–US balance of strategic intercontinental forces and the Soviet improvements in this area. Although the SS-20 intermediate-range ballistic missile was duly noticed by US intelligence agencies and mentioned from time to time, the main focus of the US media – under the influence of official information and debate – was on the SS-18 and SS-19, on the *Typhoon* SSBN and on other 'anti-US' weapon systems and not on the Soviet 'anti-European' developments which were at least as impressive and certainly much less justified. The quarrel about the *Backfire* bomber was always discussed in this period and in this context as a *possible* threat to the continental US and hardly ever as a *real* threat to Europe. In this way, several years were lost in the public opinion battle which was to develop later around the NATO TNF decision. In fact the Europeans at this time, including many experts, had difficulties in understanding the new threat presented by the SS-20.

But the Communist governments are more expert at selecting information and using it intentionally. The secrecy in decision-making is second nature for these governments, for any openness in debate before decisions are taken, especially in matters of foreign policy, would give the impression of uncertainty at the top and destroy the monolithic image which domestic propaganda wants to convey. Secrecy is also a way of preventing unpleasant facts becoming known and this limits adverse public reaction to government decisions.

One good case is the Soviet decision concerning the SS-20. Tested in 1974–75 and first deployed at the beginning of 1977, this missile programme was probably approved by the Soviet Defence Council at the beginning of the 1970s. But its existence was admitted by Brezhnev only in 1981, when the late Soviet leader decided to discuss publicly 'this rocket which is called in the West the SS-20'. If the West had applied the same rule to the *Pershing* II and GLCM, the first mention of these weapons would not appear in the world press until 1984 (with the detection of their deployment), or it might have appeared with the first test of the *Pershing* II in 1982. A US President might have begun to discuss, 'this weapon which is called by the Soviets the *Pershing* II' in 1988, that is after the completion of the programme. Conversely, had the Western rules of 'secrecy' applied in the Soviet Union, there would have been a big debate on the SS-20 around 1972–75, i.e. in the years of 'detente', of *Ostpolitik*, and of the Helsinki Conference on Security and Co-operation in Europe (CSCE). Needless to say, the outcome of such a debate and its effect on the international situation generally would have been quite different.

Another example of Communist manipulation of news concerns the Vietnam War. It is now acknowledged (by General Giap himself) that the decision to unleash operations in the South with the aim of taking over the Saigon government was made at a plenary meeting of the Central Committee of the ruling party in Hanoi in the Spring of 1959. This decision was kept secret for more than twenty years, during which time the propaganda machines of Hanoi and of Vietnam's allies tended to portray (with considerable success in the Western media) the war in the South as a 'spontaneous' insurrection of the local population, represented by 'independent' institutions such as the National Liberation Front, the Provisional Revolutionary Government and even a 'third force', all of which collapsed or disappeared in the hours or weeks following the entry of North Vietnamese troops into Saigon. The image of that war in the West would certainly have been different (and the mood in the United States different also) had Hanoi's involvement in it been better known from the beginning (and from official sources) instead of being constantly denied.

Public Opinion and International Negotiations

The second area where public opinion interferes in the conduct of governments – and the most visible – is that of negotiation. Since any conflict of interest is today a matter of negotiation, direct or indirect, *before* reaching the point of confrontation, and since the aim of negotiation is to modify the position of other governments in a desirable way, a proper means of achieving this result is to weaken the other government's determination by applying extra pressure on it through its own public opinion. Here again, this instrument works in only one direction, since totalitarian states can 'protect' their own publics from foreign information and propaganda. Even if they do not succeed completely in this task, they are not accountable to their population for their policies.

Two other factors make Western governments more vulnerable to that kind of pressure. First, those Christian values which form the stratum of Western ideology and consensus tend to portray negotiation as better than confrontation and often as an end in itself. Talks are better than arms. Governments are invited to apply their energy and patience to negotiation, arms procurement being considered 'easy' but bad. Communist governments, on the other hand, consider arms-control negotiations as part – and not the main part – of their security policy and as an instrument for achieving (by constraining the West's weapons programmes) results in terms of security which they are ready to assure anyway by their own programmes if necessary. This is the view of many Western governments too, but these must work under the pressure of public opinion which tends to see arms-control negotiations as a way of constraining their own defence efforts and as a *substitute* for a security policy instead of a complement to it.

Second, most Western governments – and hence their policies – are considered intrinsically unstable. Cabinets may change after elections or with new party coalitions, or the same cabinet may change its line on certain issues under the pressure of its constituents or circumstances. By contrast, Communist governments appear as fortresses of stability and determination. Even if the word 'never' should not be used in politics, whether in East or West, the 'never' of a Communist state seems much more credible than the 'never' of a democratic government, which can be eroded by criticism. For the same reason, the notion of an 'unacceptable' proposal has a different meaning for both

sides. In the West, a simplistic but rather common line of argument is as follows: if my government rejects as 'unacceptable' a proposal of the other side, it is taking the risk of killing the negotiations by taking too a rigid stance; I will therefore apply my right of criticism in inviting it to have a second look at this proposal. But if the other side rejects my government's proposal as 'unacceptable', something must be wrong with this proposal: it is 'unrealistic', since the other *cannot* accept it. And I will use my right of criticism in inviting my government to take, in the name of 'realism', a better account of the point of view of the other side. Communist governments, on the other hand, are not frightened of rejecting Western proposals as 'unacceptable', nor of putting forward claims which they know will be 'unacceptable' to the West. Negotiation is never considered by them as an end in itself, but rather as one way among other ways of achieving their political aims, of impressing others with their determination and in order to see whether something can be obtained somewhat short of the main goal.

Indeed, the main goal is sometimes achieved, as in the recognition of the two German States in the 1970s. This would not have been possible if Soviet diplomacy had not put forward this clearly 'unrealistic' demand for decades in its talks with the West. That is why the main task of Soviet propaganda will be relentlessly to justify all Soviet proposals or demands – especially the 'tough' ones – while encouraging in the West all the voices (the famous *trezvye golosa* of the Soviet media) who advocate a more conciliatory approach in East–West talks in the name of 'realism'. In the Kremlin's view, the Western 'realist' is one who asks his government to put forward better proposals instead of 'unacceptable' ones, or at least partially to consider some Communist claims as the true expression of Soviet concerns and interests.

Intimidation and Public Opinion
The third area of the manipulation of Western public opinion is by Soviet intimidation. It should be mentioned briefly and mainly as a potential threat, since it has not been used directly in the recent past, at least

with respect to Western public opinion and foreign policy.

Governments may, of course, be intimidated by direct pressure and extortion, but secretly. Public opinion is less easy to intimidate for fear of backlash. Crude pressure is often counter-productive, as was seen in Czechoslovakia in 1968, or more recently, in Poland. One example of such pressure (on government and on public opinion simultaneously) was the missile threat aimed at Britain by the Soviet Union during the Suez Crisis of 1956 (but Prime Minister Eden and the British public both wanted to terminate this adventure anyway). This kind of threat has not been repeated since.

Pacifism may be on the rise in the face of a potential enemy who preaches peace and disarmament, but it can only diminish if the enemy threatens war and 'punishment'. Until now most of the veiled warnings formulated by the USSR towards the Federal Republic have been about the 'danger of war' (supposedly accidental) which might result from the *Pershing* deployment and much less about any positive action which might be decided by the USSR.

Public Opinion and Foreign Policy

The fact remains that public opinion is at the same time both an instrument and a factor in the conduct of foreign policy. Although the big debate on the 'arms race' and the missile issue has taken place mainly in the West, it has undoubtedly had an impact on the policy of most governments, in both East and West.

In the West, President Reagan seems to have been more successful than his predecessor in his handling of public opinion, even though he was confronted, in the 'Freeze Movement', with formidable opposition to this policy in matters of defence and East–West relations. The motto of 'big cuts' in strategic arms seems to have been effective not only in countering the freeze argument ('cutting is better than freezing'), but also in putting the Soviet Union on the defensive and bringing them to adopt a similar concept in their own proposals. His success in selling his new weapons programmes to public opinion and to Congress has been less marked.

One lesson which can be drawn from this period is that the arguments used to appease public opinion in one country may produce the opposite result in another. Such was the case with the misguided (and confused) statement of the President on the possibility of limited nuclear war in Europe. US public opinion was happy (understandably) to learn that a nuclear war would not automatically involve US territory. Americans would like nuclear war to remain as remote as possible. Europeans see the problem otherwise: for them the best way to avoid a war (which would in any case be total for Europe) is to stress that it would be unlimited, that is without American 'sanctuarization'.

With these few exceptions, the US response to the TNF debate and the development of the Peace Movements in Europe has, on the whole, been the best it could have been in the circumstances. The 'zero option' of November 1981 was, in the eyes of many experts, a gamble. They believed then (and still believe) that NATO needed some new long-range theatre nuclear forces even in theabsence of Soviet missiles. Nevertheless, it was a clever move in terms of its effect on public opinion, since it took over the most popular slogan of the Peace Movements: 'No *Pershing*, no SS- 20'. In France the leaders of the Communist-oriented peace campaign were clearly embarrassed to have to say, after a demonstration in Paris in June 1983, that this slogan is still valid, even if it is not used any more.

At the same time, and in other Western countries, the very vigour of the Peace Movements seems to have produced a reaction and drawn attention to the limits of the influence of public opinion – or of that part of public opinion which is the most vociferous – on government decision-making. After the March 1983 elections in the Federal Republic, it was clearly realized in many quarters that legitimacy is on the side of a government duly elected by a majority of the population and that such a government is entitled to take measures unpopular with a minority, even an important minority. That is why the possibility of violent demonstrations at the end of 1983 against the *Pershing* II deployment in West Germany was considered as going beyond the legitimate expression of public opinion in a democratic system. The real test of the vitality of this system is precisely the way in which a legitimate government can execute decisions taken in conformity with the system, not the ability of a minority to reverse those decisions.

In the East, too, the Peace Movements and, more generally, the development of role of public opinion in the area of international relations has had some impact on the conduct of government. The immediate need to exploit the reactions of Western public opinion more effectively has been duly perceived and the USSR has tried in the last few years to improve the functioning of the Eastern propaganda machinery. The creation of the International Information Department in the Central Committee by Brezhnev in 1978 was intended to improve the manipulation of Western public opinion, though a sort of rivalry and redundancy has developed between this Department and the International Department under the chairmanship of Boris Ponomarev and Vadim Zagladin, professional spokesmen of Soviet foreign policy in the West. More recently, the guidelines given by Soviet Party Secretary Constantin Chernenko at the June 1983 plenary meeting of the Central Committee of the Communist Party invited the Soviet media to react more quickly in international events. He suggested that the side who gives information first conveys the dominant image of an event, imposing a judgment which the other side will find it difficult to reverse. That is precisely what happened a few weeks later with the shooting down of the South Korean airliner by the Soviet Air Force. The delay in Soviet official reaction and contradictory statements further damaged Soviet prestige, already badly shaken by this brutal action.

At another level, Communist governments have become aware of the dangers of the penetration of 'non-authorized peace ideology' in their countries. Those few Soviet citizens who wanted to create an autonomous Western-style peace movement have been severely repressed and gaoled, and the dissident views of Andrei Sakharov on the arms race and arms control have been censored and criticized. More than ever, the pacifist mood of the Soviet people has been oriented through the official Soviet Peace Committee, which is simply another channel for conveying official propaganda in matters of foreign policy. Being the only recognized counterpart of the various Western peace movements, this Committee has tried to limit the impact of the few Western 'peace marchers' authorized to enter the Soviet Union. While this task does not seem to create great problems for the Soviet authorities, it is clearly more difficult for the authorities of the satellite countries like Hungary and (particularly) East Germany. The citizens of the latter have permanent access to West German television programmes and cannot be insensitive to the turmoil created by the Peace Movements in the Federal Republic. The influence of the churches also is important there, as it is in the West but to a different degree. In East Germany the debate on peace and armaments has created the most serious trouble that has arisen between the Lutheran Church and the East Berlin authorities for many years.

Another defensive action conducted by the Soviet authorities has resulted in a change in the official Soviet propaganda about war and peace. For many years, beginning in the 1960s, Soviet military writers had advanced highly adventurous theories about nuclear war, including 'warfighting' doctrines much more destabilizing than even the most advanced ideas of US writers on this matter. War would result in the triumph of Communism; 'surprise' is decisive in using nuclear weapons; and even that a preemptive strike might be necessary in certain circumstances. (There is a good collection of such quotations in Joseph Douglass and Amoretta Hoeber *Soviet Strategy for Nuclear War*, (Stanford, Ca: Hoover International Studies, 1979)).

All those ideas have been now officially abandoned, and even criticized as no longer corresponding to the international situation. Beginning with a Brezhnev statement in 1981, the current official line is that 'only a candidate for suicide can start a war with the hope of winning such a war'.

Indeed, all the criticisms levelled at 'limited war' and 'warfighting' doctrines attributed by the Soviet Union to Americans would not have been possible without this official reappraisal of the writings of the 1960s. This reappraisal was a direct answer to the development of the Peace Movements in the West.

Certainly one can question the validity of the new and more 'peaceful' doctrine adopted by the Soviet leaders under such circumstances. What was in fact a quite unrealistic attitude in the 1960s, given the great US superiority in nuclear weapons at the time, looks much more reasonable today with the new correlation of forces. It would be unrealistic for the West to take the new mood at face value. Nevertheless, Soviet propaganda has some problems too, since it has to adjust to different needs and to address different kinds of audience. It must speak not only to Western governments, which it is necessary sometimes to intimidate, but also to Western publics, to whom the Soviet Union must appear peaceful. This creates the usual dilemma between the use of the carrot and the use of the stick. It also creates a domestic dilemma, for Soviet soldiers must be 'mobilized' and made ready to any kind of war, while the Soviet public at large must not be panicked. It is not easy to avoid contradictions in such circumstances.

Public Opinion as Both Means and Ends for Policy-Makers: II

IRIS J. PORTNY

Public opinion and policy-making enjoy a relationship of long-standing legitimacy in the eyes of the Western Alliance's political leadership. In democratic societies no other attitude can be acceptable. Yet striking the proper balance between leading and listening to the public is a continuing challenge with the relationship having become distinctly tumultuous in recent years.

It is necessary first to state four general premises:

- Governments must retain their general primacy in policy-making to ensure informed decision-making in international affairs;
- Western political leaderships and their publics do generally perceive the Soviet Union as an adversary;
- The Western Alliance's original objective – collective security – remains relevant;
- Economics cannot be divorced from security.

It follows that both economic considerations and fears of military escalation must be incorporated more fully into the security debate if the public's international priorities and perceptions are to be taken into account. Another way of stating that proposition is that the political leadership's policy objectives and world view must remain roughly compatible with the fundamental concerns of the general public.

Yet government by consensus among diverse constituent interest groups is always difficult, and diminished government and institutional authority (particularly in the US) and domestic economic stress have complicated Alliance policy-making to an extent not previously experienced during the post-war years. Renewed public fears of nuclear war have diminished even further the confi-dence afforded to Western leaderships by their publics. A general reluctance to under-take any military involvement, no doubt linked to the general unease regarding nuclear policy, has also emerged in samplings of opinion within NATO countries.

Diverse cultural, historical, political and social roots have traditionally strained co-operation among the members of the Western Alliance.[1] Yet the new bitterness characterizing trade relations and economic competition has introduced a particularly corrosive influence into the political frame-work underlying Western security co-operation. In the US this linkage has already become visible. During questioning in 1982 most US citizens (66%) considered their country's foreign policy to have a major impact upon domestic unemployment,[2] a problem ranked by both US and Western European publics alike as their major concern. Further, samplings of Western European opinions during a similar period revealed a growing suspicion, particularly among the young, that 'the US sought economic domination over Europe rather than mutual advantage'.[3] Public perceptions will thus determine governments' freedom of action in policy-making of significance to the West's vital interests.

The breadth of recent US Congressional opposition to the Administration's agreement to support the International Monetary Fund (IMF) Emergency 1983 Replenishment has reminded us how lightly foreign-policy arguments weigh against domestic economic priorities. Those responsible for formulating domestically-supportable security policies cannot remain inattentive to the implications for Western security of economic tensions among Alliance members. The effect of such irritations upon domestic attitudes towards

143

Alliance co-operation and responsibilities is not helpful.

There is widespread recognition among leadership, analysts and political observers that improvement is needed in the relationship between the West's broad security strategy and the expectations of its populace. However, the prescription for improvement has been addressed less frequently, with the solution less obvious than the problem. In any case, if governments are to be successful in defusing, even partially, public fears regarding East–West relations, they will have to devote more systematic attention to both public perceptions and public priorities.

This Paper will consider several issues of importance to the formulation and implementation of Western security policy. Omission of any discussion of the Western community's Pacific members should not be taken to imply that their concerns are any less important to Western security co-operation. It is simply that space is limited;

These issues divide broadly into three major groups:

– The growing importance to the Western policy-maker of issues *external* to the traditional sphere of foreign policy and national security decision-making, including the limited authority afforded to political leadership today, and the impact of generational attitude biases within national populations. The government's ability both to lead and to reassure its constituents has been accordingly diminished;
– Public attitudes towards East–West relations in general and military actions and trade sanctions in particular. This section will include suggestions for accommodating them in the policy process;
– Public attitudes towards the role of nuclear weapons. Again some suggestions will be included as to how the Alliance's nuclear strategy, in both formulation and presentation, might be modified to accommodate these concerns more sensitively than has been done in the past. However, the breadth of this issue exceeds the scope of this Paper; any observations offered are intended to be general and illustrative.

A New Context for the National Debate: The External Issues at Home

The decade of the 1980s finds individuals with policy authority and expertise, both within the government and outside it, with one overarching responsibility: to re-establish government authority in the handling of national security and foreign-policy issues. The breakdown in the Western consensus regarding specific policies has been widely recognized. Yet samplings of public attitudes on key issues of East–West significance, including those relating to the Soviet Union as well as allies, find the general Western public's broad concerns to be currently consistent with those of their leaders.

However, deeper currents have begun to affect the debate between the public and its political leadership. Certainly, the frequently divisive domestic debates, experienced to varying extents in Western countries, have been prompted by genuine disagreement about policy. However, the diminished authority of government in general has combined with apparent differences in generational perspectives to introduce new factors into the process of designing policies capable of attracting and sustaining domestic support.

Who is Leading? Lost Credibility, Diminished Authority

This part of the discussion will be confined to the problems of the US government. However, we should each consider the extent to which this is, in fact, a common domestic problem within our countries. Further, as traditional leader of the Western Alliance, US domestic problems become the Alliance's as well, and should be viewed in this light.

The US public, by and large, shares its government's overall objectives in East–West policies. US citizens, like their leaders, continue to regard the Soviet Union as unfriendly to US interests, untrustworthy in arms-control agreements, and the country most likely among world powers to initiate a war or generally to threaten international stability. Though concerned about the apparent lack of arms-control progress, the majority of US citizens continue to consider their government's current tough tone towards the Soviet Union to be approximately the right one to adopt. Yet, for their information about world events, most turn not to their government, but to their nightly news correspondents and journalists.[4] Moreover, for government action on foreign and security policy, a majority continues to look for increased participation in the process by their elected Congressional representatives.[5] Finally, the general perceptions in the US of the government's responsiveness to popular concerns reached its nadir by 1980.[6] The widespread scepticism regarding the candour and judgments of their elected representatives affects the ability of both US and allied officials to shape and implement security policy. When the US government offers allied officials US positions already known to be controversial at home, allied policy-makers are bound to look at them carefully. The Alliance was badly shaken by US vacillation on the Enhanced Radiation Warhead (ERW) or 'neutron bomb'. But, though a vivid example, it was not unique. Allied scepticism regarding the US ability to sustain East–West trade restrictions and sanctions has been a continuing obstacle to smooth co-operation. The West's policies must be designed at the outset to be more politically sustainable than has been the case to date.

Yet generalized credibility problems may be the 'good news' for the policy-maker. The 'bad news' follows: the volcanoes of domestic unrest which shook Western societies during the 1960s may only be dormant, not extinct. Discussing the US, analysts Seymour Martin Lipset and William Schneider have noted:

The casual observer of the American scene could be forgiven for concluding that the protest era had passed without leaving much of a residue. Even if there is little behavioural evidence of continuing dissent, opinion polls taken regularly by commercial and academic organizations report that the era of alienation did not end with the close of the Vietnam War . . . The sharp increase in negative feelings about the performance of the major institutions of American society, which first became evident during the late 1960s, did not reverse during the 1970s and early 1980s. . . . Americans today voice sentiments more like those expressed ten years ago than twenty years ago . . . alienation, distrust, lack of confidence, and attribution of low levels of legitimacy to social and political institutions .[7]

This is is hardly surprising. The US Census Bureau recently reported that the country's median age in 1980 was 30. The implications of the fact that increasing numbers of the population have grown up in a world of formative experiences and dominant values quite different from those shared by generations currently composing the majority of their political leadership are just beginning to be reviewed.

Who is Following? The Successor Generation
The children of the post-war 'baby boom' have grown up. Policy-makers and analysts have at last begun to appreciate the potential impact upon public attitudes and perceptions of this demographic shift. (The evidence for this is less than clear-cut. Szabo's study[8] uses statistical analysis to show that generational differences determine attitudes. Others, notably the Atlantic Institute in Paris, argue that other factors such as gender determine attitudes to a greater extent than generations. This author, however, continues to believe that policy-makers should pay particular attention to the perspectives and priorities brought by post-war generations to international issues.)

To Western members of this generation, the world they are discovering as they grow up is far more ambiguous in its events and in its lessons than the world experienced by their parents. To begin with, the presence of nuclear weapons has cast a shadow across all considerations of war and peace. The utility and risks of any measure of military confrontation have been evaluated in this light, particularly since no wars of decisive political outcome have been fought in their time. Concepts of economic abundance and material productivity have been tempered by the recognition of finite resources and fragile international access to them. Guarantees of access to such resources increasingly require military measures. Yet the risks of taking such military actions within a security frame-

145

work based upon nuclear weapons are omnipresent. Judgments about the importance of such access have been made accordingly. In this context it is no coincidence that interest in resource conservation and other environmental objectives has grown. The public's framework for evaluating international problems has become considerably broader than that used by much of its leadership. The Washington-based Atlantic Council suggested in its 1981 study that public perspectives have shifted so broadly within the population that a 'successor society' rather than merely a 'successor generation' may now exist.

To Eastern members of this generation, Soviet Communism offers the brutality of the Brezhnev years, but not the gore of Stalin. In both Eastern and Western Europe, the Soviet model has become less threatening to some and less appealing to others.

The ideological schism within Europe appears to have been softened:

Ideologically, if a consensus exists across Europe, it would be somewhere on the left. Young East Europeans would prefer a social democratic middle way or, to a lesser extent, a variant of the Yugoslav model. Post-war West Europeans hope for a new non-bureaucratic left future – a middle way between Sweden and Yugoslavia.[9]

Further, since there is in Western Europe little perception of war with the East as a major threat, 'the Western military alliance is not viewed with great interest or accorded a high priority by the young'.[10] The people of the United States are also becoming less interested in their country's international role and focus increasing attention on problems at home. The belief is growing that the utility of military force is becoming increasingly limited as an instrument of policy.[11] In this climate, the chances, however small, of nuclear weapons being used, whether by miscalculation or by accident, become particularly difficult for the public to accept. In an age characterized by nuclear parity between the super-powers, when even conventional military conflicts between East and West carry the strong risk of nuclear escalation, and

where threats to life often come more directly from domestic terrorist activities than from outside, it is not unreasonable for such perspectives to have developed.

If an immediate threat to the Western way of life were to be identified, it would be the termination of vital energy supplies rather than the risk of armoured attack by troops from the East. Yet the industrial democracies, particularly within the NATO framework, have been remarkably reluctant to expand the boundaries of multilateral co-operation in such a way as to provide protection against this threat. It is hardly surprising, therefore, that NATO's purpose of providing a military shield against aggression appears to be of diminishing priority in the popular mind.

If the Western Alliance is to maintain its relevance to national concerns in the coming decade its members will have to address the economic fears prevalent among their publics, and the Alliance will have to enhance its philosophical flexibility to accommodate the broadening ideological spectrum within the West.

East–West Relations: The Non-Nuclear Landscape

The General View

To Western publics and their leaders, the scene remains one of fundamental competition and tension between East and West. As revealed by a 1982 survey of transatlantic public attitudes contracted by the Atlantic Institute and the *International Herald Tribune*, Soviet activities continue to rank as the main threat to international stability.[12] Yet, as already discussed, military responses to the problems posed by Soviet actions appeal less and less to our publics.

Regardless of the reasons for increased public reluctance to support military actions as an instrument of policy, the sentiment is sharp. The same 1982 survey discovered that Soviet actions were seen as the main threat to international stability. However, a majority of West European publics also saw the US military build-up in response to Soviet actions as the next main threat.

Wariness of military involvement weighs upon attitudes towards two rather distinct

146

categories of action in East–West strategy: those actions implying potential future military involvement; and those involved in the application of economic sanctions and restrictive trade policy.

The Military Option

The continuing problems in Central America, joined recently by those in Chad, have served to remind Western policy-makers of the present domestic constraints upon the ability of Western governments to undertake direct military action on behalf of friendly but non-allied governments. The US case regarding El Salvador is relevant. In the Spring of 1982, at the time of a major US effort to secure Congressional approval of military and economic assistance for El Salvador, a Harris Survey reported that a substantial majority of US citizens (66%) felt that 'if the US does not stop Russian and Cuban efforts to set up a Communist government in El Salvador, then Honduras, Guatemala and other countries in Central America will be next'. Yet by the same substantial margin US citizens considered involvement in El Salvador to be both too similar to the US involvement in Vietnam and equally likely to expose their country to charges of intervention in the internal affairs of Central America.[13] That people were equally divided regarding whether the US was in fact supporting a centrist government there only increased public uncertainty about the wisdom of US involvement. Only a small majority (56%) of those sampled during this same time period felt there was anything the US could do about Soviet involvement in a Central American country.[14] Of those thinking that the US might well be able to take some kind of action, only 11% of those polled favoured military intervention.[15]

The Administration eventually received, after lengthy political manoeuvrings, only a portion of the 1982 assistance requested – and that portion had acquired substantial strings in the process. It is not surprising that, a year later, the conservative Republican Leader of the US House of Representatives, Robert Michel, stated his personal opposition to any expansion of US military involvement in El Salvador. Short of an attack being launched against Florida or Texas by Cuban, Nicaraguan or Salvadorean nationals, or by the Soviet Navy, it is difficult to imagine events capable of reversing US popular opposition to a military involvement in Central America. The impact of domestic preferences has already been impressed upon the list of potential policy options, regardless of the government's reluctance to acknowledge that impact.

Economic Strategy in East–West Relations

As military engagement has dimmed in its public popularity, so has the popularity of economic strategy somewhat brightened, particularly in the US. Yet with the advantages inherent in this 'softer' form of East–West confrontation (reduced risks of military involvement, lower costs in prestige suffered by the action's target) comes the distinct disadvantage to participating Western states of immediate domestic economic costs.

No action available to Western governments for pursuit of their international objectives is without some domestic cost. However, only war shares with trade policy this ability of an action taken in pursuit of a foreign-policy objective to reach directly, quickly and deeply into the public's awareness. Equity of burdens must therefore be addressed squarely in the formulation of any such multilateral policy. Domestic constituencies must not feel that they have been committed by their Government to accept an unfair share of the burdens inherent in a mutually costly, if beneficial, action. Politicians know this; the West's inability to co-operate successfully to date in trade sanctions has reflected this knowledge.

One final element introduces an unmeasurable difficulty into Western efforts to develop trade strategies vis-à-vis the East: the continuing competition for foreign markets among the industrial democracies. A residue of suspicion has been left upon the framework within which any discussions must be conducted.

How then, faced with such obvious obstacles, should policy-makers approach the process of co-ordinating actions with respect to trade policy? Like porcupines desiring to co-operate, they must be very careful. A number of principles should govern efforts to construct and implement multilateral East–West trade guidelines likely to be popularly acceptable:

– *Trade restrictions should not be proposed for the purpose of political signalling.* Western restrictions upon categories of trade with the East should have substantive and measurable impact upon the Soviet Union. If their success cannot be measured, their ability to dissuade the Soviet Union – through the imposition of costs – will also be doubtful. Moreover, without measurable impacts Western domestic constituencies will be unable to judge whether their personal sacrifices were worth the cost. (The costs of this strategy will obviously be heavier for weak economies).

– *The objectives of the restrictions should be clear at the time of their imposition.* Domestic support is considerably more difficult to secure and to sustain if the duration of trade restrictions appears indeterminate. Higher costs are more acceptable if they are to be borne only for a clearly limited time, and for an objective of interest to a majority of a country's populace.

– *Unilaterally imposed trade restrictions should be avoided as being likely to have more difficulty securing domestic support than those imposed multilaterally.* The Western Alliance is publicly justified on the grounds of shared values and mutual self-interest. If one country – so far the US – singles out a Soviet action as sufficiently threatening to justify costly trade restrictions, then there are only two possible ways of explaining to that country's public why its Allies have failed to follow suit: either its own government has erred in its judgment of the threat; or its allies no longer share the same interests. Since US–European co-operation continues to be seen as the key element in safeguarding Western security interests,[16] the explanation left in the US public's mind for their government asking to 'go it alone' in economic actions against the East is that the government has either misjudged the threat, or perhaps cares less than Allied governments about the domestic cost of restrictive trade policies. Neither explanation serves well the government advocating unilateral action.

– *For restrictions requiring multilateral implementation to be effective, they must be co-ordinated multilaterally.* One government cannot be sufficiently familiar with another's economic difficulties to be able to accommodate those difficulties within policy proposals, even if it wished to do so. Further, one government cannot judge for another the acceptable political costs inherent in the implementation of trade restrictions. Nor can one government be familiar enough with the domestic means available to an allied government to soften the impact of trade restrictions at home. Therefore trade restrictions requiring collective imposition should be developed jointly by participants, not presented to them as *fait accomplis*.

– *The restricted trade categories should, wherever possible, be limited to items of substantive military utility.* This category of item would include dual-use technology and commodities, such as the Kama River Truck plant. It ought not, however, to include oil-producing equipment and technology (in the absence of Western agreement on the criteria and objectives to be used in East–West energy-related trade) for reasons given in the previous paragraph. Nor ought it to include shoes that might be worn by soldiers, or bread to feed them.

Incorporating these principles, Western governments should be able to develop East–West trade policies with markedly more success than has been the case to date if, consistent with previous attitudes, public opinion should be supportive.

Consider the US case: the US has often been criticized by Western Europeans as avoiding US trade vulnerabilities while trampling on those of her Allies. Yet US public opinion has in fact shown willingness to accept trade restrictions whose impact would be personally felt.

In September 1982, a substantial majority of US citizens (68%) favoured trade with Russia as a 'basis for keeping peace', as long as military secrets were not included. A smaller proportion (53%) acknowledged that, in the light of Poland's continuation of martial law, it made little sense for the US to export grain to the USSR when export of US equipment for the natural gas pipeline was barred. Finally, almost half of the poll sample judged a grain embargo upon the USSR appropriate if the US wanted to 'get tough' in her efforts to encourage the lifting of martial law.[17]

Current US attitudes are consistent with those held in early 1980, after imposition of a total US embargo on Soviet trade. Weeks after the Soviet Union had invaded Afghanistan, a sampling of public opinion in the conservative farm state of Iowa revealed a majority supporting the grain embargo.[18] US public support for the embargo, particularly its grain component, withered only months later when the embargo's objectives and effectiveness had become questionable. One additional US attitude towards East–West trade has remained constant support for an embargo on high technology trade.

Nuclear Fears

Discussion of shifts in Western security strategy needed to accommodate emerging public preferences would be incomplete without specific comment on the nuclear fears which have so clearly triggered these shifts of preference.

It is self-evident that the Western Alliance's nuclear strategy has substantial problems in the public mind. Why should this be so? Simply put, our publics suspect that their leaders have ceased to share their own horror of nuclear war. As a result, prescriptions regarding nuclear doctrine or force posture are receiving severe public scrutiny. The provocations prompting these suspicions have been widely discussed during previous Institute conferences. In 1982, Harold Brown called our attention to the unintentionally casual manner in which policy-makers had come to discuss concepts of nuclear war-fighting, limited nuclear wars, and 'acceptable' levels of destruction. Henry Kissinger warned a year earlier of Western strategies that, even if successful, promise 'horrendous consequences' for the people they were

designed to protect. In 1982, Michael Howard concluded directly that the West's nuclear strategy may deter its enemies but no longer reassures its peoples.

Yet, despite storm warnings already evident in 1981, the new US Administration either did not recognize or did not fully appreciate their significance. Having campaigned in 1980 for the US Presidency on a platform including the exorcism of both SALT II and the arms-control process which had borne it, President Reagan began his tenure convinced that the US public concurred. This misjudgment of the US public, matched by inattention to allies, has since shaken the Western political structure. The US was the last country in the Alliance to feel the impact, but the MX controversy registered its arrival fully in 1982. This controversy seems likely only to intensify; its outcome remains uncertain.

The US public's dislike of nuclear weapons has remained high and fairly constant throughout the years since the nuclear attacks on Hiroshima and Nagasaki.[19] Public attitudes in Europe towards the use of nuclear weapons have generally been no warmer. One can conclude, then, that the recent uproar has not been triggered by a shift in values. A more likely explanation is that, when US nuclear superiority disappeared, it took with it the public perception that the West's threat to resort to nuclear weapons was an unarguable deterrent to Soviet military provocation of any kind. That Western nuclear strategists devoted exceptional energy to accommodating nuclear doctrine to reflect the emergence of parity subtly reinforced this public unease. However, for much of the 1970s the public controlled its unease, no doubt waiting to see if the uncertainties of parity were more manageable than they appeared at first sight. The US SALT II debate became a platform for demolishing confidence in the Carter Administration's wisdom with respect to nuclear policy. Yet, even if one discounts that particular episode, the public confidence that *any* US government could be trusted to manage nuclear planning competently on its own has disappeared. The problem of regaining general government credibility for judgments on nuclear policy and arms control remains with

Western governments. That the current US Administration's response to public pressures has continued to appear reluctant and cosmetic has not helped to calm these public fears.

Yet, even if the West develops strategies that rely less on nuclear weapons for deterrence, the US nuclear deterrent will continue to remain the central element in Western security planning. Public fears of its risks must, therefore, be calmed. Measures perceived to be of more than cosmetic nature will be needed.

Four measures suggest themselves:

– *Reduce nuclear systems which rely upon the threat of early use, particularly when their military utility is at best marginal.* At issue here are the short-range 'battlefield' nuclear systems. The US Senate has already endorsed this approach. NATO's Nuclear Planning Group announced plans to reduce short-range nuclear weapons in Europe (by a further 1,400) on 28 October 1983, though the decision drew much less public attention than it merited. In a July 1983 vote, during debate on the FY 1984 Defence Budget, Senators approved an amendment by Senator Nunn to deny the Administration's request for funding for a modernized 155mm nuclear artillery shell. Funding was earmarked instead for improved conventional munitions. Arguing for his amendment, Senator Nunn stated, 'We must invest funds in creating a larger firebreak between conventional and nuclear warfare and in decreasing a great overreliance on the early use of nuclear weapons as a key to NATO deterrence'.[20] Sixty-seven Senators supported Nunn; only thirty dissented. The debate, unusually well attended by Senators on the floor, has enhanced general US appreciation of the problem. Expressing similar sentiments, in 1982 the North Atlantic Assembly (NAA) parliamentarians recommended reductions of short-range nuclear systems, noting that such an action could only improve the political climate surrounding deployment of the cruise and *Pershing* II missiles. NATO's publics need to see action demonstrating government commitment to reduce reliance on nuclear weapons, accompanied by greater caution regarding the risks arising from their modes of deployment.

– *Reduce reliance where possible upon the roles played by land-based nuclear systems of either strategic or intermediate range.* Only sea-based and some air-breathing systems operate on empty battlefields. The visibility of almost all land-based systems serves as a symbolic reminder of the general risks of nuclear war. Once reminded, the observer remembers also that the symbol is a target.

– *Restore public confidence in the nuclear arms control process.* Nuclear modernization – perhaps, indeed, deterrence itself – is not acceptable to the public when pursued outside a durable, productive arms-control framework. The impression must be avoided that, whether by intent or coincidence of timing, existing arms-control agreements are being chipped away while negotiations on new ones are stalled. For example, if the US is to initiate bilateral discussions regarding possible Soviet SALT I violations (as appears to be her intent) then largely acceptable, previously negotiated but as yet unratified agreements, such as the Threshold Test Ban Treaty (TTBT), should be submitted for ratification. Similarly, if START is stalled, then smaller and more limited agreements, such as a bilateral one-year freeze of testing of new MIRVed land-based strategic systems, should be attempted. Western public confidence in US and allied arms-control motivations cannot withstand stagnation of present arms-control efforts accompanied by the continual erosion of the framework which preceded them.

– *Avoid official pronouncements, and offhand comments by government officials, suggesting that policy-makers are paying more attention to ways to fight nuclear wars than to deter them.* Recommending the new procurement of nuclear systems acknowledged to be exceptionally vulnerable to an attack only exacerbates the public's fears. Loose talk of shovels and sandbags as survival systems exacerbates the problem.

Taken together, or perhaps even individually, these measures would begin to restore public confidence that their leaders are pursuing policies designed to protect them from nuclear war, not during one. There is no evidence as yet that a candidate's position on nuclear weapons and arms control has been the determining factor in a voter's willingness to support him or her. Perhaps this situation will continue. Nevertheless, public doubts and fears, already widespread, seem likely to persist and will have immeasurable impact upon the credibility of policy-makers in all areas of security policy if not addressed.

Conclusion

This discussion may appear to have detailed, in large part, not a two-way street joining the policy-makers and their publics, but a one-way street, all from the public's direction. This is not so. As stated at the outset, in democracies the relationship between policy-makers and their publics must see both performing as speaker and audience, depending upon the circumstances. The political leaderships, and their supporting government staffs, are charged with the responsibility both to lead their publics as well as to represent their concerns. In ordinary times it should not be necessary for those with policy responsibility continually to measure their constituencies' preferences. Indeed to do so would be impractical and would often produce firm public preferences when too little is still generally known.

Yet these are not ordinary times. These are times of transition and flux in demography as well as in circumstance. Such times require that closer attention be paid to what would otherwise be routine information about our societies, and about people's attitudes. Fundamental attitudes do not change from year to year. However they do change, and have been changing, with the decades. In large part, governments have been preoccupied with meeting continuing crises at their own level of concern and responsibility; they have been lax about checking on what has been happening behind them. Gaps have developed between the policy-maker and the public – gaps in perception, gaps in priorities, gaps in objectives. Western governments are still far short of a crisis point in relationships with their publics, but it is not too soon for

steps to be taken to ensure that the interests of both groups are better aligned. For democracies to function properly, this is essential.

Consider the possible implications of a failure to do so. The US nuclear guarantee is, and has always been, the cornerstone of Western co-operative actions. Yet the people of the United States, suspicious that their Allies are exporting their own unemployment to the US through unfair trade practices and policies, might some day come to question the rationale of accepting any degree of nuclear risk to protect countries perceived as insensitive to US domestic economic difficulties. Similarly, the leaders of the United States must recognize the implications of the fact that the US can no longer safeguard Western interests through essentially unilateral largesse. The surplus of US economic and military resources which characterized most of the post-war period no longer exists. Thus, the importance of multilateral co-operation – with inevitable domestic implications for each participating country – must be considered fully during policy debates. US leaders must afford the domestic constraints of their Allies the same respect demanded for their own problems. The 'two-way street' of political discourse and compromise in international considerations has become a requirement for policy both within the Western countries and among them.

Finally, an additional difficulty confronts the West's political leaderships if their policies do not reflect improved co-operation and responsiveness to domestic concerns. Dissatisfied constituents are more prone than they once were to listen to the propaganda and alternative critiques of their government's opponents, both at home and abroad. In this age of vast national and international information networks, governments will almost never be in a position to regain their ability to determine the information to which their publics will have access in the field of foreign affairs, but governments can develop present policies to increase people's confidence that their leaders are generally responsive to their concerns.

At this time of increasingly diverse domestic values and perspectives, improvements in the relationship between governments and the governed will certainly not eliminate contention over policies; but strengthening communications channels between the public and their leaders will make the inevitable disagreements considerably more manageable than they seem to be at the moment

NOTES

[1] For an excellent discussion of this issue see Stanley R. Sloan's paper 'Sources of Differing American and European Attitudes toward East–West Relations: Implications for the Atlantic Alliance', presented to the Conference entitled 'Toward a New East–West Balance', Knokke, Belgium, 9 May 1981 (unpublished).

[2] John R. Rielly (ed.), *American Public Opinion and US Foreign Policy 1983*, released by the Chicago Council on Foreign Relations, February 1983, p. 23.

[3] The Atlantic Council, *The Successor Generation*, (Washington DC: The Atlantic Council, 1981).

[4] *Op. cit.* in note 2, p. 36.

[5] *Ibid*, p. 33–4.

[6] Seymour Martin Lipset and William Schneider, *The Confidence Gap: Business, Labor and Government in the Public Mind* (New York: The Free Press, 1983), p. 25.

[7] *Ibid*, p. 3.

[8] Stephen F. Szabo, *The Successor Generation: International Perspectives of Postwar Europeans* (London: Butterworths, 1983).

[9] *Ibid.*, p. 171.

[10] *Ibid*, pp. 172, excerpted from discussion on pp. 167–73.

[11] *Op. cit.* in note 3.

[12] Survey conducted for the *International Herald Tribune* and Atlantic Institute, released October 1982.

[13] Harris Survey released 1 April, 1982.

[14] CBS/*New York Times* poll, released March 20, 1982.

[15] *Ibid.*

[16] *Op. cit.* in note 12.

[17] Harris Survey, released 29 September 1982.

[18] CBS/*New York Times* poll, released 21 January 1980.

[19] Carl Ladd, 'The Freeze Framework', *Public Opinion*, August/September 1982, pp. 20, 41). (In November 1946, Gallup found that 20% cent of the populace thought their country 'should stop making atom bombs and destroy all those we have now.' A plurality in 1950 favoured efforts to reach an agreement with Russia to control the atom bomb 'before we try to make a hydrogen bomb', and in 1958, a plurality endorsed a US–Soviet treaty banning nuclear weapons testing.)

[20] *US Congressional Record*, Proceedings of 13 July 1983, pp. S9852–S9862.

The Role of the Third World in the East–West Relationship: I

DR MOHAMMED AYOOB

In order to understand the interaction between the Third World, on the one hand and the 'East–West Relationship' (a euphemism for super-power relations), on the other, one must first clearly delineate super-power objectives in the international arena as well as try to build a coherent picture of the most pressing needs of third-world countries, and particularly their governments. For the central theme in super-power–Third World relations is the interaction of the former's objectives with the latter's requirements – economic, military and political.

Despite the largely adversary character of US–Soviet relations, it is relatively easy to categorize their objectives and accord them certain priorities. It becomes a more difficult task when one attempts to do the same for the vast collectivity called the third-world. However, third-world states do share certain basic characteristics: economic underdevelopment, weak state structures, weak political institutions, narrowly-based regimes, intra-regional antagonisms (which are quite often the product of colonially-drawn boundaries); easy permeability by external forces, and the weak linkage of their security concerns with those of the security of the international system as a whole. Taken together, these characteristics provide a remarkable degree of similarity to the most urgent demands they make in the context of their relationship – both individual and collective – with the super-powers.

As far as the super-powers are concerned, their major international concerns can be grouped into three categories, and in the following order of importance: the maintenance of the central strategic balance in a form sufficiently stable not to upset the technological and military equilibrium in such a fashion as to make it unacceptable to either super-power; the management of intra-alliance and inter-alliance relations in such a way as to provide a degree of cohesion within the Alliances (NATO and the Warsaw Pact) which is sufficient for the maintenance of a common stance on issues considered vital to the stability of the strategic balance and to the interests of the super-powers; and competition for power and influence in the 'grey areas' of the globe, viz. the Third World, to demonstrate their global reach as well as to prevent the adversary super-power from gaining 'unfair advantage' on the global political chessboard. (In addition to this general requirement of 'global power politics', specific considerations, like access to oil and strategic minerals, strategically located waterways and the need for bases, also determine super-power policies towards the Third World.)

It becomes clear from this categorization that, while the competition for power and influence in the Third World is important to the super-powers to maintain their image as 'global powers' and to gain access to certain scarce and strategically important resources, it is an objective or interest that certainly has a lesser priority for them than the maintenance of the strategic balance (which is vital for the maintenance of systemic security and for their status as super-powers) and the management of intra-alliance and inter-alliance relations. Since the security of the major European states and of the two Alliances are inextricably intertwined with the maintenance of systemic security (as defined by the super-powers), it is obvious that intra-alliance and inter-alliance relations take priority over even the most salient and critical third-world issues. This is the major reason why conflicts within the Third World are considered permissible by the super-powers, while those in Europe are totally ruled out.

The Concerns of Third-world States

When one turns to the Third World and looks at the minimum common concerns – which also form the basic concerns – of most third-world states or regimes, one is struck by the highly introverted nature of these concerns. These are related to three broad but inter-related issue-areas. The first is the problem of internal security, which includes both the security of state structures as presently constituted and the security of regimes which preside over these structures. The second is the problem of external security, largely the produce of regional antagonisms, often themselves the product of colonially-drawn boundaries which have created artificial states and have in many cases given rise to irredentist or separatist phenomena (in this context the links between problems of external and internal security are obvious). The third is the problem of distorted economic development – and, in most cases, of mass poverty – which are related to the colonial experience and the social and economic structures created or augmented by that experience, as well as to the way the international economy (and, therefore, the national economies in the Third World) continues to function today, exacerbating the gap between rich and poor countries and between rich and poor within individual third-world states. (There is an obvious link here between economic and social issues and the problems of security.)

From this categorization, it becomes clear that the inequality of the encounter between the super-powers and third-world states, individually or collectively (which is in any case obvious if one uses any of the traditional indices for the measurement of power), is further exacerbated by the great need on the part of many third-world regimes to acquire super-power patronage (in one or more of its dimensions – economic, military and political) and by the inability of most third-world states – in fact, of whole regions – to affect more than marginally the issues that are considered vital by the super-powers and which are central to the international system as it is

presently constituted. Therefore, the super-power–Third World relationship has been, for the last three decades and more, largely a one-way street, with the former defining broadly the importance of third-world regions, conflicts and issues, as well as setting limits to their own involvement or intervention in them.

Given the peripheral nature of the Third World to vital East–West concerns, the super-powers have tended to permit, even to encourage, conflicts in third-world regions in order to serve their own purposes. Not that local issues prompting such conflicts (both intra-state and inter-state) have been lacking in the Third World. However, these have been exacerbated as a result of super-power intervention, an intervention designed, at least in part, to let off steam thus helping to cool the temperature around the core issues chiefly relevant to the central balance and vital to super-power interests. Conflicts in the Third World are, therefore, considered permissible by the super-powers, as long as they do not threaten to draw them into direct confrontation with each other. The only conflict in the Third World currently with this potential is the Arab-Israeli conflict (or, more appropriately, the problem of Israel in the Middle East), but this has a unique dimension to which we shall return later. The problem of the white minority regime in South Africa also has this potential, although the current saliency of that issue is considerably less than that of its counterpart in the Middle East.

There are, of course, a number of other reasons that lead the super-powers to tolerate and, quite often, to encourage conflicts in the Third World. These include a whole range of interests from arms sales, through the demonstration of 'credibility' to allies, to ensuring access to strategic raw materials. But what is important for our purpose here is to note the one-way nature of the super-power–Third World relationship on this score. This stems, as I have argued earlier, from the inability of third-world countries – even the largest, the most powerful or the most closely allied of them – to affect the central equation in the international system in a significant way. Thus the super-powers have had the best of

154

both worlds in this relationship so far. On the one hand, they have been able to insulate their own (and inter-alliance) relations from the uncertainties and insecurities prevalent in the Third World. On the other, they have been able to play out their rivalry and competition – even by means of proxy wars – in the 'grey areas' of the globe, and in doing so they have been able to test, among other things, the 'capability' and the 'will' of the adversary power and the limits of its political and military tolerance – all this, of course, at the expense of third parties.

The Third World and the Super-power Balance

This is a pattern that has lasted for three decades. As a result people have come to expect that it would have developed a life of its own and that this pattern of interaction could continue indefinitely *barring radical changes, or expectations thereof, in the super-power balance.* This is an understandable and, one must admit, a realistic position, except that it does not give enough weight to the qualifying clause at the end of the statement.

During the last three decades the central balance has remained insulated from the instabilities and insecurities in the Third World and the crises and conflicts on the periphery because of the basic stability of that balance. However, since this stability has been largely dependent upon technological factors, the existing equilibrium – given the escalatory nature of modern technology since the Industrial Revolution – is inherently fragile. Indications are already beginning to surface – whether in President Reagan's 'Star Wars' speech or in Andrei Gromyko's increasingly alarmist pronouncements – that the technological equilibrium may be in much greater danger of being upset, even if temporarily, than one has come to expect over the last thirty years.

What is even more important, perceptions in Washington and Moscow are taking on more and more alarmist hues. Therefore, even if a technological disequilibrium of major proportions does not actually occur, the increasing apprehensions among super-power policy-makers that it might do so

towards the end of the present decade could introduce (and is probably introducing already) an element of grave uncertainty in their calculations. These apprehensions could distort reality or could even turn into self-fulfilling prophecies. In either case, if present trends continue, they can be expected to introduce serious problems in super-power relations and increase sharply the uncertainties surrounding the central balance.

If this scenario unfolds in the second half of the 1980s – and it is not improbable, given the present noises coming out of both Washington and Moscow – it might provide the Third World – with all its conflicts and its insecurities – with the opportunity to impinge upon the super-power equation much more dramatically than it has been able to do so far. This would not happen because of any inherent change in the nature of the Third World or in its concrete importance to the super-powers. It would result from the 'state of nerves' that super-power policy-makers can be expected to suffer from when they begin to work on the assumption that the central balance is on the verge of serious disequilibrium as a result of technological escalation. In a state of great nervous tension over the likely effects of strategic imbalance (whether actual, projected or merely perceived), super-power policy-makers are likely to exaggerate out of all proportion the significance of their continuing competition and involvement in the Third World. This could provide the Third World with a convenient entry point from which it (or particular segments of it) might be able to affect the course of the super-power relationship in the late 1980s and early 1990s to a much greater extent than it has been able to do during the last three decades.

The Quest for Autonomy

There is another factor which might affect the nature of the Third World's interaction with the super-powers. This is what I call the 'quest for autonomy' on the part of at least some of the more important third-world states and their regimes. The initial impetus for non-alignment, particularly as it was given substance in Indian foreign policy under Nehru, came to a large extent from the aspiration of certain third-world elites to act independently of super-power control in the international arena. This was seen as a necessary corollary of political decolonization. However, the limits to such aspirations were set by the varying degrees of technological, economic and military dependence, of even the largest and most powerful third world countries on the super-powers and their European allies. Although institutionalized in the Non-Aligned Movement, the initial thrust of non-alignment towards genuine autonomous action and development was considerably blunted by the prevailing realities of dependence and inequality within the international system.

These aspirations for autonomy received a fillip in the early 1970s from the Vietnamese success in preventing the US from achieving her political objectives in Indochina. But, once again, the example lost its force when Vietnam found herself stuck in the Indochinese (particularly Kampuchean) quagmire and was sucked into the Sino-Soviet conflict. The Iranian Revolution of 1979 exalted this aspiration for autonomy to the status of an ideology, not merely by proclaiming that Iran's foreign policy would be based on the dictum 'Neither East nor West', but even more by legitimizing the destruction of the old order and its replacement by a new one based on an authentic, indigenous political phenomenon – radical, populist Islam. While the post-revolutionary rulers of Iran have, over the last four and half years, had to make considerable adjustments to, and compromises with, the prevailing realities within the international system, enough of the ideological kernel of the Islamic Revolution remains to make it still sufficiently attractive to those forces which see their future linked to such autonomous political transformations in the Third World, and particularly in its Muslim component.

It is probably too early at this stage to pass final judgement on this quest which underlies all reasonably successful and popular ideologies in the Third World, from nationalism to radical Islam. While the political manifestations of this aspiration have been disturbing for the super-powers – notice the initial US denunciation of non-alignment and the initial Soviet refusal to accept the legitimacy of a 'Third Way', as well as the temporarily traumatic effect of Vietnam on US society – they have failed to affect, except in a marginal way, the East–West relationship. If the search for autonomy (which, as Iran demonstrated, in order to be successful must encompass social, cultural and economic as well as political dimensions of national life) becomes the central issue of third-world political development in the next decade, it may be able to make some impact on issues of vital super-power concern. Short of that, however, while events such as the Iranian Revolution may cause considerable concern in the US and USSR periodically, their life-span as live issues in super-power calculations is bound to be limited. Again, while such episodes may have a cumulative effect on the super-powers' psyche over a period of time, unless there is a sustained momentum in the Third World towards 'autonomist' goals, the immediate effect of each of these episodes on the super-power's relationship and on their interaction with the Third World, individually and collectively, is likely to be ephemeral in character.

The Middle East and Southern Africa

However, there are two regions ('crisis areas', if you like) which, even short of a serious disequilibrium in the central balance or of a serious quest for 'autonomy' in the Third World, have the capacity to affect the super-power relationship in the 1980s and 1990s more than other parts of the Third World. These are the Middle East and Southern Africa. Although both these regions are rich in scarce resources (oil on the one hand, strategic minerals on the other), this is not the major reason for their importance to, or their greater leverage *vis-à-vis* the super-powers. Of course, the oil and the minerals are important in a resource-hungry world (particularly the developed part of it), but what is more important is the fact that the dominant conflicts in both these regions, and particularly one of the principal parties to each of them, have major links with important constituencies within one of the super-powers, viz the United States. This has meant that a societal consensus within the

US has already evolved (in the case of the Middle East) or is in the process of evolving (as in the case of Southern Africa) which commits (or is expected to commit) the US in such a fashion as to link the two conflicts symbiotically with the central concerns of US policy-makers.

This is clear in the case of Israel in the Middle East. It is less clear in the case of South Africa. But, if the Israeli experience and the current policy of the Reagan Administration towards South Africa are any guide, the US–South African relationship (ostensibly portrayed in the form of a 'strategic consensus' against the Soviet Union) can be expected to follow in the path of US–Israeli relations. The reasons which prevailed in the case of the US commitment to Israel have little to do with the Soviet 'threat' to the Middle East (although, of late, they have been portrayed, at least partially, in those terms). They were primarily related to the nature of the Israeli state, for Israel is – in terms of her ideological origins, her pattern of colonization in Palestine, the organization of her society and polity, the composition of her elite (even under *Likud*), and her links with strong and important European and American constituencies – a European state. The comparisons with South Africa are striking, once you substitute southern Africa for Palestine and Afrikaner for *Likud* in the above statement.

It is true that US affinities with South Africa have not taken on such salience as they have done in the case of Israel, but an important reason for this is the fact that South Africa – despite the rhetoric of the African states – has not faced such grave challenges to her legitimacy as Israel has done from within the region she inhabits. Once these challenges escalate, the affinities are likely to be brought into sharper focus.

Moreover, because of the nature of these two states and of their regimes, the Israeli-Arab conflict and the escalating tensions between the South African regime and the majority of its population (as well as the front-line states) are not really third-world conflicts in the sense that the term is applied to other conflicts, like those between India and Pakistan or between Ethiopia and Somalia. For, while both Israel and South Africa are *in* the Third World, they are not *of* it. It is this factor which explains the tremendous inequality in the power equation between Israel and South Africa, on the one hand, and their adversaries, on the other, the great leverage both Israel and South Africa have with at least one of the super-powers, and the strong linkage (existing and potential) between the security of these two states and issues considered vital to the super-power. The importance of the Middle East and southern Africa to the super-powers is therefore largely a function of the importance of Israel and South Africa (in a quite fundamental way, based on a firm societal consensus) to the US – an importance which rivals that of Western Europe and, in the case of Israel, might have even surpassed it.

This has provided the regional pro-Western actors with a large margin of manoeuvre and advantage over their challengers – particularly since, despite Soviet surface-to-air missiles in Syria and Cuban troops in Angola, there is no similar societal consensus in the Soviet Union in favour of her local clients in the Middle East or southern Africa. In the final analysis, they are expendable as far as the USSR is concerned, and all are fully aware of this fact. Moreover, given the fundamentally 'third-world' character of these societies – in terms of political organization, technological advancement and economic management, – they are, at least at present, no match for the European-dominated societies of Israel and South Africa.

But this short-term advantage for her allies is likely to be a major long-term disadvantage for the US herself, particularly since, as a global power, the major thrust of her diplomatic activity in the Third World is aimed at winning friends and influencing people. This objective, irrespective of the stability of the central balance, is likely to remain; any perceived, projected or actual disequilibrium in the central balance is only going to make it an even more pressing necessity. However, if as is now the case in the Middle East and possibly could be the case by the late 1980s and early 1990s in southern Africa, the US is left with the principal 'pariah' states as her principal allies in the two strategically important and most conflict-prone regions in the Third World, her diplomatic and political thrust is bound to be considerably blunted, particularly if viewed in a long-term time frame. While the US might be able to win ephemeral diplomatic victories (more 'Camp Davids' for example) anti-Americanism in a deeper sense is expected to grow particularly within societies that are undergoing rapid mass politicization. That such feelings are barely below the political surface even in third-world countries most friendly to the US was demonstrated very dramatically by the burning down of the US Embassy in Pakistan in November 1979 at a time when the military rulers in Islamabad were engaged in crucial negotiations with the US for arms assistance to their country.

While it is true that for the super-powers the competition for influence in the Third World takes a tertiary position to the maintenance of the strategic balance and issues of intra- and inter-alliance relationship, nonetheless, if the US is in this game of global competition, she should realize the long-term advantages she has conceded to the Soviet Union by backing the wrong (though 'winning') horses in both the Middle East and southern Africa. In fact, it is the US posture in the Middle East that has allowed the Soviet Union to get away with the invasion of Afghanistan relatively easily at the bar of Muslim opinion in the world. For, as long as Israel is in occupation of Arab territories (including Arab Jerusalem), and as long as the US is perceived to be conniving at this, Soviet excesses in Afghanistan will be seen in less harsh a light than would have been the case otherwise.

It is in this context that policy-makers in the US need to be aware of the principal contradiction between their objectives (extending US influence and countering Soviet influence), on the one hand, and Israeli and South African objectives, on the other. For the latter, it is imperative that they demonstrate to the US that in their respective regions they are the *only* strategic assets and the *only* dependable allies that the US has. What better way to demonstrate this than to drive all their regional antagonists into the arms of the Soviet Union? Israel would welcome (would indeed facilitate the process of) King Hussein turning to the USSR, just as South Africa would not be averse to seeing President Kaunda turn in the same direction (she has already seen to this in the case of the leading African nationalist organization in South Africa). It is for the US to decide whether she wants to achieve the same objective. If not, then she must reassess drastically the direction and long-term effects of her policy towards both the Middle East and southern Africa. This reassessment becomes particularly pressing for the US at this juncture because the Soviet Union has, during the second half of the 1970s, reached a stage in terms of her global reach – both politically and militarily – that the US had achieved in the 1950s. In the 1980s, therefore, the USSR is in the process of committing the same blunders of over-extension, arrogance and insensitivity to regional concerns, that the US had committed in the 1960s in the Third World.

However, in the 1980s the US may not be able to emulate the Soviet success of the 1960s in capitalizing upon American blunders by capitalizing in turn upon Soviet mistakes. For invariably the latter would be mitigated, if not totally condoned, at least in the Middle East and southern Africa, by the much more glaring US sins of omission and commission in these two most conflict-prone areas of the Third World. It may very well be that the US will have to live with this (at best unsatisfactory, at worst quite explosive) situation for the next few decades, because of the consensus in her society in support of Israeli objectives on the one hand and, potentially, South African objectives on the other. Alternatively, the US leadership must work hard in the 1980s at changing this consensus in favour of one that is not merely even-handed but is more in keeping with long-term Western interests (and there is much greater recognition of this in Western Europe, especially as regards the Middle East) in the two critical regions of the Third World. For, while the Third World may not be as central to super-power concerns as the strategic balance of intra- and inter-alliance relationships, political and military manoeuvrability on a global scale has become the hallmark of super-power status. In fact, this is what distinguishes the super-powers from the great powers of the pre-war era. In the absence of a serious US reassessment of her policies towards the Middle East and southern Africa, her global manoeuvrability may become increasingly compromised by the time we enter the 1990s. One can be reasonably sure that this in turn would be reflected in popular perceptions – particularly in the Third World – regarding the status of the US as a global super-power.

Conclusion

The major reason why the US has been, and continues to be, at a disadvantage *vis-à-vis* the Soviet Union in her relationship with strategic regions of the Third World is her inability to come to grips with that segment of the political dynamics of the Third World which is independent of super-power control or even of sustained super-power influence. As the events of the last two decades indicate, this has been a growing and increasingly important segment of the Third World's political dynamics and is related to the processes of social and political change within third-world societies and regions as well as to their capacity, however uneven and limited, to respond to the challenges facing them without reference to the interests or promptings of external powers and forces.

This inability on the part of US decision-makers and policy analysts is related to their preoccupation with the effects of these dynamics on the super-power balance, rather than with their causes. As a result, their perceptions of third-world political realities often become very distorted. In fact, it is because of the inability of the US to understand the motivations of third-world actors (and to fashion her policies accordingly) that the Soviet Union appears to US policy-

makers to be the major cause as well as the major beneficiary of regional instabilities and conflicts. Such a conclusion, more often than not, prompts the US to design her response in terms of what she perceives to be a 'Soviet threat' to her position – be it in Central America, the Middle East or southern Africa. In the process, not only are the basic issues lost sight of, but the US, because of her lack of empathy for the concerns of third-world actors, falls far short of even her proclaimed principal objectives, namely the containment or erosion of the Soviet position in important third-world regions. In fact, because of the mistaken assumptions in the US and the policies that flow from them, quite often the Soviet position is strengthened rather than weakened. Where the Soviet position is eroded, it is the result, once again, of autonomous factors at work within the Third World rather than of US policies.

The only way for the US to reverse this trend is to concentrate the formidable analytical capabilities of her policy-making apparatus on deciphering the fundamental causes of conflict and instability in the Third World and on discerning the primary reasons for the deep-seated anti-American and anti-Western feelings in strategic areas of the Third World like the Middle East. Only then might she be in a position to initiate policies which are more responsive to the central concerns and dilemmas of important third-world actors. In the absence of such attempts at empathy and understanding, and with the consequent continuance of linkages between the US and, for example, the 'pariah' states in the Middle East and southern Africa, the US will continue to remain, at least as far as long-term trends are concerned, in a position of disadvantage in the super-power competition for influence in large parts of the Third World, including some of its most strategically important regions.

159

The Role of the Third World in the East–West Relationship: II

PROFESSOR HELIO JAGUARIBE DE MATTOS

Features of the Third World

As is well known, the expression 'Third World' opposes the underdeveloped societies, mostly of the southern hemisphere (South), to the market industrialized societies, mostly of the northern hemisphere (North, or 'First World') and the centrally-planned economies, the self-labelled 'socialist' regimes (sometimes called the 'Second World').

The Third World is a vast and rather complex cluster of countries, presenting so many varieties that it is more easily characterized by its negative aspects, connected to general underdevelopment, than by specific common traits.[1] Diversity in the Third World concerns quantitative aspects, such as territorial size, population, or total or per capita gross national product (GNP), as well as qualitative features, such as cultural origins and patterns of national development. Some, like China and Cuba, are both second-world centrally-managed societies and third-world countries at the same time. Others, like some of those in Latin America, are both characteristically Western societies *and* third-world countries. Most of the OPEC countries, on the other hand, have higher GNPs than many first-world countries, but remain, even in terms of their economic structure, typical third-world societies.

Therefore, in order to consider sensibly the immense variety of the Third World, it is necessary to differentiate the countries of the group according to some basic typological variables. Most relevant among these are the ones which concern (1) levels of development, (2) levels of national viability, (3) cultural origins and characteristics, and (4) levels of international activity.

In terms of comparative development, the Third World may again be divided into four main groups. At the top are societies with a comparatively high level of industrialization and overall development (Argentina, Brazil, Mexico) but which we place in the Third World mostly for socio-political reasons. At the bottom are extremely poor agricultural societies (Ethiopia, Bangladesh). In the middle are, on the one hand, several semi-industrialized societies (Chile, Colombia, Egypt) and, on the other hand, the generally underdeveloped but oil-rich societies of the OPEC group.

In terms of national viability, a three-level division differentiates countries with high general viability (Brazil), with medium viability (Peru) and with low national viability (Central American countries).

Cultural origins and characteristics constitute an important variable but in a more indirect sense. They relate to the way in which societies with different cultural traditions (Buddhist, Islamic, animist) react to the processes of modernization.

A variable which is particularly important for the subject of the present study is the level of international activity. This tends to reflect the three previous sets of variables. As might be expected, societies with a comparatively high level of development, a high level of national viability and cultural origins and traits favourable to their modernization tend to present a higher level of international activity than societies with the opposite traits.

In terms of their levels of international activity, third-world societies present three basic positions: (1) internationally active (Brazil, India); (2) regionally active (Venezuela, Egypt, Vietnam) and (3) reactive (most of the remaining countries). This variation in international activity is not a peculiar feature of third-world societies; it corresponds to a general differentiation of international behaviour, applicable to all

160

countries.[2] Yet, as is to be expected, internationally active third-world countries will tend to play a more modest role than large first-world powers, such as Japan or West Germany, not to mention the super-powers. Compared with second-world countries, however, some internationally active third-world countries, such as Brazil or India, have more independent activities and influence than any in the socialist group, except, of course, the Soviet Union.

In terms of regional activity, the relationship between third-world countries and comparable countries in the two other worlds presents a different picture. Regionally active third-world countries, such as Colombia and Venezuela in Latin America, Egypt, Israel and Saudi Arabia in the Middle East, Nigeria in Africa, and Vietnam in south-east Asia, are more active in regional affairs than some first-world countries, such as Italy or Holland, or some second-world countries such as Hungary and Czechoslovakia. In the latter case, this is due to the differences between the Western and the Soviet international systems. Most third-world countries belong, economically, to the periphery of the Western (American) international system. Because such countries enjoy a certain amount of international autonomy, it is possible for them to preserve a corresponding degree of politically independent activity at international or regional level. By contrast, the countries of the Soviet bloc tend to enjoy greater economic autonomy, but have very little political independence, with the possible exception of Romania.

To an extent, the greater regional activity of certain third-world countries (*vis-à-vis* comparable first-world countries) is due to the fact that the latter are predominantly European societies, well integrated into their region. They have developed a comprehensive regional machinery for the mutual adjustment of interests, and therefore depend much less on conventional diplomatic or formal inter-state negotiations.

The East–West Dimension

The East–West relationship presents a typical inter-imperial character in which each of the two super-powers is an imperial centre, with its own periphery. Such a condition brings about a double imperial pattern: (1) the inter-imperial pattern, opposing (in a conflict/co-operation relationship) the American bloc to the Soviet bloc; and (2) the intra-imperial pattern, opposing, in each bloc (in an asymmetric co-operation/conflict relationship) the respective super-power to its periphery.[3]

This brief study cannot analyse the characteristics of the two imperial systems. It is enough to stress that the Soviet bloc is politically tight but permits a considerable degree of economic autonomy to the dependent countries, which thus form a multi-layered periphery. The American bloc, on the other hand, is relatively tight in economic terms but politically flexible, forming also a multi-layered periphery. Moreover, in the American bloc centrality is functionally differentiated: strategically, it is concentrated in the US; economically, centrality is shared by the US, although unevenly, with the other members of the OECD.

The two imperial systems tend to cover the world, but they have not yet succeeded – and may never succeed – in encompassing all countries. China, for example, has reached an independent condition of regional primacy.[4] Other countries, to a greater or lesser extent, have managed to retain international autonomy: Argentina and Brazil in Latin America; Nigeria in Africa; India, Iran and Pakistan in Asia.

International relations take place according to two main variables: variables of position; and variables of international activity. In terms of position, countries vary from formal alignment with one of the super-powers to formal non-alignment, with some *de facto* intermediate positions. As already noted, in terms of international activity countries present three different levels: internationally active, regionally active, or simply reactive.

The Reactive Case

Reactive countries constitute by far the largest group numerically. They, too, tend to be characterized by negative rather than positive specific traits. Because of the modesty of their resources and their lack of major international interests and means for efficient international action, they do not pursue relevant objectives in the international arena.

They simply tend to react, mostly within their own boundaries, to external events which may affect their domestic interests.

Within this broad group of reactive countries, it is necessary to pay particular attention to those where crucial national issues tend to have important external consequences. They include countries trying to break colonial ties and to acquire or consolidate their national independence (most African and many Asian countries) and countries that are trying to overcome oppressive oligarchies, allied to and supported by powerful external forces (as in Central America). In both cases, the direct or indirect interference of powerful external forces confronts these states with challenges that far surpass their capacity to withstand them. To match such challenges requires the revolutionary mobilization of all possible human and material domestic resources and a large measure of compensatory external aid.

The United States, the inheritor in many ways of the legacy of European nineteenth-century colonialism, is the current political *status quo* power in the world. She is the leading economic force in the international market, with consequential economic *status quo* interests. Internationally she is an untypical society, in terms of her historical formation and experience, including strong ethnic-cultural biases. Because she is associated with *status quo* forces and interests all over the world outside the Soviet bloc, she feels herself menaced or negatively affected by all revolutionary movements which are not anti-Soviet.[5] This explains, in general terms, the animosity of the United States towards the anti-colonial movements of national liberation in Asia and Africa after World War II, as well as her past and current antagonism with respect to the anti-oligarchical movements of social-political liberation in Latin America, particularly in Central America. The Soviet Union, independently of other covert or overt motivations and of her own ethnic-cultural biases, tends naturally to support such anti-colonial and anti-oligarchical liberation movements. Marxism–Leninism, as the Soviet official ideology and as theory and praxis of social change, reinforces that inclination.

Until the early 1960s, the Soviet Union retained the image of a socialist society, devoted to the international promotion of socialism. Yet the erosion of her ideological credibility,[6] which began with the practices of Stalinism and was generally discredited by the 1970s, has not yet reached some countries and social groups (as in Central America) actively engaged in revolutionary efforts, located far from the Soviet Union herself and receiving, in several forms, decisive support from her.

This is also true of Marxism–Leninism. In Western European countries Marxism has been submitted, in theory and in practice, to general critical revision, strongly opposed to its former Leninist version, and reoriented to a humanistic and democratic reading of the writings of Marx (by, for example, Gramsci, Horkheimer, Irving Fetscher, Berlinguer). By contrast, some militant revolutionaries, mostly non-European and educated in the Leninist tradition, have kept their theoretical and practical faith in the older body of Marxism–Leninism. This is typically the case of the Sandinista '*comandantes*'[7] and of many leaders of the guerrillas in El Salvador. It is also true of the leading actors of the Cuban regime. All these elements combine to produce a profound distortion in the perception and understanding of contemporary revolutionary movements.

Seen from the viewpoint of the US politico-military establishment and conservative interests, revolutionary movements in reactive countries outside the Soviet bloc tend to be perceived as predominantly conditioned by direct or indirect Soviet interference. Isolating the affected countries from Soviet interference and reinforcing incumbent governments militarily and economically is supposed, from that viewpoint, to be the way to suppress revolutions and maintain public order. Even when such order is acknowledged to be socially unjust and arbitrarily repressive, authoritarian regimes are preferable to any sort of Soviet-influenced leftist regimes not only for the US but supposedly also for the natives.[8]

This viewpoint and the political behaviour it tends to encourage is loaded with consequences. Assuming indirect interference (through proxy states such as Cuba, or, allegedly, Nicaragua) or direct Soviet interference as the basic cause of revolutionary movements, the United States compels such movements to rely increasingly on Soviet or proxy aid in order to compete with American intervention. Such a process thus reconfirms the doctrine that the Soviet Union is the ultimate cause of troubles all over the world, and so in turn reinforces the need of local movements to appeal for yet more Soviet aid. At the same time, such a self-fulfilling prophecy strengthens the ideas and positions of Marxist–Leninist radicals in national and social revolutionary movements at the expense of progressive democratic leaders.

The ultimate effects of such doctrine and practices are extremely negative, both for the societal development of third-world countries trying to get rid of oppressive colonial or oligarchical forces, and for the strategic interests of the United States which they are supposed to be protecting. Compelling third-world societies living under oppressive regimes to choose between an increasingly intolerable *status quo* and reliance on Soviet aid (implying, as it must, closer alignment with the Soviet Union) induces such societies to take the latter option. This ultimately increases the human and material resources and the geopolitical and strategic advantages of the Soviet bloc.

One of the most paradoxical aspects of that picture is the fact that the United States, through her doctrine and practice of pretending that Soviet interference is the primary cause of disturbances in the Third World, is consistently increasing the extent of Soviet influence, at the precise historical moment when the Soviet regime is internationally most discredited, as much in the Third World as elsewhere. It should also be added that the initial romanticism surrounding the Cuban Revolution in Latin America and other areas of the Third World has been succeeded – without denying its many extraordinary achievements – by a colder appraisal of Cuba's lack of economic success, her growing dependence on Soviet aid and her increasing dependence on internal repression.[9] In such conditions, American demonological anti-Sovietism is becoming the most powerful

force for the expansion of Soviet influence in the Third World.

Latin America

As a region, Latin America reproduces on a smaller scale the complexity and variety of national conditions that obtain in the Third World.[10] There is the contrast between dwarf states in Central America and the Caribbean and very large states, such as Brazil. There is the same contrast between extreme poverty (Haiti) and rather high levels of overall development (Argentina). The same sets of typological variables are applicable also to the region: (1) levels of development; (2) levels of national viability; and (3) levels of international activity. For the purposes of this brief study it is sufficient in the case of Latin America to concentrate on two typological variables – the levels of overall development and the levels of international activity of Latin American countries.

Levels of Development and Activity

In terms of levels of development, the Latin American countries may be divided into three groups: (1) higher comparative level of development (Argentina, Brazil and Mexico); (2) middle level of development (Chile, Colombia, Cuba, Ecuador, Peru, Uruguay and Venezuela); and (3) lower comparative level of development (Central America, the Caribbean countries, Bolivia and Paraguay).

In terms of the three levels of international activity, one can differentiate the following groups: (1) internationally active (Brazil and Cuba); (2) regionally active (Argentina, Mexico, Venezuela and Colombia); and (3) reactive (the other countries of the group). Such a classification, as with most others, presents some borderline cases that might be given an alternative treatment. Argentina, for instance, by virtue of her overall weight, her capability and her eventual willingness to confront a large world power (Britain in the Malvinas War) and her eventual interference in international affairs, might qualify for the classification of 'internationally active'. However, as many Argentinian scholars are the first to acknowledge,[11] after the first Peron government in the 1950s the country has tended to play a role more reactive than active in the broad international arena, while having a decisive influence, if not always amounting to active interference, in regional affairs. On the other hand, Nicaragua, since the advent of the Sandinista government, has moved from the level of international reactiveness to play a relevant sub-regional role in Central America. That notwithstanding, her classification here as a 'reactive country' reflects the fact that her current Central American role is much more determined by external conditions and pressures than by inward propensities.[12]

Confronted with the East–West competition, the Latin American countries present a picture which is also similar to that which occurs in the Third World as a whole. One country, Cuba, has a formal commitment with the Soviet bloc. Less formally, this was the case with Granada; to a smaller extent Surinam and, ambiguously, Nicaragua, are also inclined to favour that bloc. No country is formally committed to the US bloc. Many Central American countries are, however, *de facto* linked to the US camp: Honduras, Guatemala, El Salvador, the Dominican Republic and Haiti. Chile, Paraguay and Uruguay also fit into this classification. The rest of the countries, although belonging to the periphery of the US system, tend to adopt a more qualified position. They stress, with greater or lesser emphasis, their independent line and their commonality of interest with the Third World in general and with Latin America in particular. But they point out at the same time their Western character and, explicitly or implictly, their ultimate allegiance, in case of a world confrontation, to the US camp.

Considered in a general way, Latin America has moved from a close alignment with the US up to the Second World War to the tentatively non-aligned position of today.[13] This trend has had very little to do with Soviet influence. That influence has been of a basically reactive nature. The transition of Latin America from close alignment with the US to non-alignment reflects important changes in the international position of both Latin America and the US.

The larger Latin American countries have generally become more developed and more complex societies since the 1930s, but particularly after the Second World War. As a consequence they have moved from an almost exclusive trading relationship with the US to an increasingly diversified participation in international trade, with Japan and the European countries playing a rapidly expanding role. Intra-Latin American trade has also grown. Some of the countries of the region are now rapidly expanding their trade with other third-world countries. The United States, on the other hand, no longer has absolute world trading or military primacy, having to balance her strategic strength with the Soviet Union and to accept that growing proportions of world trade are taken by Japan and the Western European states.

In such conditions, the conflictual/co-operative East–West relationship – now demonstrating declining co-operation and increasing conflict – has created for the non-aligned countries of Latin America, and particularly for the larger ones, increasing space for more independent international behaviour, without actually bringing them to a closer economic or political association with the Soviet Union. In economic terms, an important reason for this has been the lack of a large reciprocal demand by the USSR for their respective exports. An exception to this has been the case of Argentine grain, now predominantly exported to the Soviet Union. Yet even Argentina is finding great difficulty in making equivalent purchases from the Soviet Union.

In political terms, Latin American non-aligned countries have not come closer to the Soviet Union, both for domestic political reasons (most of them have been under right-wing military governments in the last decade) and because of their objective lack of interest in any closer political association with the Soviet Union. They have realized that, forming as they do a peripheral part of the US international system, they could not preserve or expand their room for international manoeuvre if that were to run against important US strategic interests. A clear example of that is given by Argentina during the Malvinas War. Although the US finally gave its formal and effective support to Britain, Argentina nevertheless rejected effective support from Cuba and the Soviet Union, except perhaps in accepting some operational intelligence.[14]

Central America

Contiguity to the US, extreme weakness, powerful US economic and military interests relating to the security of the Caribbean and the link between the Atlantic and the Pacific Oceans, have helped to make Central America and the Caribbean areas of overt American intervention since the early nineteenth century. The subsequent annexation of Puerto Rico, the occupation of Cuba and the opening of the Panama Canal, together with the seizure of the Canal Zone, reinforced such a tendency.

In the more recent past, US intervention in Central America has tended to assume a permanent form through the combination of military and economic aid oriented to maintain, as agents of US interests, the local oligarchies and their associated National Guards against the will of the local peoples.[15] The paradigm of that system was the US intervention in Nicaragua to repress the nationalist revolution in the 1920s led by Augusto Cesar Sandino. Organizing and training a National Guard under Anastasio Somoza, the US succeeded in defeating the Revolution, in getting Sandino assassinated and in maintaining the Somoza dynasty in power until the victory of the new Sandinista Revolution in 1979. Similar procedures in Guatemala led to the successful CIA expedition of Castillo Armas, which overthrew constitutional President Jacob Arbenz in 1954 and led to the installation of a US-supported military regime.

As is to be expected, the military-oligarchical regimes imposed on Central America by US intervention are hated by the local peoples. There have been many popular attempts, usually crushed by the National Guards with US support, to overturn them.

These tiny Central American countries are poor agricultural societies, with a strong social stratification. This is reinforced by the fact that the peasants are Indians (except in Costa Rica), while the small urban middle class is predominantly of Spanish descent.

Economic and political control is exercised by a few oligarchical families, intimately associated with the military leadership.[16] In such conditions, there is very little room, if any, for reformist movements. The dominant groups and interests will rigidly preserve the *status quo*, maintaining it by a combination of ruthless repression and the eventual co-optation of moderate middle-class opponents. The opposition forms around middle-class intellectuals, who tend to acquire a Marxist–Leninist orientation in the universities and, given the circumstances, naturally develop very radical ideas. Such ideas lead in the direction of socialist revolution, with a built-in propensity to follow Marxist–Leninist views and practices, strongly imbued with anti-American feelings.

Yet the Soviet Union, in spite of what she might be expected to see as socially favourable local conditions, has always played a very cautious role, rarely taking initiatives and involving herself more in a reactive than in an active way. Central America is too close to the US geopolitically and economically, and too far from the Soviet Union, to encourage the USSR to pursue an active role. Cuba, which became the first country in the region to take a formal pro-Soviet position, is herself an example of Soviet reluctance to interfere in the area. The Castro Revolution started as a radical national-democratic movement which gradually mobilized the support of all social groups without any discernible tendency to become a Marxist–Leninist movement and to join the Soviet camp. In his famous speech 'History will absolve me', Fidel Castro promised land reform with State indemnity to the owners. And the initial policies of the Castro regime, consistent with his former statements, were of a socially oriented nationalism, maintaining private property under the guidance of the state.

Only three years after the Revolution, in December 1961, did Castro proclaim himself a Marxist–Leninist. Whatever may have been his own personal route to such convictions, it is quite clear in terms of public policy that the Cuban Revolution adopted that position under a double necessity: (1) to force the protective involvement of the Soviet Union as the only way to prevent a direct US intervention; and (2) to create, internally, the irreversibility of the Revolution.[17] The sovietization of the Cuban Revolution was a defensive choice by Fidel Castro, made without any encouragement by the Soviet Union – indeed against Soviet intentions – through a sort of irresistable political *chantage* which publicly compelled the USSR to incorporate Cuba into her camp.

Soviet behaviour, in the subsequent development of the Central America drama, has maintained the same cautious orientation. The Sandinista Revolution was a completely domestic movement, gradually mobilizing all sectors of Nicaraguan society against the dictatorship of Somoza, including finally even the bourgeoisie. As in the case of Cuba, Soviet aid occurred *after* the victory of the Revolution and, at least initially, as part of an international assistance package provided by the European democratic countries. It was the increasingly aggressive position of the Reagan Administration that led the USSR and her allies, at the desperate request of the Nicaraguan Government when confronted with the imminence of American intervention, to supply Nicaragua with military equipment and advisers.

Concluding Remarks

The US self-fulfilling prophecy of Soviet intervention in third-world revolutions is nowhere more typical than in Central America. It is true that most of the leaders of Central American revolutionary movements have adopted Marxist–Leninist convictions and practices. It is equally true that local conditions tend strongly to lead to a right/left polarization, bringing about, with the victory of the revolutions, regimes with socialist characteristics. Yet the sovietization of the local regimes and of their international alignment has always been the result of external circumstances, independent of Soviet action, in which US behaviour has represeted the strongest and sometimes the unique factor.

There are two main reasons for that situation. One, economic, is the acknowledgment by the revolutionary leaders, independently of their personal ideological convictions, that Central American countries have much to gain in keeping within the international market and much to lose in becoming members of the Soviet bloc. The other, political, is their clear understanding of the strategic dangers of joining the Soviet camp.

The poor example of the Cuban economy is observed by all Central American leaders. In the case of Nicaragua, the Sandinista Government aims at building a socially-regulated market economy connected, although in a selective way, with the world market.[18] The Sandinistas are clearly doing all they can to prevent a final break with the US and are very sure that alignment with the Soviet Union would neither be accepted by the Soviet Union nor tolerated by the United States. Cuba may be a unique case for a country of the area, because of the unprecedented conditions in which joining the Soviet bloc came about and it is acknowledged that Cuba might well be deprived of effective Soviet protection. If that is the case with Cuba, how much the less likely that the USSR will permit herself to be trapped into the protection of small, weak and poor countries, in an area where she has much to lose and little to gain and where she confronts extremely difficult operating conditions.

Both the Sandinista Government and the guerrillas of El Salvador (if they should come to rule the country) aim at some kind of mixed economy, with strong production and regulatory state intervention, but preserving as far as possible a significant private sector and keeping the economy selectively connected to the world market. Internationally, they aspire to neutralist non-alignment, retaining important ties to the European democracies and the rest of Latin America. This has been acknowledged by the countries of the Contadora Group.

The trouble in the area has been, and is still, the insistence of the United States, even under liberal Administrations, such as President Carter's, on assuming that the Soviet Union is directly or indirectly responsible for the local revolutionary movements. It is hard to know to what extent such theses are actually believed by their proponents. Seen from any moderately informed and objective viewpoint, the doctrine of Soviet deliberate interference in Central America is so obviously false that the more likely explanation for it is that it provides the United States with a justification for intervening, militarily if convenient, in an area where she has important strategic interests.

Given the inevitability of revolutions in Central America, for social domestic reasons, and the constant propensity of the US to escalate her intervention in the area, there is a continuous danger that things may get out of control, leading to events that may seriously destabilize the precarious balance of the world.

NOTES

[1] On the formative process of the Three Worlds, see Irving L. Horowitz, *Three Worlds of Development* (New York: Oxford UP, 1966); on the international aspects see George Liska, *Alliances and the Third World* (Baltimore: Johns Hopkins Press, 1968); for a Latin American view see Luciano Tomassini (ed.), *El Diálogo Norte–Sur – Una Perspectiva Latinoamericana* (Buenos Aires: Belgrano, 1982).

[2] See Marcel Merle, *Sociologie des Relations Internationales* (Paris: Dalloz, 1976), particularly Part 3, ch.1. For a systemic view see also James N. Rosenau (ed.), *International Politics and Foreign Policies*, (New York: Free Press, 1969).

[3] See 'The New International System', in Helio Jaguaribe, *Political Development* (New York: Harper & Row, 1973), pp. 357 ff, and *idem*, 'The New Interimperial System', Karl Deutsch *et. al*, (eds), *Problems of World Modelling* (Cambridge: Ballinger, 1977), ch. 10; see also George Liska, *Imperial America* (Baltimore: Johns Hopkins Press, 1976), and Amaury de Riencourt, *The American Empire* (New York: Dial Press, 1968).

[4] See Liska, *op. cit.* in note 3; for current positions, see Edmond Lee, 'Beijing's Balancing Act', *Foreign Policy*, Summer 1983, pp. 27–46.

[5] See George Liska, *Career of Empire* (Baltimore: Johns Hopkins Press, 1978).

[6] On the theoretical aspects of Soviet Marxism see Leszek Kolakowski, *Main Currents of Marxism*, (Oxford: Clarendon Press, 1978), vol. III, chs 1–5; on social conditions, see Allen Kassof (ed.), *Prospects for Soviet Society* (New York: Praeger, 1968); see also, for dissidents' views, Roy A. Medvedev, *On Socialist Democracy* (New York: Norton, 1977) and Ota Sik, *Quale Comunismo?* [Italian translation], (Roma: Laterza, 1977).

[7] See Ruy Mauro Marini, 'The Nicaraguan Revolution and the Central American Revolutionary Process', *Contemporary Marxism*, no. 3, Summer 1981, pp. 62–6.

[8] See Ambassador Jeane Kirkpatrick, 'Dictatorship and Double Standards', *Commentary*, November 1979, and 'US Security in Latin America', *Commentary*, January 1981; for a Latin American analysis of such policies see the studies of Luis Mara, Roberto Bouzas and Riordan Roett, in Helio Jaguaribe (ed.), *La Política Internacional de los Años 80*, (Buenos Aires: Belgrano, 1982), pp. 81–160.

[9] For the most comprehensive and objective appraisal of the Cuban revolution see Jorge I. Dominguez, *Cuba – Order and Revolution*, (Cambridge: Harvard UP, 1978); on the economic aspects of Cuba, see CEPAL, *Cuba: Estilo de Desarrollo y Políticas Sociales* (Mexico: Siglo XXI, 1980); for present positions, see Sergio Roca, 'Cuba Confronts the 1980s', *Current History*, February 1983, pp. 69–73.

[10] For a general picture of Latin America see Jaguaribe, *op. cit.* in note 3, chs 19–22; see also *idem*, 'A America Latina no Sistema Internacional', in Henrique Rattner (ed.), *A Crise da Ordem Mundial* (Sao Paulo: Simbolo, 1978).

[11] See Carlos Perez Llana, *Reinsercion Argentina en el Mundo* (Buenos Aires: El Cid, 1983).

[12] See Sergio Ramirez, 'Sandinismo, Hegemony and Revolution', *Contemporary Marxism*, no. 3, Summer 1981, pp. 23–6.

[13] See Jaguaribe, 'A America Latina no Distema Internacional', *op.cit* in note 10.

[14] For an objective and comprehensive view of the conflict see Carlos Moneta, 'El Conflicto de las Islas Malvinas: su papel en la Politica Exterior Argentina y en el Contexto Mundial', mimeo (Caracas: SELA, 1982).

[15] See Susanne Jonas, 'An Overview: 50 Years of Revolution and Intervention in Central America', *Contemporary Marxism*, no. 3, Summer 1981, pp. iii–xxiv; see also, in same journal and issue, James F. Petras, 'Economic Expansion, Political Crisis and US Policy in Central America', pp. 69–88.

[16] See Edelberto Torre-Rivas, 'Seven Keys to Understanding the Central American Crisis' *Contemporary Marxism*, no. 3, Summer 1981, pp. 49–61; for the present situation see Richard Millet, 'Central American Cauldron', *Current History*, February 1983, pp. 69–73.

[17] See Dominguez, *op. cit.* in note 9, particularly chs 5–9.

[18] See CEPAL, *Nicaragua: El Impacto de la Mutación Política* (Santiago: CEPAL, 1981).

Conference Report

DR ROBERT O'NEILL

Our choice of starting point in this Conference, the Soviet Union, was dictated by the nature of our principal interests: policy guidelines for the West and those other states which are concerned about Soviet capacities to do them harm. In their cogent and persuasive Papers, Professors Brzezinski and Bialer have given us a consistent view of the Soviet Union which is both disturbing and calming. Two elements of their analyses are particularly compelling: first the one-dimensional nature of Soviet power which is emphasized both by the strengthening of her military might and, as Bialer puts it, by 'the profoundly adverse trends in their domestic economic, social and political environment'; and second, the Great Russian domination of the multi-national Soviet Union, whereby 115 million Russians have control over the other 155 million Soviet citizens.

These factors handicap the Soviet Union as a competitor of the West in all dimensions save the military, and even there questions arise because of the dilemma of choice: between expanding the defence establishment directly in the coming decade and increasing large-scale investment in defence industrial capability to support future military growth. Bialer, in his Paper, offers us the prospect that the Soviet Union will not be able to maintain both at the levels of the 1970s and judges that the leadership will opt for investment in future defence industrial capabilities. These same factors also exercise an extremely confining influence on the degree to which the Soviet political, social and economic systems can be liberalized or mellowed. Hence, in the judgments of Brzezinski and Bialer, Western policies aimed at these ends have poor prospects of success.

But are we allowing ourselves to be overimpressed by this comforting vision of internal crisis and decay in the Soviet Union? Our own societies are not exactly in perfect order.

It may be that there is a state of competitive decline existing between the two superpowers. Perhaps therefore we ought to adopt a little caution, first with regard to the degree of crisis that we expect to occur in the Soviet Union and second with regard to the level of superiority which the West might hope to maintain in social, economic and technological sectors.

In foreign policy, the interesting question arising from the Papers by Bialer and Brzezinski is: can the Soviet outward thrust be halted on the present frontiers of containment, where they exist, or be kept limited to existing spheres of influence, where containment has never applied? The old problems of the Russian and Soviet expansion eastwards, namely where to stop or why to stop at all, have been replaced by the newer one of having to calculate whether the gains of expansion, direct or indirect, will be worth the likely consequences. In this sense particularly, Bialer carries conviction in his view that the principal question for this decade is not what Soviet leaders will do, but rather what the Western Allies will do. The old Russian habit of solving external problems by absorbing them in effect into her own frontiers may not have gone with the post-1945 changes – witness Afghanistan but over the past thirty-five years she has been given many signals to stop. Where these signals have been backed by credible force, prudence has gained the upper hand in the Kremlin. The Soviets may be difficult to live with but they are not stupid.

When we come to look at Soviet means for fulfilling her foreign-policy goals, the panoply available to her is certainly narrow. As far as effective diplomacy is concerned, the Soviet Union is poorly equipped. Professor Ayoob in his Paper gives us the view, from a standpoint that is obviously not pro-Western, of the USSR in the 1980s 'com-

168

mitting the same blunders of over-extension, arrogance and insensitivity to regional concerns that the US had committed in the 1960s'. Similarly, economic aid and trade are short levers in the hands of the Soviet leadership. In one area which we did not discuss much in this Conference, namely that of espionage and other covert operations, the Soviet Union is not so badly suited. In our considerations of the control of illegal technology transfers we took note of her major drive for technological intelligence. Unfortunately we also have to take note of a major Soviet capability to acquire Western political and military secrets, and to conduct operations in both political and military senses.

The Military Balance

No equivocation was expressed from the view that the Soviet Union's major tool for influencing events beyond her borders is military power. There was, however, considerable divergence of views in the two committees looking at the East–West military balance as to whether the Soviet Union can use this military power to any decisive effect.

Despite a good deal of talk involving the numbers of the changed US–Soviet balance, many tend to disparage the significance of numbers in themselves, and indeed agree with the thesis of Bo Huldt's Paper that a 'balance' could be drawn only in the light of a particular political and strategic perspective. From the Soviet point of view it might plausibly be maintained that the tremendous Soviet build-up could be justified in the light of the total forces the USSR would face if attacked.

The Western perspective necessarily would be different. Terms like 'superiority' have strategic significance only in terms of the concrete abilities conferred to accomplish political objectives. Accordingly, what matters is whether there is *political* significance in the possession of a margin of nuclear superiority; and what military options might be conferred or denied by the loss of a US margin or the acquisition of advantage by the Soviet Union.

There is unlikely to be any consensus on whether nuclear superiority confers political leverage. The Soviet Union seems to have been particularly aggressive during a period of US nuclear monopoly; at the same time, in periods of intense crisis, it may be that American superiority was taken for granted by US decision-makers. In the future, they will not be able to act with such freedom. There were calls in the Conference for a reacquisition of a measure of nuclear superiority and this call is echoed in Major-General Odom's Paper.

Discussion of this paper divided on the predictable lines of whether the acknowledged Soviet build-up had resulted in developing new strategic options for the Soviet Union, or simply closing off options to the US. Some at the Conference tended to look on the latter development as a healthy one and even prescribed a European nuclear force as a means of replacing the waning US extended deterrent (as to whose waning there was, so long as 300,000 American troops remained in Europe, some dissension).

But it was conceded that were the Soviet Union actually to acquire new strategic options by virtue of her build-up, this trend would be cause for serious concern. In this regard, there may well be a connection between the new-found Soviet ability to harass US reinforcement of Europe by threats in the Caribbean and around the Gulf. Without security in these two now vulnerable areas, a successful NATO defence of Europe could not, perhaps, be conducted. Therefore Soviet increases in strength have changed the calculus for US vital interests, although at the same time the establishment of a new equilibrium in the Far East has reduced the demands for US capabilities there.

In summary, there was agreement in the Conference that an important strategic factor had changed: the Soviet Union had carried off a programme of considerable military expansion. But there was no agreement as to whether this was motivated by a desire to open up new strategic options and even, if so, whether the arrival of parity and various local superiorities could be translated into political gains. Parity, said one participant, is a formula for war; but beyond suggesting a more aggressive defence for NATO there was little discussion of what counter-balancing moves the US might make.

Indeed, even if it were possible for the US to regain strategic superiority, this result would not necessarily reassure Europe and thereby fulfil one of the true functions of the US extended deterrent. Arms-control progress and attention to the role of public and political opinion within the Alliance remains important. It is in any case doubtful whether superiority can be achieved, except by the route of defensive systems which could ultimately prove to work against the West's interests by decoupling or by neutralization when they were inevitably acquired by the Soviet Union also.

There was, however, no general concurrence with calls for an arms-control restraint on further Soviet force expansion. Whatever their political significance, Soviet advances are real and, from an American perspective, the 'balance' had altered unfavourably. Should the United States aim at superiority and not merely maintenance of parity remains the most important, albeit unresolved, question.

For many, NATO forces appear simply as an expensive trip-wire for nuclear retaliation. Radical military reforms could reduce costs and increase effectiveness. The alternatives for NATO posture might be: a thin and over-stretched facade; a Maginot Line defensive system; a defensive system in substantial depth; and a force suited for pre-emptive attack. The first, it was said, is what we have. A Maginot Line would cost too much. Defence in depth would not be accepted by the Germans. And pre-emptive attack is politically impossible. One solution of the problem might be a modification of defence in depth with a tough shell near the inner-German border.

Political Aspects of East–West Relations
Perhaps the principal political issue debated at the Conference was the extent to which the policies of the Soviet Union, both towards Eastern Europe and towards the rest of the world, could be influenced by Western measures – political, economic and social. In his Paper Zbigniew Brzezinski warns us to expect little result. Theo Sommer, in his contribution, is more optimistic about achieving a mellowing within the Soviet Union and points to continuing benefits to Eastern and Western Europeans as a result of detente.

Six topics were discussed by the first of two committees examining relations between the two halves of Europe: Western aims *vis-á-vis* Eastern Europe, going even as far as possible revision of the Yalta Agreement and settlement of the German question; the scope for change in Eastern Europe; differentiation of policy to be applied to East European governments; the relative utilities of positive and negative incentives; the roles of international financial institutions; and private exchanges.

On revising Yalta, intensive debate ensued between those who believed that the West should not accept the division of Europe as permanent and those who pointed to the potential instability of a multiplicity of independent nation states in Central Europe, with wider implications for the central balance. On German reunification, it was contended on the one hand that the Soviet Union might offer the bait of reunification in order to neutralize the Federal Republic. On the other, it was argued that the question of reunification was closed and that the USSR would not risk this course in any event.

Little optimism was felt in the committee for the possibility of inducing change in Eastern Europe. At best the fruits of such Western policies would be marginal although, of course, over a long time, the margins would accumulate. Differentiation of treatment of Soviet and East European governments by the West was regarded as still of importance, yet approaches to Eastern Europe had to be accompanied by parallel exchanges with the USSR if they were to be significant. Strong support was expressed for the utility of privately sponsored exchanges in promoting reform and pluralization, although scepticism was expressed as to whether the benefits flowed further than to the immediate Eastern participants.

The second committee reminded us that we have to ask the right basic question: should the goal of the West *in fact* be transformation of the East?

Many at the Conference replied, in effect, with a qualified 'no'. Western attempts to produce such transformation *en bloc* would lead to instability in Eastern Europe, which in turn would leave the states and peoples within that region worse off than before. Eastern Europe was historically different from Western Europe even before its post-war dominance by the USSR and, as such, it may not be particularly well suited to Western European notions of democracy.

The opposing viewpoint was also heard, particularly regarding the Polish situation. If the Soviet Union had not had to worry about Western reaction to the various Polish crises, Soviet tanks would have rolled into Warsaw. Others argued that the basic question to be answered was how should the West act to bring about the inevitable changes in the East with the least confrontation possible, or how should the West cope with the changes when they occurred? While there were no clear-cut answers to those questions, there seemed to be a consensus for a differentiated policy, which attempts to preserve stability on the one hand while encouraging the possibility for evolutionary change on the other.

Yet the future may hold *revolutionary* changes in and for Eastern Europe rather than evolutionary ones. The Soviet Union's likely response to such changes is essentially unpredictable. She might simply muddle through or down, sensing inevitable decline in her empire; she might consider alternatives (e.g. changing her German policy); or she might tighten the screws, as she has in the past. Faced with a revolutionary situation in Eastern Europe, the West might itself tighten the screws on Eastern Europe and the USSR. We have to recognize that Eastern Europe is of *secondary* importance to the US, whose policy is much less oriented now – as a result of the experience of the 1970s with Eastern Europe (loan default) and the USSR (failure of detente) – towards helping Eastern Europeans and, therefore, easing burdens on the Soviet Union.

By contrast, Western European policy is primarily concerned with stabilizing Eastern Europe for the sake of the Continent as a whole, but Eastern Europe is so volatile and irrational that it may well be impossible to recommend a single Western policy. Differentiation, on the other hand, might simply postpone the eruption, as in the case of the Polish debt problems in the 1970s, and make the inevitable crisis worse once it finally occurred. Perhaps an issue-by-issue, year-by-year, approach to Eastern Europe and *no* across-the-board policies is the only valid option open to the West.

There were those who argued in favour of giving first priority to arms control in any attempt to improve East–West relationships, contending that more possibilities for agreement exist in this area than others. Furthermore, some initial arms-control agreement may be necessary in Europe before current tensions can begin to subside, especially since the USSR puts such emphasis on military power and has reason to fear (e.g. through modernization of theatre nuclear forces) the possibility of the West under-cutting her. Other participants expressed considerable scepticism regarding this potential role for arms control. They doubted that arms control, although valuable as a means of making the balance of military forces more stable, would have much effect on the political and societal changes desired for Eastern Europe. Confidence-building measures, for example, are probably more important '*in* the West than *for* the West'. The West should perhaps first put its own house in order, while continuing to maintain cultural and intellectual ties to Eastern Europeans through what were going to be dangerous, unpredictable times.

Economic Aspects of East–West Relations

Discussion of economic aspects at the Conference revolved around three issues: the economic effects on the Soviet Union of sanctions; the political consequences of such effects; and the political feasibility of application of sanctions by democratic societies. There was general agreement that some economic impact on the USSR could be achieved, particularly by removing subsidies. There was less agreement as to whether these effects would be realized significantly over either a short or a long term. The aim of such measures should be to compel the USSR to make a choice between the military and civil sectors, even though the presumption exists that she will choose to invest in the military; she would however be forced to operate at a lower level of aggregate investment.

Given that these economic effects are possible at least in moderate degree, the question of political consequences thus becomes paramount. There was general agreement that it was too much to expect that modification of Soviet behaviour would result from either short- or long-term actions. The motivation for a long-term policy, such as resource denial, should rest upon preserving the direct security interests of the West rather than inducing any great change in Soviet behaviour. For the short term, politically specific, conditional and 'liftable' sanctions might be useful to demonstrate concern at individual Soviet actions. There was a division of opinion as to the applicability of such measures to Eastern Europe, for fear of the degree of tension that would be induced in the East–West relationship. Some insisted that introduction of instability was desirable while others, with equal vehemence, insisted that a high degree of instability would be politically unacceptable to Western Europeans because of the potential human costs. Few were prepared to defend the thesis that co-operation with the Soviet Union would mellow her system and behaviour.

The political feasibility of regulatory measures is likely to be limited not so much at the international level but at the national. Bureaucratic and industry-government disagreements as to the value of particular exports are rife; international agreement is at best problematic in the face of such domestic disputes.

There was some agreement that a common policy should be developed to eliminate subsidies and 'windfall profits taxes' on premiums that the Soviet Union either paid or received. Yet we should beware the political fallacy, namely, 'I can prove that my opponent's practical solutions will not work, therefore my plan will'. While many agree that detente did not work, this is no guarantee that embargoes will.

Technology Transfers

With respect to the strategic implications of technology transfers, three issues dominated the debate: the extent of the Soviet Union's attempts to acquire Western technology; the consequences of such acquisitions for the military balance between East and West; and the problems of establishing effective controls over the flow of technology to the Soviet Union.

There was consensus on the first point: the West faces a serious new threat. The Soviet Union has systematically developed a major programme for gaining high technology and technological intelligence from the West. In recent years this programme has facilitated a quantum jump in the sophistication of Soviet weapon systems. In some cases the Soviet Union may have been able to exploit the acquired technology to a higher level than had the original developers.

Opinions varied as to how far those trends had tipped the military balance in the Soviet favour, but there was consensus that the consequences were serious. Maintenance of an advantage at least in terms of lead-times is of critical importance to the West's ability to offset superior Warsaw Pact numbers, and there is clear evidence that some of these lead-times are being reduced substantially.

Debate sharpened on how to prevent this situation from further deterioration. Opinions differed on whether only the horse's head was out of the barn, whether the horse was half-way out, or whether the tail was through the doorway, making its closure pointless. Many factors complicated the effectiveness of controls. These include: the dual applicability of many advanced-technology items to civil and military purposes; the need for smaller nations without large domestic markets to seek foreign customers in order to sustain their new high-technology industries; the great difficulties in deciding whether a particular technology was of significant utility; the political pressures which could be generated by interested manufacturers; further sales to the Soviet Union by third countries, especially neutrals such as Sweden and Switzerland, and some developing countries; Soviet membership of international organizations relating to high technology; and the existing method of decision-making in COCOM, namely unanimity. At least there was final consensus that, despite the difficulties, stricter controls were necessary, but it is hard to define how strict the controls should be.

172

Wider Elements of East–West Relations

In addition to those direct elements of East–West relations, the Conference examined wider aspects such as the impact of the Third World and the role of public opinion in shaping events and policies.

With regard to the Third World, debate focused on the causes of regional instability, the extent of the influence of developing countries over the super-powers (and *vice versa*), the utility of third-world allies and partners (particularly in the sense of the old American political adage – an honest man is one who, when once bought, stays bought), and the positive and negative attractions of the Third World for the super-powers.

Sharp contention raged over US failure to support national liberation movements, with critics claiming that US policies forced political reformers into the arms of the Soviet Union while the defenders claimed that the United States was upholding the true interests of the Third World against Soviet attempts to disrupt and spoil. The most important concern for the West generally was the exploitation of regional conflict by the Soviet Union to distract the US from central issues and to divert resources away from more important commitments. This concern is of the greatest relevance to the Middle East and Central America, and carries implications for the security of Western Europe as well as the United States.

In discussing public opinion as means and ends for policy-makers, the starkly differing natures of totalitarian and democratic states in this dimension were recognized at the outset. As Michel Tatu pointed out in his Paper, the *raison d'être* of democratic states was the broadest possible identification between individual and collective values. Public opinion in totalitarian states was not irrelevant – nor totally immune to Western influence – but it was a means rather than an end.

In the Conference, debate focused on four issues:

– *The problems of democratic states when the use of force was involved.* How could public opinion be mobilized and sustained when the government decided that force was necessary? How could informed public opinion be created on issues which were paradoxical and complex? What was the significance of selectivity and timing in the release of information? Several participants stressed the need to create a direct relationship between any conflict and the national public involved. It is becoming more difficult for democratic countries to fight wars in distant countries, and the South Atlantic crisis of 1982 contains both positive and negative lessons. Military members and journalists clashed on the question of how to balance the advantages of an uncensored press, subject to commercial pressures, with the need for security and protection of soldiers' lives. Journalists argued that censorship of information in these circumstances brought only short-term military advantages and could easily be abused. How, it was asked, could the need to create support and sustain a consensus be reconciled with the need for truth? Military members replied that operational necessity compelled the use of limited censorship.

– *Changes in Western public attitudes due to heavy reliance on nuclear weapons.* Iris Portny argues in her Paper that a change has taken place in American public opinion in this regard, hence the Alliance should begin to redefine its emphasis. The immediate concerns and perspectives of the public must be better understood and responded to. Although there was not complete consensus on the shift in public opinion – or indeed about whether a coherent and consistent public opinion existed – this analysis was regarded as being true also for Britain. There was considerable support for the proposal that government and public concerns needed to be harmonized. However, we must recognize the danger that governments will accommodate policy to the whims of less informed publics.

– *The role of private organizations and pressure groups in shaping public opinion.* Although there was little concern that such groups might be ideologically inspired, several participants criticized their simplistic and selective use of information, and pointed to the need to counter this practice at local levels. The difficulty of presenting complex nuclear issues to the general public was seen as a major challenge.

- *The elusive nature of the concept of 'public opinion'.* It can be taken to mean the views of a majority of the electorate, views as expressed in opinion polls, the views of the educated and articulate sector of society, or the climate within which debate took place. It can be argued that democratic governments are affected principally by the views of the educated public, and hence the United States, with the most highly educated electorate, stands the most exposed of Western nations to the forces of public opinion. This argument, one hopes, is one for understanding the political dynamics of Western societies rather than for the closure of universities.

The Western Alliance in the 1980s

Few, if any, of the measures discussed here and in the Conference can be made effective, as Henri Simonet reminded us in his Paper without cohesion and determination in the Western Alliance. He gave us guidelines for improving these qualities in the political, economic, strategic and wider international dimensions. Perhaps the most salient of his observations is that the Alliance 'must be able to rely on a single strategic vision of the world'. We all know that this single strategic vision, which existed once, is now no longer to be found. If it remains lost, the consequences will be severe. To re-establish it will take major efforts and reassertion of a broad Atlanticist vision; it will also call for sacrifices from governments in terms of domestic support. In a Presidential election year, we may look in vain for much change in this regard in the United States. But this prospect is no reason for the other allies to stand pat: in taking a lead, they can both weaken the countervailing pressures on the Administration and reassert the positive value of the European contribution to the Alliance.

In the light of all these deliberations, what can be said of the prospects we face in conducting our relationship with the East in the 1980s? The challenges will be severe and their outcome is difficult to predict but we will be best served by continuing efforts to improve the effectiveness of our military forces, coupled with a more alert, flexible and engaged diplomacy than of recent years, supported by carefully and jointly regulated economic interaction with the East.

Index